Theory of Decision under U[image_ref id="1" /]

This book describes the classical axiomatic th
as well as critiques thereof and alternative theories. It focuses on the meaning of
probability, discussing some definitions and surveying their scope of applicability.
The behavioral definition of subjective probability serves as a way to present the
classical theories, culminating in Savage's theorem. The limitations of this result as
a definition of probability lead to two directions – first, similar behavioral definitions
of more general theories, such as nonadditive probabilities and multiple priors, and
second, cognitive derivations based on case-based techniques.

Itzhak Gilboa is a professor in the Berglas School of Economics, Tel-Aviv University, Israel, and a professor in the newly established Department of Economics
and Decision Science, HEC, Paris. Earlier, he became a chaired professor at North-
western University in 1992, visited at the Department of Economics, University of
Pennsylvania (1995–1997), and was a professor at Boston University (1997–1999).
Professor Gilboa also served as a Fellow at the Cowles Foundation at Yale University from 2001 to 2007. The recipient of a Sloan Fellowship, among other awards,
he has published articles in the leading economic theory journals, primarily on
decision under uncertainty. Professor Gilboa coauthored *A Theory of Case-Based
Decisions* with David Schmeidler (Cambridge University Press, 2001). He received
his Ph.D. from Tel-Aviv University in 1987.

Econometric Society Monographs

Editors:

Andrew Chesher, University College London
George J. Mailath, University of Pennsylvania

The Econometric Society is an international society for the advancement of economic theory in relation to statistics and mathematics. The Econometric Society Monograph Series is designed to promote the publication of original research contributions of high quality in mathematical economics and theoretical and applied econometrics.

Other titles in the series:

G. S. Maddala *Limited dependent and qualitative variables in econometrics*, 0 521 33825 5
Gerard Debreu *Mathematical economics: Twenty papers of Gerard Debreu*, 0 521 33561 2
Jean-Michel Grandmont *Money and value: A reconsideration of classical and neoclassical monetary economics*, 0 521 31364 3
Franklin M. Fisher *Disequilibrium foundations of equilibrium economics*, 0 521 37856 7
Andreu Mas-Colell *The theory of general equilibrium: A differentiable approach*, 0 521 26514 2, 0 521 38870 8
Truman F. Bewley, Editor, *Advances in econometrics – Fifth World Congress* (Volume I), 0 521 46726 8
Truman F. Bewley, Editor, *Advances in econometrics – Fifth World Congress* (Volume II), 0 521 46725 X
Herve Moulin *Axioms of cooperative decision making*, 0 521 36055 2, 0 521 42458 5
L. G. Godfrey *Misspecification tests in econometrics: The Lagrange multiplier principle and other approaches*, 0 521 42459 3
Tony Lancaster *The econometric analysis of transition data*, 0 521 43789 X
Alvin E. Roth and Marilda A. Oliviera Sotomayor, Editors, *Two-sided matching: A study in game-theoretic modeling and analysis*, 0 521 43788 1
Wolfgang Härdle *Applied nonparametric regression*, 0 521 42950 1
Jean-Jacques Laffont, Editor, *Advances in economic theory – Sixth World Congress* (Volume I), 0 521 56610 X
Jean-Jacques Laffont, Editor, *Advances in economic theory – Sixth World Congress* (Volume II), 0 521 48460 X
Halbert White *Estimation, inference and specification*, 0 521 25280 6, 0 521 57446 3
Christopher Sims, Editor, *Advances in econometrics – Sixth World Congress* (Volume I), 0 521 56610 X
Christopher Sims, Editor, *Advances in econometrics – Sixth World Congress* (Volume II), 0 521 56609 6
Roger Guesnerie *A contribution to the pure theory of taxation*, 0 521 23689 4, 0 521 62956 X
David M. Kreps and Kenneth F. Wallis, Editors, *Advances in economics and econometrics – Seventh World Congress* (Volume I), 0 521 58011 0, 0 521 58983 5
David M. Kreps and Kenneth F. Wallis, Editors, *Advances in economics and econometrics – Seventh World Congress* (Volume II), 0 521 58012 9, 0 521 58982 9
David M. Kreps and Kenneth F. Wallis, Editors, *Advances in economics and econometrics – Seventh World Congress* (Volume III), 0 521 58013 7, 0 521 58981 9
Donald P. Jacobs, Ehud Kalai, and Morton I. Kamien, Editors, *Frontiers of research in economic theory: The Nancy L. Schwartz Memorial Lectures, 1983–1997*, 0 521 63222 6, 0 521 63538 1
A. Colin Cameron and Pravin K. Trivedi *Regression analysis of count data*, 0 521 63201 3, 0 521 63567 5
Steinar Strom, Editor, *Econometrics and economic theory in the 20th century: The Ragnar Frisch Centennial Symposium*, 0 521 63323 0, 0 521 63365 6
Eric Ghysels, Norman R. Swanson, and Mark Watson, Editors, *Essays in econometrics: Collected papers of Clive W. J. Granger* (Volume I), 0 521 77297 4, 0 521 80407 8, 0 521 77496 9, 0 521 79697 0

Continued on page following the index

To my family

(David included)

Theory of Decision under Uncertainty

Itzhak Gilboa
Tel Aviv University, Israel, and HEC, Paris

CAMBRIDGE UNIVERSITY PRESS
Cambridge, New York, Melbourne, Madrid, Cape Town, Singapore,
São Paulo, Delhi, Dubai, Tokyo, Mexico City

Cambridge University Press
32 Avenue of the Americas, New York, NY 10013-2473, USA

www.cambridge.org
Information on this title: www.cambridge.org/9780521741231

First published 2009
Reprinted 2010

A catalog record for this publication is available from the British Library.

Library of Congress Cataloging in Publication Data

Gilboa, Itzhak.
Theory of decision under uncertainty / Itzhak Gilboa.
    p. cm.
Includes index.
ISBN 978-0-521-51732-4 (hardback)
1. Decision making.   2. Uncertainty (Information theory)   I. Title.
QA279.4.G556   2009
003´.54 – dc22   2008042408

ISBN 978-0-521-51732-4 Hardback
ISBN 978-0-521-74123-1 Paperback

Contents

Preface   *page* xiii

I   Intuitive Definitions   **1**

1 Motivating Examples   3

2 Free Will and Determinism   5
   2.1   Can Free Choice Be Predicted?   5
   2.2   Is the World Deterministic?   6
   2.3   Is Free Will Observable?   6
   2.4   The Problem of Free Will   7
   2.5   A Rational Illusion   10
   2.6   Free Will and the Decision Matrix   12

3 The Principle of Indifference   14
   3.1   Will a Canonical Space Help?   14
      3.1.1 The Canonical State Space   14
      3.1.2 Difficulties with a Uniform Prior on [0, 1]   15
      3.1.3 Conclusion   16
   3.2   What's Special about the Coin?   17
      3.2.1 Symmetry   17
      3.2.2 Smooth Beliefs   18

4 Relative Frequencies   20
   4.1   The Law of Large Numbers   20
   4.2   The Problem of Induction   21
      4.2.1 Hume's Critique   21
      4.2.2 Goodman's Grue-Bleen Paradox   22
      4.2.3 Kolmogorov Complexity and Its Dependence
          of Language   23
      4.2.4 Grue-Bleen Again   26
      4.2.5 Evolutionary Explanations   31
   4.3   Problems with the Frequentist Approach   34

5 Subjective Probabilities   37
  5.1   Linda the Bank Teller   37
  5.2   Pascal's Wager   38
  5.3   Classical versus Bayesian Statistics   40
    5.3.1 Basic Definitions   40
    5.3.2 The Gambler Fallacy   41
    5.3.3 Exchangeability   42
    5.3.4 Confidence Is Not Probability   44
    5.3.5 Classical Statistics Can Be Ridiculous   45
    5.3.6 Different Methods for Different Goals   46

II   Behavioral Definitions   **49**

6 A Case Study   51
  6.1   A Characterization Theorem for Maximization
       of Utility   51
  6.2   Proof   53
  6.3   Interpretations   55
    6.3.1 A Few Definitions   56
    6.3.2 A Meta-Scientific Interpretation   59
    6.3.3 A Normative Interpretation   62
    6.3.4 A Descriptive Interpretation   63
  6.4   Limitations   64
    6.4.1 Semiorders   65
    6.4.2 Other Ways to Measure Utility   71

7 The Role of Theories   72
  7.1   Theories Are Always Wrong   72
  7.2   Theories and Conceptual Frameworks   74
  7.3   Logical Positivism as a Metaphor   76

8 Von Neumann–Morgenstern's Theorem   78
  8.1   Background   78
  8.2   The Theorem   79
  8.3   Proofs   83
    8.3.1 The Algebraic Approach   83
    8.3.2 A Geometric Approach   84
    8.3.3 A Separation Argument   85
  8.4   The Three Interpretations   86

9 De Finetti's Theorem   89
  9.1   Motivation   89
  9.2   The Theorem   90
  9.3   A Proof   91
  9.4   The Three Interpretations   92

10	Savage's Theorem	94
10.1	Background	94
10.2	States, Outcomes, and Acts	96
10.3	Axioms	97
	10.3.1 P1	97
	10.3.2 P2	97
	10.3.3 Notation	99
	10.3.4 Null Events	99
	10.3.5 P3	100
	10.3.6 P4	102
	10.3.7 P5	102
	10.3.8 P6	103
	10.3.9 P7	104
10.4	The Result for a Finite Outcome Set	105
	10.4.1 Finitely Additive Measures	105
	10.4.2 Nonatomic Measures	107
	10.4.3 The Theorem	108
10.5	The Case of a General Outcome Set	108
10.6	Interpretations	109
10.7	The Proof and Qualitative Probabilities	110
11	The Definition of States	113
11.1	Causality	113
	11.1.1 Newcomb's Paradox	113
	11.1.2 States as Functions from Acts to Outcomes	114
	11.1.3 A Problem	115
11.2	Hempel's Paradox of Confirmation	116
	11.2.1 Are All Ravens Black?	116
	11.2.2 A State-Space Formulation	117
	11.2.3 What Is a Confirmation?	117
	11.2.4 A Resolution	118
	11.2.5 Good's Variation	118
	11.2.6 What Do We Learn from This?	119
11.3	Monty Hall Three-Door Game	120
12	A Critique of Savage	123
12.1	Criticizing Critiques	123
	12.1.1 An Example	123
	12.1.2 The General Lesson	124
12.2	Critique of P3 and P4	125
	12.2.1 Example	125
	12.2.2 Defense	126
	12.2.3 State-Dependent Utility	127
	12.2.4 The Definition of Subjective Probability	128
	12.2.5 When Is State Dependence Necessary?	129

12.3 Critique of P1 and P2   130
      12.3.1 The Basic Problem   130
      12.3.2 Reasoned Choice versus Raw Preferences   131
      12.3.3 Schmeidler's Critique and Ellsberg's
              Paradox   132
      12.3.4 Observability of States   136
      12.3.5 Problems of Complexity   137

13 Objectivity and Rationality   138
   13.1 Subjectivity and Objectivity   138
   13.2 Objective and Subjective Rationality   139

14 Anscombe–Aumann's Theorem   142

III Alternative Behavioral Theories   **145**

15 Choquet Expected Utility   147
   15.1 Schmeidler's Intuition   147
   15.2 Choquet Integral   149
   15.3 Comonotonicity   150
   15.4 Axioms and Result   151

16 Prospect Theory   154
   16.1 Background   154
   16.2 Gain–Loss Asymmetry   154
   16.3 Distortion of Probabilities   156
   16.4 Rank-Dependent Probabilities and Choquet
         Integration   158

17 Maxmin Expected Utility   160
   17.1 Convex Games   160
   17.2 A Cognitive Interpretation of CEU   161
   17.3 Axioms and Result   163
   17.4 Interpretation of MMEU   163
   17.5 Generalizations and Variations   165
   17.6 Bewley's Alternative Approach   165
   17.7 Combining Objective and Subjective Rationality   166
   17.8 Applications   168

IV Cognitive Origins   **171**

18 Case-Based Qualitative Beliefs   173
   18.1 Axioms and Result   173
   18.2 Four Known Techniques   175
   18.3 The Combination Axiom in General Analogical
         Reasoning   177
   18.4 Violations of the Combination Axiom   179

19 Frequentism Revisited 180
   19.1   Similarity-Weighted Empirical Frequencies 180
   19.2   Intuition 181
   19.3   Axiomatization 182
   19.4   Empirical Similarity and Objective Probabilities 184

20 Future Research 188

References 191
Index 199

Preface

This book comprises lecture notes for a graduate-level class in decision under uncertainty. After teaching such classes for many years, it became more difficult to squeeze all the material into class discussions, and I was not quite sure about the appropriate order in which the issues should be presented. Trying to put everything in writing, and thereby finding at least one permutation of topics that makes sense, is supposed to help me forget less and confuse the students less. As a by-product, the notes may be useful to students who miss classes or who wish to know what the course is about without having to show up every week.

The graduate classes I normally teach are geared toward students who want to do research in economics and related fields. It is assumed that they have taken a basic microeconomic sequence at the graduate level. In teaching the class, I hope that I can convince some students that decision theory is a beautiful topic and that this is what they want to do when they grow up. But I'm fully aware of the fact that this is not going to be the case for the majority of the students. I therefore attempt to teach the course with a much more general audience in mind, focusing on the way decision theory may affect the research done in economics at large, as well as in finance, political science, and other fellow disciplines.

The present notes contain relatively few proofs. Interested students are referred to books and papers that contain more details. The focus here is on conceptual issues, regarding which I find that each teacher has his or her own interpretation and style. The mathematical results are a bit like musical notes – they are written, saved, and can be consulted according to need. By contrast, our presentation and interpretation of the results are akin to the performance of a musical piece. My focus here is mostly on the interpretation I like, on how I would like to perform the theory, as it were. I comment on proofs mostly when I feel that some intuition may be gained from them and that it's important to highlight it.

These notes are not presented as original thoughts or a research paper. Many of the ideas presented here appeared in print. Some are very old, some are newer, and some appeared in works that I have coauthored. I try to give credit where credit is due, but I must have missed many references, of which I may or may not have been aware. The discussion also includes other thoughts that have not appeared in print and that originated in discussions with various people, in particular with David Schmeidler. When I recall precisely that a certain idea was suggested to me by someone, I do mention it, but there are many ideas for which I can recall no obvious source. This doesn't mean that they are original, and I apologize for any unintentional plagiarism. At the same time, there are also many ideas here that I know to be peculiar to me (and some to David and to me). I try to warn the reader when I present something that I know many colleagues would dismiss as complete nonsense, but, again, there must be incidences in which I was not aware that such a warning was due, and I apologize for such omissions as well.

I enjoyed and was enriched by comments and references provided by many colleagues. Peter Wakker has been, as always, a fantastic source of knowledge and critique. Nicolas Vieille also made extremely detailed and insightful comments. I learned a lot from comments by Daniel Algom, Massimo Marinacci, and Teddy Seidenfeld on particular issues. The final version also benefited greatly from the detailed comments of Edi Karni, George Mailath, Marion Oury, and two anonymous reviewers. Doron Ravid and Arik Roginsky were of great help in the final stages of the preparation of the manuscript. I am very grateful to all these colleagues for their input.

PART I

INTUITIVE DEFINITIONS

SCOPE OF THIS BOOK

This book is about decision theory under uncertainty, namely, asking how do, and how should, people make decisions in situations of uncertainty. You probably already know the standard answer in economics, namely, that people do, and should, maximize expected utility. I don't think that this is a bad answer if we know what "utility" and "probability" mean.

The difficulty is that we often don't. Both concepts are problematic. We will discuss the notion of utility at various points, but these notes basically revolve around the meaning of probability. We ask, what is meant by saying "the probability of event A is p"? There are obviously many other ways to organize the material presented here, and, in particular, one can start with the meaning of utility. The present organization is but one way to relate the various topics to each other.

Naturally, the main question around which this book is organized has implications regarding its scope and content. There are important and interesting recent developments in decision under uncertainty that are not discussed here. In particular, there is relatively little discussion of nonexpected utility theory under risk, namely, with given probabilities, and almost no reference to models of choices from menus and to various models of behavioral economics. On the first topic (and, in particular, on cumulative prospect theory), the reader is referred to Wakker (2008), which also covers much of the classical theories covered here.

The first chapters are devoted to intuitive definitions of probabilities. We start with a few motivating examples and see how three intuitive definitions cope with these examples.

CHAPTER 1

Motivating Examples

Let us start with a concrete question such as what is the probability of another war in the Middle East erupting before December 31 of the current year? Of course, the focus should not be on this particular problem, but on the way we address it and, in fact, on its meaning. Similarly, I could ask you what is the probability of a stock market crash in the NY Stock Exchange during the next month. In both examples we have to define precisely what is meant by "war," or "stock market crash," so as to make the question well defined. Assume that we've done that. How would you approach the problems?

I believe that these are very complicated questions, not only because they have to do with complex processes, each involving many factors, but mostly because they are conceptually hard to deal with. To appreciate the difficulties, it may be useful to contrast this class of questions with three others. For concreteness, consider the following four questions, which, I will later argue, are in increasing order of conceptual difficulty:

1. I'm about to toss a coin. What is the probability of it coming up head?
2. I consider parking my car on the street tonight. What is the probability that it will be stolen overnight?
3. I am about to undergo a medical operation. What is the probability that I will survive it?
4. What is the probability of war in the Middle East this year?

It will prove useful to analyze these questions in light of the type of answers we can give them. From the very early days of probability theory (mid-seventeenth century), three ways of assigning probabilities to events can be documented. The first, sometimes called the "classical" approach, suggests that equal probabilities be assigned to all outcomes. The second, the "frequentist" approach, holds that the probability of an event should be the relative frequency with which it has been observed in the past. Finally, the "subjective" approach offers the mathematical machinery of probability theory as a way to model our vague beliefs and intuitions.

We will discuss these three methods in more detail. (In fact, the discussion of the subjective method will cover the entire classical theory of subjective expected utility maximization.) But before we do that, a word on free will may be in place.

CHAPTER 2

Free Will and Determinism

2.1 CAN FREE CHOICE BE PREDICTED?

In considering the four questions mentioned in Chapter 1, it is sometimes suggested that the fourth is conceptually more difficult than the others because it involves decisions of human beings, who have goals and desires, beliefs and ideas, and perhaps also free will. Can we hope to predict the behavior that results from all these? Will such prediction not be in conflict with the notion that individuals have free will?

These questions should bother anyone interested in the social sciences. If humans have free will, and if this means that their behavior cannot be predicted with any accuracy, we would have to declare social science an impossibility. The fact that we study economics probably indicates that we believe that some prediction is possible.[1] Indeed, the question of free will is usually not brought up in the context of the second question, namely, whether my car will be stolen. But cars are stolen by humans, and therefore any prediction regarding the car theft should also cope with the question of free will.

The fact is that there are many generalizations that are true of human beings and many predictions that can be made about them with a high degree of certainty. Whether individuals have free will or not, it is safe to predict that a $100 bill will not be lying on the sidewalk for 5 days in a row without being picked up by someone. Moreover, the individual who chooses to pick up the bill may well feel that she has free will in general, and even that she exercises it in this very act. This subjective experience of free will does not contradict our prediction.

By contrast, it may be very difficult to predict certain natural phenomena even if they do not involve the decision of any cognate entity to which free will can be ascribed. Combining the two, it appears that whether the behavior of a certain system can or cannot be predicted with confidence has little to do with the question of free will.

---

[1] This type of inference, from observed choices back to the beliefs that led to them, is what Part II of the book is about.

2.2 IS THE WORLD DETERMINISTIC?

A question that arises in the context of free will, but also in other contexts relating to probability and randomness, is whether the world we live in is deterministic, namely, one in which past events fully determine future ones. In the context of probability, the most popular version of determinism is causal or material determinism, which holds that knowledge of the laws of physics, coupled with exact knowledge of location and velocity of each particle, would suffice to fully determine the future. According to this view nothing is truly random, and probability can be used only when we do not have enough information or sufficient calculation capabilities.

This view is quite compelling in many situations. When I toss a coin, we all believe that an exact measurement of the angle at which my finger hits the coin, of the power exerted, and so forth could suffice for a precise calculation of the outcome of the toss. Indeed, if I let the coin simply slide from my finger down to the table, no one would accept the toss as "random," because it will be very easy to compute its outcome. Slightly more vigorous tosses, the claim goes, will differ from the languid slide only in degree, but not in kind.

However, it is clear that we can measure initial conditions only up to a certain accuracy. Even if we can exactly compute the outcome of a toss of a coin, it would be impossible to collect all the information needed to predict more complicated phenomena such as the exact impact of an earthquake or the result of a vote in Congress. This impossibility is not only a matter of practicality. Heisenberg's principle of uncertainty states that there are limits to the degree of accuracy with which mass and momentum can be simultaneously measured. Even within the scope of Newtonian physics, Chaos theory shows that deterministic systems can be sufficiently complex that all the information that can be gathered in reality will not suffice for complete prediction.[2]

One may model the world as deterministic, by introducing sufficiently many hidden variables (such as the world's future). But this model will be observationally equivalent to another model in which the world is nondeterministic. It follows that, as far as we will ever be able to know, the world is not deterministic.

2.3 IS FREE WILL OBSERVABLE?

Free will is a private phenomenon. I, for one, believe that I have free will, and I experience the exercise of free will whenever I make conscious decisions. I trust that all my readers also feel that they have free will. I can ask you to take a

---

[2] To be more concrete, even if we devoted all our resources to the production of measurement devices, the information gathered will be insufficient for perfect prediction. To complicate matters further, the measurement devices would be part of the system and would require to be measured themselves. (This brings to mind some of the discussions of Maxwell's demon, who can presumably decrease entropy of a system that does not contain itself.) That is, the impossibility of prediction that one can derive from Chaos theory goes a step beyond the commonsensical notion of "practicality."

few minutes, think whether you feel like turning the light on (or off), and then make a decision about it. You'd probably report a sensation of exercising free will and a feeling that you could have chosen differently. However, I do not have direct access to your sense of free will. I will not be able to distinguish between two individuals, one who feels that she has free will and another who only claims that he has, but who actually behaves in an automatic way without considering alternative courses of action. To put it bluntly, I know that I have free will, but whether anyone else has free will is a meaningless question.

This well-known observation is partly the reason that economists do not think that they should be interested in the phenomenon of free will. If it is un-observable, why should we care about it? If people make the same buying and selling decisions whether they do or do not have free will, who cares about the latter? Furthermore, one can argue that no scientific field should concern itself with the question of free will: observational equivalence implies that no amount of data, regarding economic behavior or otherwise, will ever suffice to deter-mine whether an individual has free will. Free will is a metaphysical concept.

However, the sensation of free will, the subjective experience that one can choose among different options or could have chosen otherwise, is observable. Admittedly, only my own sensation of free will is directly observable to me, and that of others, only by their report. But this is the case with many psychological phenomena. Let us therefore refine our discussion: when we mention "free will" here, we refer to *psychological free will*, namely, the sensation of choice among several possible alternatives. This phenomenon has to do with our definition of the decision matrix and is therefore relevant to our analysis of our own decisions.

2.4   THE PROBLEM OF FREE WILL

We have hopefully agreed by now that (i) free will does not preclude prediction and (ii) the world is not deterministic. It would appear that free will should not bother us: whether people experience this sensation or not, there are no deterministic theories with which it may conflict. And the metaphysical notion of "real" free will certainly cannot conflict with observations. We can therefore go about our business, providing predictions of people's choices, without taking a position on the freedom of their will, whether this freedom is metaphysical or psychological. I claim, however, that a problem persists.

Much of the philosophical discussion of free will through the ages focuses on its conflict with determinism – causal determinism, as discussed earlier, or other notions, such as theological determinism, namely, the claim that the Almighty has already determined the future or at least that some entity (such as Fate) knows the future. Some recent contributions, relying on modern science, accept the view that determinism is the main challenge for the existence of free will. Penrose (1997) argues that the uncertainty at the level of elementary particles (Heisenberg's principle) may suffice to evolve into uncertainty about people's decisions, thus salvaging the notion of free will. Searle (2004) claims that our understanding of neurobiology at present does not yet prove that the brain is deterministic and that, consequently, free will is an illusion, though he speculates that neurobiological research will get to this point.[3]

But to show the difficulty with free will one need not assume that *all* decisions are *predetermined*. It suffices that *one* decision be *known*. The logic is similar to suggesting a counterexample to a conjecture. The existence of one counterexample suffices. Similarly, if we can find one instance in which we have an undeniable sensation of free will on the one hand and practically certain knowledge of our choice on the other, we will have to admit that the sense of free will is illusory, at least in this example. In principle, one such example would suffice to put the notion of free will in doubt. In practice, I maintain that such examples abound.

Consider the following example: Sir Isaac Newton stands by a large window on the fourth floor. He contemplates the possibility of jumping out of the window. Should he jump, he considers two possibilities: he may hover in the air, enjoying the view, or crash to the ground. Being a rational decision maker, Newton contemplates the possibility of jumping and, given his knowledge of physics, concludes that crashing to the ground is a practical certainty. He now considers his own decision and decides not to jump. In so doing, he feels that he has made a decision and that he has exercised his free will. He could imagine choosing differently, and he decided not to.

Suppose that we are sitting with Sir Newton in his office throughout this process. Our limited knowledge of physics suffices for us to conclude, as does Newton, that a jump will result in a crash. With a lesser degree of certainty, but still quite confidently, we are willing to predict that Newton will not jump. We have seen many people next to many windows, and for the most part, they prefer to stay in their rooms. In short, we know Newton's choice with a high degree of certainty.[4]

But what about Sir Isaac Newton himself? Surely he knows himself at least as well as we know him. If we could conclude, based on our knowledge of human nature in general, that Newton will not jump, so can he. In fact, he is even in a privileged position to make predictions about himself.[5] Let us examine his reasoning process. A reasoned decision is supposed to take into account

---

[3] For a survey covering many other recent contributions, see Kane (2005).

[4] You may prefer to use the term "belief" in this context. The point is that this is a high degree of belief, which is probably as high as we can hope for in the social sciences and higher than our belief in, say, the weather forecast for the day after tomorrow. I do not think that the notion of free will can hinge on events that are possible but improbable, such as zero-probability events. One argument against a zero-probability event is aesthetic. It seems cheap. The other is more pragmatic: a zero-probability event will not be worth contemplating for even a negligible amount of time. The rational arguments given next can be restated when "knowledge" is replaced by "belief with very high probability."

[5] Some people have suicidal tendencies, but the majority do not. Our knowledge about Newton, based on statistics on a larger population, is less accurate than his own. Thus, for the majority of individuals it is true that they know that they are not suicidal with a higher degree of certainty than an outside observer would. Since we seek an example, we are justified in assuming that Newton is in this majority.

rules and regularities that are known to be quite accurate, to help us think about the consequences of our choices. We could imagine Newton drawing a decision tree and using all his knowledge to assign probabilities to the various branches in the tree, in particular, to cross out branches that he knows are practically impossible. This is how Newton concluded that, due to the gravitational force, he will not hover in the air should he jump. But, by the same logic, Newton can now cross out the branch "I jump" just as he previously crossed out the branch "I hover in the air" (conditional on jumping). By the time he finished the analysis there is no longer any decision to be made. Newton knows what his decision will be in the same sense that he knows what the outcomes of different decisions would be. When was a decision *taken* in this process? And how can Newton report an experience of free will if he cannot imagine a logically consistent world in which he chooses differently? How can we make sense of his claim "but I *could* have jumped"?

The paradoxical nature of free will stems from the co-occurrence of (i) the ability to imagine possible worlds that differ in terms of our choices and (ii) the fact that often our choices are practically known to us before we make them. Let me elaborate on these.

(i) Whatever free will is, it is closely related to the ability to conceive of different possible worlds, differing only in one's choice and its consequences. The ability to think of such different worlds, if not simultaneously then at least in the process of making a single decision, is essential to rational choice. And this ability is essential to, and maybe even a definition of, the sensation of free will. I feel that I exercise free will when I raise my arm, but not when my heart beats. The reason is that when consciously deciding to raise my arm, I can simultaneously imagine two worlds, one in which the arm is raised and the other in which it isn't. By contrast, I have never felt my heart stopping to beat, let alone decided to do so, and I cannot imagine a choice that would lead to this state of affairs. I therefore cannot argue that I exercised free will in letting my heart beat.

To see this point more clearly, suppose that you program a robot that will automatically make all the choices I make. Next, you allow the robot to speak and you want it to utter the statement "I hereby exercise free will" at the right moments, say, when I make such statements. Let us be slightly more demanding and require that the robot print out reasonable justifications for its choices. To this end, you will have to endow the robot with some reasoning ability and with the ability to distinguish between its own acts and the environment in which it lives. When facing an act, the robot will have to play around with some propositions of the form "If I do a, then the outcome will be x" and "conclude" that it prefers act a to act b. The robot will have to print several different such conditional statements for us to agree that it has exercised free will.

(ii) We typically know many things about ourselves. We know decisions that we have made, and we often have pretty good guesses about certain decisions that we are going to make. I know that I'm going to prefer coffee to tea. I know that I prefer not jumping out of the window to jumping. As a rational decision maker, I gather data and make inferences. I cannot help observe regularities around me, and my own decisions in the past are included in the environment I study. Moreover, it is essential for rational choice that I learn things about myself. I need to know my "technical" capabilities, such as how fast I can run and how good my eyesight is. It will also be useful to know something about my mental capacities, such as how good my memory is and to what extent I follow my new year's resolutions. For this last purpose, I need to know my own choices in circumstances in which I felt that I was exercising free will. Finally, learning regularities about myself can be useful in predicting other people's behavior.

Let us consider the robot again. Will it know its own choices? Since you are programming it, you may try to avoid such knowledge. It is possible to restrict the inferences made by the robot to external events and to abort any calculation that refers to the robot's own choices. This will be somewhat artificial. Moreover, it will be inefficient, because the robot will not be able to use its own past decisions as guidance. Every time it will be offered coffee or tea it will have to make a calculation afresh. But the main difficulty with such a robot will be that it will not be as rational as I am. There will be some obvious inferences that it will fail to draw. Our own reasoning engines do not stop when it comes to our own choices in the past. We do learn about ourselves, and someone who fails to see obvious regularities in her own behavior is typically viewed as irrational.

We conclude that rationality makes two fundamental demands: first, we have to consider possible worlds that differ in terms of our choices. Second, we have to observe obvious regularities about ourselves, just like about any other relevant phenomenon. Taken together, we obtain the contradiction: we often need to consider as possible worlds that we know are impossible. Thus, the sensation of free will depends on our ability to suspend knowledge that we have about ourselves. Importantly, both the consideration of multiple possible worlds and the knowledge that some of them are impossible are dictated by rationality.

2.5   A RATIONAL ILLUSION

At the risk of belaboring obvious points, let me emphasize the following: not every decision will be known to the decision maker or to an outside observer before it has been taken. As long as the decision maker does not know what her choice is going to be, her sense of free will does not require that she suspend any knowledge she might have. In such a case the problem mentioned previously does not exist.

For example, assume that I have to choose between two quantities of a desirable good. We may think of tens of thousands of dollars or of years left to live – the point is that I truly prefer more to less. Consider now the following three choices:

(i) $\sqrt{17}$ or $(27/13)^2$
(ii) 2^3 or 3^2
(iii) 0 or 1.

In case (i) there is no difficulty. Reading the problem, it is not obvious to me which of the two numbers is larger. I therefore have to compute the outcome of both of my choices and then find out which one I prefer. An outside observer may have completed the calculation earlier and may already know what my choice will be. But I do not, and therefore my sense of free will does not contradict any knowledge I have at the time of starting my deliberation.

By contrast, case (iii) is one in which I know, more or less as soon as I read the problem, what my choice will be. I don't need a lengthy computation to figure out the meaning of 0 and 1. This is akin to Newton's problem, who stands by the window and has to decide whether to jump out or not. (The analogy is stronger if the numbers designate years one has to live, and 0 describes immediate death.) In both cases one needs to understand the two options and what they entail, but this understanding is quite trivial. The calculation that $1 > 0$ is about as immediate as the realization that jumping out of the window would result in death.

Case (ii) is brought as an intermediate case, suggesting that we cannot think of cases (i) and (iii) as qualitatively different. There is a range of difficulty levels, and a reasonable account of rational choice should describe a process that applies in all three cases. Thus, in all three cases we would like to assume that the decision maker makes a tentative assumption that she takes one option and thinks about the outcome. Then she does the same for the other option(s) and then she can make a reasoned decision. In case (i) there is no conflict with knowledge of her own choices, whereas in case (iii) there is. In cases such as (i) the decision maker may believe that she has free will, but in cases such as (iii) she has to admit that this was an illusion.

Efficiency of decision making might suggest that we need not compute our optimal choice anew every time. We may develop habits and rules that simplify our lives. It would therefore be tempting to categorize all decisions into two classes – the habitual decisions, such as in case (iii), in which there is no freedom of choice, but also no subjective sensation of free will; and the reasoned decisions, such as case (i), in which there is freedom of choice, but no a priori knowledge of what this choice is about to be. If such a dichotomy were possible, free will would not be such a pervasive problem: it would never clash with knowledge of one's own choice.

This, however, is not the case. Moreover, this could not be the case for rational individuals. First, however habitual a choice is, a rational individual should be able to ask herself whether she indeed wishes to stick to her habit. As soon as the question is posed, the individual will have to admit that she does know her choice, yet that she has a sensation of free will. Second, there will invariably be intermediate cases that are not regular enough to require no thought, yet sufficiently regular for the individual to know her own choice.

Rationality requires that we gather information and learn about the environment, our selves and our future selves included. Thus, we cannot escape knowledge of certain choices of ours. But rationality also requires that we be able to question these choices from time to time, and this means suspending our knowledge of our own choices. To conclude, free will is an illusion that is inherent to rationality.

2.6   FREE WILL AND THE DECISION MATRIX

The basic formal model of decision under uncertainty is the decision matrix – a matrix in which rows designate acts; columns, states of the world; and entries, outcomes. The matrix is interpreted as listing all possible acts (or plans, strategies, or courses of action) that the decision maker can choose among, all possible states of the world, namely, circumstances that are not up to the decision maker to choose, and the outcomes that would result from every possible pair of act and state.

The distinction between the acts, over which the decision maker has control, and states, over which she hasn't, is one of the pillars of rational choice. Many mistakes in everyday life have to do with an inappropriate distinction between acts and states. For instance, if the decision maker believes that she can affect that which she cannot, we would say that she engages in wishful thinking. If a state of affairs can indeed be affected by the decision maker, it is not a "state of the world" in the sense of decision theory. Rather, it is a result of the decision maker's act and the "pure" state of the world.

On the other hand, it will be equally irrational for a decision maker to assume that she cannot choose certain acts that are, in fact, available to her, as would be the case if she knows her decision before thinking about it. Thus, the decision matrix should have acts, over which the decision maker has control but not beliefs, and states over which she has beliefs but not control.

It is relatively simple to write down the states of the world in such a way that one has no control over them: one starts out the acts one can choose from and then writes down the states of the world as Nature's strategy in a game. Such a strategy specifies Nature's reaction to the decision maker's choices, and it can be thought of as a function whose argument is the choice. As such, the decision maker chooses the act, which is the argument of the function, but cannot affect the choice of the function itself, namely, the state of the world (see the discussion in Section 11.1).

A guarantee that the decision maker has no knowledge (or belief) about the acts is more complicated and cannot be obtained simply by an appropriate definition of acts or states. Here what is required is the mental ability to suspend one's knowledge about one's own decision, that is, the ability to believe in the illusion of free will. Failing to do so will result in one's inability to reconsider one's choices.

The classical notion of a decision matrix relies on the distinction between acts and states. This distinction may bring to mind the "Serenity Prayer" of the American pastor Reinhold Niebuhr, which reads, "God, give us grace to accept with serenity the things that cannot be changed, courage to change the things that should be changed, and the wisdom to distinguish the one from the other" (see Niebuhr, 1976). (According to his widow, the prayer was written in 1943.) The things we cannot change are the states of the world. We should accept them, namely, cope with the fact that they are possible and estimate their likelihood irrespective of how desirable they are. The things we can change are our acts. We should have the courage to change our choices, which requires not taking as given knowledge that we have about ourselves from the past. And having the wisdom to distinguish between acts and states is one of the main challenges in approaching any decision problem.

CHAPTER 3

The Principle of Indifference

The principle of indifference, also known as the principle of insufficient reason, is attributed to Jacob Bernoulli, and sometimes to Laplace. Simply stated, it suggests that if there are n possible outcomes and there is no reason to view one as more likely than another, then each should be assigned a probability of $1/n$. Quite appropriate for games of chance, in which dice are rolled or cards shuffled, the principle has also been referred to as the "classical" approach to probability assignments.[1]

However, this principle has to be used with great care. Early examples include the event "two consecutive tosses of a coin will come up head." If we know nothing about the coin, one may try to apply the principle and conclude that this event has probability 50%, but then the same argument would apply to any two outcomes of the two tosses. However, this type of counterexample can be ruled out by referring to the structure of the problem and arguing that there is sufficient reason to find three outcomes more likely than one.[2]

More serious problems arise when we apply the principle to everyday problems, which are often not endowed with sufficient symmetries. For instance, assume that I ask you what is the probability that it will rain tomorrow. If you think of the two outcomes, "rain" and "no rain," you come up with the probability of $1/2$. But if the possibilities are "rain," "snow," and "no precipitation," the probability drops to $1/3$. Typically, one can partition the state space in a multitude of ways, resulting in the principle of indifference assigning practically any desired probability to the event in question.

3.1 WILL A CANONICAL SPACE HELP?

3.1.1 The Canonical State Space

A possible attempt to avoid the arbitrariness in the choice of the events involves a list of "all" possible states of the world. This is not a completely foolish

---

[1] Where "classical" probably means "as in the early letters of Pascal and Fermat."

[2] See Arrow (1951), who quotes Keynes, attempting to deal with difficulties raised by von Kries as early as 1886.

idea. One can imagine all the finite sentences in English that make sense as propositions about the world. A state of the world may be defined as a truth function, namely, a consistent assignment of the values 0 (false) and 1 (true) to these propositions. The logically consistent assignments are some subset of $\{0, 1\}^{\mathbb{N}}$, and thus one gets no more than (the cardinality of) a continuum of states of the world. The resulting state space can be viewed as "canonical." One can make the plausible assumptions that we only care about states we can comprehend and that our comprehension is limited to what can be described by sentences in English. Under these assumptions, the state space generated by providing truth values to all meaningful propositions can describe all that matters to us. By the very definition of these states we have not ruled out any possibilities (apart from those we anyway cannot comprehend).

The canonical state space, comprising sequences of the binary digits 0 and 1, can almost be identified with the points in [0, 1], whose binary expansions are also sequences of 0s and 1s. This embedding is not one to one because the binary rational numbers have more than one representation. For instance, $0.01111\ldots = 0.1000\ldots = 1/2$. To clean up the analogy, one may enrich [0, 1] by distinguishing between pairs of representations of the binary rationals, map states into the Cantor set (replacing 1s by 2s and viewing the result as a ternary expansion of a number in [0, 1]), or just shrug one's shoulders in the face of countably many glitches.

In any event, the formal resemblance of the canonical state space to the interval [0, 1] invites a continuous version of the principle of indifference, which would assign a uniform prior to the interval [0, 1]. But this assumption will not be innocuous (as is, allegedly, the definition of the state space itself). It will not be justified either. At least two technical points are well known in this context.

3.1.2   Difficulties with a Uniform Prior on [0, 1]

First, if we have a random variable X on [0, 1] and we know nothing about it, we cannot assume that it has a uniform distribution on [0, 1] and pretend that we made a natural choice. Indeed, if X takes values in [0, 1], so does $Y = X^2$.[3] Clearly, X and Y are in a one-to-one relationship. If we know nothing about X, we know nothing about Y as well. But then, if we are justified in assuming $X \sim U(0, 1)$, we are equally justified in assuming $Y \sim U(0, 1)$, which is incompatible with $X \sim U(0, 1)$. In fact, for each $\alpha > 0$, one may consider $Z_\alpha = X^\alpha$, and again, any two variables Z_α and Z_β are in a one-to-one relationship. Hence, we know nothing about each of them. But at most one of them can have a uniform distribution. Selecting such a distribution for one such

---

[3] I remember encountering this example in DeGroot (1975), which is a textbook. I'm unaware of the historical origins of this particular example. The first example of this nature is probably Bertrand's paradox, dating back to 1888 (Bertrand, 1907). It involves the selection of a chord in a circle, which can be done in three different ways, all appearing to be straightforward applications of the uniform distribution, but all leading to different answers.

variable appears ad hoc, a far cry from a reasoned way of assigning probabilities to events.

Second, the richness of the canonical state space $\{0, 1\}^{\mathbb{N}}$ is not exhausted by different densities on $[0, 1]$. Consider a sequence of i.i.d (independently and identically distributed) tosses of a coin with parameter p. That is, a sequence of i.i.d. random variables X_i, each assuming the value 1 with probability p, and the value 0, with probability $(1 - p)$. Under this assumption, for every $p \in (0, 1)$, the probability of each particular state (sequence of tosses) is 0. Hence the countably many binary rationals can be ignored, and we can identify the canonical space with $[0, 1]$. The process defined by the sequence of tosses induces a measure on (the Borel σ-algebra on) $[0, 1]$. If $p = .5$, the resulting measure is Lebesgue's measure λ: the interval $[0, 0.5)$ corresponds to the event $X_1 = 0$, and it has a probability of $0.5 = \lambda ([0, 0.5))$. The interval $[0.25, 0.5)$ corresponds to $(X_1 = 0, X_2 = 1)$, and it has a probability of $0.25 = \lambda ([0.25, 0.5))$, and so forth.

Consider now the same process, only this time with $p = .3$. Now we will have another probability $\lambda_{.3}$, which satisfies $\lambda_{.3} ([0, 0.5)) = 0.7$, $\lambda_{.3}([0.25, 0.5)) = .21$, and so forth. The measure $\lambda_{.3}$ evidently differs from λ. But more than that can be said: due to the law of large numbers, we know that $\lambda_{.3}$ is concentrated on sequences that have a limit frequency of 0.3. That is, if we define

$$A_p = \left\{ \sum_i \frac{x_i}{2^i} \mid x_i \in \{0, 1\}, \quad \frac{1}{n} \sum_i^n x_i \xrightarrow[n \to \infty]{} p \right\},$$

we obtain, for every p, $\lambda_p(A_p) = 1$, because, in the process governed by p, there is probability 1 that there will be a limit frequency of 1s in the sequence and that this limit frequency will be p. At the same time, we have $A_p \cap A_q = \varnothing$ for $p \neq q$. Hence we obtain a continuum of pairwise disjoint sets, $\{A_p\}_p$, and a continuum of corresponding measures, $\{\lambda_p\}_p$, and it is not obvious which one of them has a claim to the title "the natural probability on $[0, 1]$." What complicates our life further is the recognition that the choice among the measures $\{\lambda_p\}_p$ is irreversible: once we chose one of them, say, λ_p, to be our prior probability, no amount of evidence will ever hint that we might have made the wrong choice and that some q would have been more appropriate than p. Since, for $p \neq q$, $\lambda_p(A_q) = 0$, any Bayesian update of λ_p will leave us with a zero posterior probability for the event A_q, which should have been the certain event were q the appropriate value of the parameter.

3.1.3   Conclusion

It appears that the principle of indifference allows for a large degree of arbitrariness, and probability assignments based on it will be fundamentally ad hoc. Whereas the arbitrariness is evident with a finite state space, it is sometimes believed that a continuous model, either because it reflects a canonical state space, or due to the richness of the real line, may minimize this arbitrariness and suggest a uniform distribution as a natural candidate for beliefs. This, however, is not the case. The real line conceals in its depths continua of pairwise incompatible conjectures, each of which may present itself as a natural choice and challenge the uniform distribution's claim to primacy.

3.2   WHAT'S SPECIAL ABOUT THE COIN?

The principle of indifference cannot be applied in general. It appears very problematic as soon as we go beyond the first motivating question (tossing a coin) to the others (insurance, medical operation, or war). Thus, even if we could justify it in the case of the coin toss, it will not be terribly relevant to most economic problems. And in problems such as the tossing of a coin, the principle can be replaced by empirical frequencies. It is therefore tempting to declare that it makes no sense, and leave it at that.

And yet, many of us would feel that in the case of the coin, even if the principle of indifference is not completely compelling, it is not as nonsensical as in the case of the war. Someone who assigns a probability of 50% to war erupting simply because there are two possibilities, "war" and "no war," will be the butt of many jokes. Someone who assigns probability 50% to an unknown coin coming up head will appear reasonable. Why?

I have no satisfactory answers to this question. Here are two attempts.

3.2.1   Symmetry

The coin presents us with a symmetric problem. Head and tail appear to be symmetric. Given this symmetry, it seems natural to assign probabilities that are also symmetric, namely, equal.

But what is "symmetry"? If we take a broad definition, namely, that things look very similar after the application of some transformation, we may be too permissive. Consider the war example again. Admittedly, for most of us "war" and "no war" are not symmetric, because there are many things we know about each such outcome that have no counterpart with the other. But let us assume that a Martian comes down to Earth and is asked about the probability of war. The Martian knows nothing about what war entails, what it takes to wage a war, and so on. Rather, for the Martian "war" is some proposition p, while "no war," its negation $\neg p$. In a logical universe consisting only of $\{p, \neg p\}$, the two propositions are symmetric. The operator of negation maps p to $\neg p$ and vice versa. If this is all the Martian has to rely on, will he be justified in assigning p the probability 50%?

Some may argue that this is indeed a reasonable assignment of probabilities, at least as long as no additional information is provided. This approach would also suggest that, if we don't know what "cloint" and "biseb" mean, we should believe that a randomly selected cloint is a biseb with probability 50%, due to the symmetry between bisebs and non-bisebs. Another approach would be to deny the validity of this assignment of probabilities, arguing that there is not enough symmetry in the war or in the biseb examples to warrant the application of the principle of indifference.

Is there more symmetry in the coin example than in the war example? Perhaps. A coin tossed in the air undergoes a rotation that is an element in a group of functions, of which the rotation by 180° has a unique role of being its own inverse (but not the identity). It is possible that the additional structure in the coin example may help explain why it is intuitively considered to be sufficiently symmetric for the principle of indifference to apply.

3.2.2   Smooth Beliefs

Another explanation goes back to Poincaré (see a discussion and additional citations in Machina, 2004). Consider a roulette wheel. The wheel is spun, and the ball bounces about and lands on a particular number. What is the probability that the number will be odd?

Assume that the roulette wheel is fair and that it contains only the numbers 1–36. In this case, the probability of an odd number should be 50% by definition. Next, suppose that the wheel isn't necessarily fair. Perhaps the set of numbers 11–20 has a much higher probability than either the set 1–10 or the set 21–30. Still, the splitting of the range to consecutive red–black numbers implies that each color gets a fair share of each region of the roulette. More formally, if you believe that the process is governed by a density with a bounded derivative, and you keep splitting the wheel into smaller and smaller holes, the probability of the odd-numbered holes will converge to 50%. This can also guarantee bets that have almost objective probabilities. Two agents might have very different subjective probabilities, but they may still agree that with a fine enough partition, the probability of "red" is indeed 50%. For the two agents to agree on this fact, their beliefs should be smooth with respect to the same underlying measure, which is much less demanding than to assume that they would have the same beliefs.

The coin is similar to the roulette wheel in that in both cases it is too complicated to calculate the result of the experiment (the toss or the spin). Indeed, if I take a coin out of my pocket, bet against you that if lands head up, and then simply put it down on the table, head up, you'd argue that I was cheating. If I flip it carefully exactly once, I'd still be cheating. The toss is considered fair only if the coin appears to be making sufficiently many rotations in the air. You will win the bet if the final number of rotations is odd (even), and I, if it is even (odd). With a "smooth enough" distribution function over the number of rotations, and if the mass of the function is on large numbers of rotations, we can assume that the overall probability of head, as well as of tail, is 50%.

Similar arguments seem to apply to shuffling a deck of cards, to sampling the time from one's computer, and so on. In all of these examples, the randomizing device is supposed to be sufficiently complex so it cannot be predicted with great accuracy, and the outcome space can be viewed as subdivided into small segments, which are lumped together to obtain the events whose probabilities are claimed to be equal. Indeed, in all of these examples the randomization device would not appear fair if the division is not fine enough, as in the case of betting on a deck of cards that is barely shuffled, or on the first digit of the hour. It is not entirely obvious that there are convincing examples of the principle of indifference that are not of this class.

CHAPTER 4

Relative Frequencies

4.1 THE LAW OF LARGE NUMBERS

The principle of indifference can, at best, help us in assigning probabilities only in our first example. We agree that it is not going to be very reasonable to say, in Example (2) in Chapter 1, that the probability of the car being stolen is 50%, because either it is or it isn't stolen. Rather, one would like to resort to experience and say that the fact that most cars that are parked on the street overnight are not stolen implies that we have to assign a probability lower than 50% to theft. Moreover, the percentage of experiments in which a car was indeed stolen (where an "experiment" is defined by a car–date pair) should be the definition of the probability of theft.

This definition is related to the law of large numbers, dating back to Jacob Bernoulli (1713), and stating that when we observe i.i.d (independently and identically distributed) random variables, X_i, their average, $\bar{X} = \frac{1}{n} \sum_i X_i$, converges to their expectation.[1] In order to use the law for the estimation of probabilities, one considers a sequence of "experiments," or observations, say, cars that may or may not be stolen. For each such experiment we may define an indicator (Bernoulli) random variable X_i, which assumes the value 1 if the event has occurred and the value 0 if it hasn't. Assuming that the random variables are i.i.d. implies that we think of the experiments as repeated "under the same conditions": for each of them there is the same probability of success, regardless of the outcome of past experiments.[2] Applying the law(s) of large numbers to such a sequence of i.i.d. indicator variables, one finds that the relative frequency of occurrence of the event in question (which equals the average of the variables) converges to the probability of the event (which equals the expectation).

---

[1] I assume that readers have seen precise formulations of some laws of large numbers. See, for instance, Feller (2005) and Halmos (1950).

[2] If by "the same conditions" we also mean the same *initial* conditions, independence of the events follows. If, to the contrary, past realizations were to affect conditional probabilities of future ones, one may argue that the experiments were not done under the same conditions.

The laws of large numbers can therefore be used to estimate probabilities: if an experiment is repeated under the same conditions, and we observe that for a large n, the relative frequency $\bar{X}$ equals $\hat{p} \in [0, 1]$, this number $\hat{p}$ may be a good estimate of the probability p of the events in question (assumed to be identical across experiments). Moreover, statistics offers us ways to quantify the proximity between the observed empirical frequency $\hat{p}$ and the true, unknown expectation. Relying on the central limit theorem, which allows us to approximate the distribution of $\bar{X}$, the statistical machinery can tell us how close we are to the true probability for various degrees of confidence.

Observe, however, that this procedure of estimating probabilities cannot serve as a definition of the concept of probability to begin with. The law of large numbers relies on the notion of probability in several ways. First, it assumes that every X_i has a certain probability p of assuming the value 1. Second, the law assumes that the variables are independent, a term that is defined in a probabilistic setup. Third, the law is stated in terms of probabilities (guarantees a high probability of being close to the expectation, or converging to it with probability 1). If we are not sure what is meant by "the probability of an event," none of these claims has a clear meaning.

But the law of large numbers can be turned on its head and be used to inspire a definition of probability. This is, in fact, the most intuitive definition of probability. If you say that the probability that your car is stolen is 1%, and you're asked to explain the meaning of this statement to a child, you'd probably say, "out of 100 identical cars, one will be stolen," or if you're more careful, "if I had 10,000 such cars, I'd expect that about 100 of them will be stolen."

This is often referred to as the "frequentist" approach to defining probabilities: when we say that an event A has probability p, what we mean to say is that if you were to consider a repeated experiment in which A may or may not occur, the relative frequency of occurrence would be approaching p as the number of repetition tends to infinity.

4.2 THE PROBLEM OF INDUCTION

4.2.1 Hume's Critique

The notion that empirical frequencies in the past will tell us what probabilities for future events are might strike one as odd. How do we know that the same "probabilities" that can represent the past also apply to future events? Suppose, for example, that a coin is tossed infinitely many times and that during the first 1,000,000 tosses it appears to behave completely randomly, but thereafter it comes up head in each and every toss. Any statistical procedure that we may use over the first million observations will not warn us that the coin changes its behavior later on. Can we trust past relative frequencies, then?

The bad news is that we cannot. The good news is that this is an old problem, common not only to all sciences, but to everyday human reasoning. David Hume famously argued that induction has no logical basis. In Hume (1748, section IV) he writes,

> The contrary of every matter of fact is still possible; because it can never imply a contradiction, and is conceived by the mind with the same facility and distinctness, as if ever so conformable to reality. *That the sun will not rise to-morrow* is no less intelligible a proposition, and implies no more contradiction than the affirmation, *that it will rise*. We should in vain, therefore, attempt to demonstrate its falsehood.

Every scientific field attempts to make generalizations and to predict the future based on the past. As such, it is engaging in inductive reasoning.[3,4] Similarly, when I sit down on a chair, trusting that it will not break under the weight of my body, I use inductive reasoning, even if I tested the chair just a minute before sitting down. There is therefore some consolation in the fact that in performing inductive reasoning despite its apparent arbitrariness, we are not alone. And, more importantly, it is hard to imagine any scientific work, or even everyday existence, without some form of induction.[5]

4.2.2   Goodman's Grue-Bleen Paradox

One could hope that in the two and a half centuries since Hume, some progress would be made and that the problem of induction would be better understood. This did not happen. Quine (1969a) writes,

> I do not see that we are further along today than where Hume left us. The Humean predicament is the human predicament.

Worse still, the heightened sensitivity to language typical of twentieth-century analytical philosophy produced Goodman's "grue-bleen" paradox (Goodman, 1954), which showed that the legitimacy of inductive reasoning is even shakier than we used to think. The paradox goes as follows.

Assume that a scientist wishes to test the theory that emeralds are green, contrasted with the theory that they are blue. Testing one emerald after the other, she concludes that emeralds are indeed green.

Next assume that another scientist comes along and wants to test whether emeralds are grue as opposed to bleen. "Grue" emeralds are emeralds that appear to our eyes green if tested until time T, but appear blue if they are tested

---

[3] The notion of prediction of the future can also construed subjectively, relative to one's state of knowledge. With this interpretation, even historians may engage in prediction. Assume, for example, that new letters of Napoleon are found, and historians are asked to speculate about their content. Should they agree to do so, they would be using inductive reasoning again.

[4] While mathematics is purely deductive, the work of the mathematician involves inductive reasoning as well. As long as a mathematical problem is not solved, and it is a source of subjective uncertainty to mathematicians, they are likely to search for conjectures and attempt proof techniques based, to some degree, on their past experience.

[5] David Schmeidler often quotes Kenneth Arrow, who said once in a seminar something along the lines of, "Now here we have a serious problem that we have to face. Let's face it. And now let's move on." In essence, that's all we can say in face of Hume's critique.

after time T. "Bleen" emeralds are defined symmetrically. Choose a time T in the future and observe that the scientist will find all emeralds to be grue. She will therefore conclude that after time T, all new emeralds to be tested, which will most likely be grue as those tested up to T, will appear blue to our eyes.

Testing the hypotheses that emeralds are green versus blue seems perfectly reasonable. Testing for grueness versus bleenness appears weird at best. Yet, how can we explain our different reactions? The two procedures seem to be following the same logical structure. They both appear to be what the scientific method suggests. Why do we accept one and reject the other?

A common reaction is to say that if emeralds are tested and found green, there is no reason to suppose that, all of the sudden, new emeralds will start appearing blue. But one may claim, by the same token, that after all tested emeralds appeared grue, there is no reason for new emeralds to switch, at time T, and become bleen. Our common sense suggests that "green" and "blue" are simple predicates, whereas "grue" and "bleen" are complex predicates. But this is true only if one assumes "green" and "blue" as primitives of the language and defines "grue" and "bleen" in terms of "green" and "blue." If one were to start out with "grue" and "bleen" as the primitive terms, "green" and "blue" would appear to be the complex terms.[6]

Thus, Goodman's paradox has shown that not only does inductive reasoning lack logical foundations, it is not even clear what is meant by this process. Even if we are willing to accept the claim that "The thing that hath been, it is that which shall be," it is not clear what future corresponds to a given past as its "natural" continuation.

Goodman's green-blue paradox is taken by many to be a philosophical puzzle that has little implications for working scientists. Indeed, if we were interested only in coins tossed and dice rolled, we could probably assume it away. However, when we come to questions such as the probability of war, it is not quite obvious how we should generalize past experiences. Since events such as wars never repeat themselves in exactly the same way, there will often be more than one natural way to encode past events.

Having said that, I have recently come to the conclusion that Goodman's paradox is an artifact of a very particular choice of language. It will be simpler to explain this, however, after we discuss complexity a bit more formally.

4.2.3 Kolmogorov Complexity and Its Dependence of Language

A possible justification of the process of induction is the preference for simplicity. When several theories are just as accurate at explaining past observations and just as general in terms of the scope of predictions they can generate, preference for the simplest theory has been promoted both normatively and descriptively. As a normative argument, namely, that we should prefer simpler theories to more complex ones, the claim is attributed to William of Occam

---

[6] See also Sober (1975).

(see Russell, 1946). As a descriptive argument, that is, claiming that this is how people tend to select theories, it dates back to Wittgenstein's tractatus at the latest. He writes, "The procedure of induction consists in accepting as true the *simplest* law that can be reconciled with our experiences" (Wittgenstein, 1922, 6.363). The basic argument would be that it is simpler to assume that the world will continue to behave as it has in the past, and thus we are justified in believing, for example, that the sun will rise tomorrow. While we do not know that the sun will rise, we can at least explain why, of all the theories that conform to past observations, we chose one that predicts that the sun will rise tomorrow as well.

One important lesson of Goodman's grue-bleen paradox is that our notion of simplicity depends on our language. This lesson has also emerged in a different literature, discussing Kolmogorov's complexity. Kolmogorov was trying to define "randomness." Assume that you observe a finite sequence of binary digits, 0 and 1. When will you say that the sequence is random? Surely, if you see 0000..., you will assume that you observe a constant phenomenon, roughly the opposite of randomness. If you were to observe 010101..., you would admit that you are not observing the realization of a constant process, but you will not think of it as random. In fact, such a process has a simple pattern, and it may be described by a finite automaton.[7] Even when you consider sequences that cannot be generated by a finite automaton, you may feel that they are not random, as in the case of 0100110001110000111l.... What would be a general definition of "not random" or of "exhibiting a pattern"?

The measure known as *Kolmogorov's complexity* (see Kolmogorov, 1963, 1965, Chaitin, 1966) is the following: given the finite sequence, consider all Turing machines that can generate it.[8] There will always be such machines, and, at worst, one can think of the rather silly machine that goes from one state to the next, where each state writes down the appropriate digit and moves on to the next state. Now select one of the "smallest" machines that can generate the sequence: a machine with a minimal number of states or a machine whose description (also as a sequence of binary digits) is the shortest. If the smallest machine is rather small, relative to the original sequence, we can say that we found a simple pattern in the sequence and that it is therefore not random. If, by contrast, the smallest machine is long – say, almost as long as the sequence itself – we will have to admit that no pattern was found, and this could serve as a definition of randomness.

The reason that Kolmogorov's definition uses the concept of a Turing machine is that this is considered to be the formal definition of an "algorithm," that

---

[7] A finite automaton has finitely many states, a transition function between them, which determines the next state given an input character, and a behavior function, as, in our case, the decision to write 0 or 1. For formal definitions of finite automata, Turing machines, and other computational models, see, for instance, Aho *et al.* (1974).

[8] A formal definition of a Turing machine is too cumbersome to be included here. It can be thought of as an automaton with finitely many states that is also equipped with an infinite tape on which it can write and from which it can read.

is, a well-defined sequence of instructions.[9] Turing machines are known to be equivalent, in terms of the algorithms they can describe, to several other computational models, including modern computer languages (provided that the computer can store unbounded numbers). For the purposes of the present discussion, one may replace the notion of a Turing machine by, say, the computer language PASCAL. It is easy to imagine short PASCAL programs that can describe (i.e., produce) the sequences $0000\ldots, 010101\ldots, 010011000111\ldots$, even if we were to continue these sequences for quite a while and make them very long. The fact that the PASCAL program remains short relative to the sequence it generates captures the nonrandomness in the sequence. Importantly, by using PASCAL programs (or Turing machines), we are not restricting our attention to a particular type of patterns – say, cyclical ones. Any pattern that can be described algorithmically is captured by the notion of a program. The pattern $0110101000101000101000\ldots$, having 1 in entry i if and only if i is a prime number, will also be described by a short program no matter how far we extend the sequence.

Kolmogorov's complexity can be applied to the philosophy of science, as suggested by Solomonoff (1964). Coupling the notion that people prefer simple theories with Kolmogorov's measure, one obtains a model of theory-selection, predicting which theory people will prefer given a certain body of evidence. It can also be used to understand everyday phrases such as "understanding a poem": understanding a work of art, similarly to understanding data, implies being able to generate most of it (or at least its important aspects) by a concise algorithm.

The notion of Kolmogorov's complexity highlights the role of language in measuring complexity. This is one advantage of formal modeling – it imposes a certain discipline that brings to light potentially subtle points. A formal model that describes how complexity is measured forces one to realize that the computer language one uses will factor into the definition. The simplest theory, when described as a Turing machine (with states, a transition function, and so on), need not be the simplest theory when described as a PASCAL program. When trying to fit numerical data, the simplest theory stated in the language of polynomials may not be the simplest when stated in the language of trigonometric functions. Moreover, the computer model also explains the role of definitions. When a certain concept is used often, it is efficient to define it using a new word, just as a programmer may decide to define a sequence of instructions as a procedure in the program.

At the same time, Kolmogorov's complexity may not always be an intuitive measure of complexity. A purist definition of the complexity of a theory would count each and every bit needed to describe it, so that all constants used in the theory will be spelled out in binary expansions and the digits used to describe

---

[9] This definition is known as Church's thesis. It is not a formal mathematical conjecture, because an "algorithm" is not a formal entity. In fact, in accordance with Church's thesis, an algorithm is defined as a Turing machine, or as an equivalent computational model.

them will be counted as part of the theory's complexity. One may find that theory A, that is,

$$y = 1.3096203x,$$

is as complex as theory B, stating that "if the integer value of x is prime, then $y = 2x$; otherwise, if the integer value of x is divisible by 7, then $y = x$, and otherwise $-y = -x$." It may be counterintuitive that bits that are used to describe the constant 1.3096203 in theory A have the same complexity cost as the bits describing the arcane logic of theory B. A tempting alternative is to count only the bits that describe a program's "logic," and allow any arithmetic operations on registers that contain numbers, regardless of the size of the numbers. But this leaves open the possibility that large numbers will be used to encode instructions of the program, thus "concealing" some of its complexity.

Let us conclude with a hopeful comment. The general claim that simplicity judgments depend on language is qualified by the observation that languages with the same expressive power have compilers translating from one to the other. Specifically, for two languages l and l', let $C_{l,l'}$ be a program, written in l', that accepts as input a program written in l and generates as output an equivalent program written in l'. Let $c_{l,l'}$ be the length of the minimal description of such a compiler $C_{l,l'}$. It follows that if the minimal length of a program (representing a theory) A in l is m, the minimal representation of A in l' cannot exceed $m + c_{l,l'}$. Hence, for very two languages l and l', there exists a constant $c = \max(c_{l,l'}, c_{l',l})$ such that for every theory A, the complexity of A as measured relative to l and the complexity of A as measured relative to l' cannot differ by more than c.

The order of quantifiers is of importance here: given two theories A and B, one can always come up with a language l, in which one theory is simpler than the other. On the other hand, given any two languages l and l', one finds that if theory A is sufficiently simpler than theory B in one language, A has to be simpler than B also in the other language.

4.2.4   Grue-Bleen Again

A formal analysis of Goodman's paradox may show that there is something artificial in Goodman's argument. Basically, in order to make Goodman's claim, one needs to use a language that does not allow direct reference to specific values, but only to functions. Here is one possible account.

Denote time periods by $\mathbb{N} = \{1, 2, 3, \ldots\}$. At each time i there is a value $x_i \in \{0, 1\}$, which has been observed for $i \leq T$, and is to be predicted for $i > T$. The value x_i should be thought of as the color of the emerald tested at period i. For example, $x_i = 0$ may denote the observation of an emerald that appeared blue (i.e., in the blue wavelength), and $x_i = 1$, that appeared green. The model can be extended to an arbitrary set of observations at no additional cost. As usual, finite sets can be encoded as sequences of binary digits, so that the present formulation does not involve any significant loss of generality. It is important, however, that the present analysis does not necessitate additional observations or embedding the problem in a larger context.[10]

Let $F = \{0, 1\}^{\mathbb{N}}$, the set of functions from time periods to observations, denote all possible theories. We focus here on generalizations from the past to the future, but the same apparatus can be used to analyze any projection problem, that is, any generalization from a set of observations to a superset thereof.[11]

It will be useful to restate the problems of induction explicitly within the formal model:

(i) **How can we justify generalization:** Suppose that a function $f \in F$ matches all past data; that is, $f(i) = x_i$ for all $i \leq T$. How do we know that f will continue to match the data for $i > T$?

(ii) **How do/should we perform generalizations:** Suppose that $f, g \in F$ are such that $f(i) = g(i) = x_i$ for all $i \leq T$, but $f(i) \neq g(i)$ for some $i > T$. How do we know whether f or g should be used for prediction?

(iii) **What is a natural generalization:** In the setup given earlier, which of the two theories may qualify as a "simpler" theory or otherwise a "natural" choice?

Hume (1748) posed the first problem and argued that no logical justification of generalization is possible. This has been recognized as a problem we have to live with. But once we agree that there is no logical necessity that a function f will continue to match the data in the future, we are faced with the second problem, namely, that there are many possible ways to project past observations into the future. Which one should we choose?

We argued that one may resort to simplicity as a justification for inductive reasoning. Simplicity provides a criterion for selection of a theory f among all those that fit past observations. Indeed, everyday reasoning and common scientific practice implicitly deal with problems such as (ii), and statistical inference does so explicitly. It appears that simplicity, again, is the key to induction, as suggested by Wittgenstein. It is an insightful description of our natural tendency to choose theories in everyday and in scientific reasoning, and it is a prominent principle for model selection in statistics.

Simplicity does not always offer an unique theory that is clearly the obvious candidate to generalize the observations. For instance, given the observations 01, one may be unable to make a reasoned choice between the competing generalizations 011111 ... and 010101.... Yet, each of these latter sequences

---

[10] Some resolutions of Goodman's paradox do rely on a wider context, such as Goodman's own theory of entrenchment.

[11] Goodman was, of course, correct to point out that a prediction problem can be viewed as a special case of a projection problem. At the same time, the opposite embedding can also be done: if we enumerate observations by the time at which they were revealed to us, a projection problem can be thought of as the problem of predicting what our next observation will be, even if we believe that the content of the observation has been determined in the past. As mentioned earlier, in this sense historians can also engage in prediction even if they discuss only the past.

offers a natural continuation (as is evident from the informal way in which we described them in the previous sentence). On the other hand, a sequence such as 011010 allows, again, for a variety of generalizations.

It follows that if we accept the preference for simplicity, Problem (ii) can easily be solved as long as, among all theories that conform to observations, there is one that is much simpler than all the others. But Problem (ii) will remain a serious problem if the data do not allow such a theory to emerge. Indeed, when the data appear "random," the simplest theories that conform to the data are going to be many equally complex theories. Generally speaking, our confidence in a generalization will be a matter of degree, depending on quantifiable magnitudes such as the randomness in the data, the theory's simplicity, and the simplicity of competing theories.

Given this background, we can finally consider Goodman's paradox. Goodman posed problem (iii), suggesting that it is not always obvious what is the most natural generalization or which is the simplest theory that fits the data. This problem is not always a "paradox." It is often a very real problem, and serious experts may indeed debate how should past observations be generalized. However, in Goodman's emeralds example Problem (iii) appears paradoxical: we all feel that "green" is a natural generalization whereas "grue" is a ridiculous one, but we are hard-pressed to explain why. In the rest of this section I wish to explain why Problem (iii) is not a serious problem in the case of the emeralds, but I do not wish to dismiss it altogether. To reiterate, I find that this problem is a very important one in general, and there is nothing paradoxical or perplexing about its very existence. At the same time, we need to explain why it seems silly when emeralds are concerned.

Goodman considers emeralds that have so far been observed to be green. That is, he considers a long sequence 111.... According to the preceding discussion, as well as to our intuition, there is but one reasonable way to extend this sequence, namely, to consider the function $f_{green} : \mathbb{N} \to \{0, 1\}$ that is the constant 1, namely,

$$f_{green}(i) = 1 \qquad \forall i \in \mathbb{N}. \qquad (4.1)$$

Goodman contrasts this function with another function $f_{grue} : \mathbb{N} \to \{0, 1\}$ defined by

$$f_{grue}(i) = \begin{cases} 1 & i \leq T \\ 0 & i > T \end{cases}. \qquad (4.2)$$

The standard argument is that we should prefer f_{green} over f_{grue} on the basis of simplicity. If we were, say, to describe f_{green} and f_{grue} by PASCAL programs, f_{green} will have a shorter description than will f_{grue}.[12] But here Goodman asks

---

[12] You might wonder why we should select PASCAL as our language. The discussion of Kolmogorov's complexity implies that the choice of the language is immaterial here: for every language that is equivalent to PASCAL, there is a T_0 such that for $T \geq T_0$, f_{grue} is more complex than f_{green}.

that we realize that one need not assume "green" and "blue" as primitives of the language. If, instead, we use "grue" and "bleen" as primitives, we find that f_{grue} is "grue whenever tested," whereas f_{green} is given by "grue if tested at time $i \leq T$ and bleen otherwise," in which case "green" and "blue" are the complicated functions.

Stating Goodman's argument formally would highlight the problem. Define also the functions f_{blue} and f_{bleen} in the symmetric way, namely,

$$f_{blue}(i) = 0 \qquad \forall i \in \mathbb{N} \tag{4.3}$$

and

$$f_{bleen}(i) = \begin{cases} 0 & i \leq T \\ 1 & i > T \end{cases}. \tag{4.4}$$

Goodman suggests that we consider the definitions of f_{grue} and f_{bleen} in the language of f_{green} and f_{blue}, that is,

$$f_{grue}(i) = \begin{cases} f_{green}(i) & i \leq T \\ f_{blue}(i) & i > T \end{cases}; \qquad f_{bleen}(i) = \begin{cases} f_{blue}(i) & i \leq T \\ f_{green}(i) & i > T \end{cases}, \tag{4.5}$$

and contrast them with the definitions of f_{green} and f_{blue} in the language of f_{grue} and f_{bleen}, namely,

$$f_{green}(i) = \begin{cases} f_{grue}(i) & i \leq T \\ f_{bleen}(i) & i > T \end{cases}; \qquad f_{blue}(i) = \begin{cases} f_{bleen}(i) & i \leq T \\ f_{grue}(i) & i > T \end{cases}. \tag{4.6}$$

Goodman is absolutely right to argue that (4.5) is just as complex as (4.6). But his formulation does not allow us to compare the complexity of (4.2) and (4.4) with that of (4.1) and (4.3).

In other words, Goodman refers to the pairs of predicates "green whenever tested" and "blue whenever tested" versus "grue whenever tested" and "bleen whenever tested," and argues that the choice among them is arbitrary. That is, he refers to functions in F. But he does not refer to the *values* that these functions assume, 0 and 1. When he refers to an observation of an emerald as green, he does not treat it as observing the value 1, but as observing that at time i the data were consistent with a certain theory f. That is, he claims that we observed $f(i)$ (for some f). He does not allow us to say that we observed 1.

Of course, whenever $f(i) = 1$ for some function (predicate) f, one may replace 1 by $f(i)$ and obtain a valid description of the observations. But one should not be surprised if complexity considerations do change as a result of this substitution. Indeed, one lesson we learned from Goodman's paradox is that the measurement of complexity depends on language. In a natural language, where the values 0 and 1 have explicit references, or proper names, the preceding function f_{green} is simpler than f_{grue}. But if we are not allowed to use names for the specific values, and we can only refer to them indirectly as the values assumed by generalized functions, then indeed f_{green} and f_{grue} may appear equally simple. In other words, Goodman's paradox relies on a very peculiar language, in which there are names for functions but not for the specific values they assume.

Should Values Have Names?

There are several reasons for which one may require that our language have names for specific values, namely, for observations. The first and perhaps most compelling is, why not? A true and fundamental problem cannot be alleviated by the introduction of terms whose observational content can be defined by already-existing ones.

To see this point more clearly, observe that one may define values by using variables. For instance, given that the function f_{grue} (or f_{green}) is in the language, one would like to be able to set

$$x = f_{grue}(1); \qquad y = 1 - f_{grue}(1)$$

and thereafter use also the variables x and y in the description of theories. This would be a rather awkward substitute to using the values 0 and 1, but even this would not allow us to state the paradox. The paradox relies on a ban on references to observations either as specific values or as variables assuming such values.

A second reason to include names for values is that they would enable the modeling of inductive reasoning, namely, the process by which particular sense data are generalized to predicates such as "green whenever tested" and "blue whenever tested."

This point may be worth elaboration. Goodman's formulation actually does not allow us to say "the emerald tested at time t was green." We can only say, "The emerald tested at time t was of the type green-whenever-tested." The fact that this is not obvious is precisely because we don't expect to see grue emeralds. Since all emeralds so far tested were found to be green, we perform the inductive step and thus tend to confuse "green" with "of the type green-whenever-tested," that is, the specific value and its generalization.

Suppose, by contrast, that we try to forecast the weather. Every day we may observe rain or no rain. If it rained on day t, we may say that $x_t = 1$, or even that day t was "rainy." But we do not say "day t was of the type rainy-at-each-i." Because rain is not as regular a phenomenon as the color of emeralds, it would be unlikely to confuse "my hair is getting wet" with "this is an instance of the theory that my hair always gets wet."

Observe that having names for values does not presuppose that our perception or memory is infallible. In referring to the value 1, there is no claim that this value, observed yesterday, is in some deep sense the same as the same value observed today. These two values need not be instantiations of the same atemporal entity, "the 1." And there is also no need to assume that we correctly recall previous observations. All that is needed for the naming of constants is that at a given time t, we be able to look back at our recollections of past observations and categorize them as "same" or "different." In fact, we may assume without loss of generality that the first observation was 1 and then understand the value 1 as "the same as the first observation, to the best of my recollection and judgment" whereas 0 would be "different from the first observation [...]." It is hard to imagine a formulation of the problem of induction that denies the reasoner this basic ability. Even if we accept the claim that observations are theory laden (Hanson, 1958), the inability to compare observations renders induction vacuously impossible.

Whether one finds it natural to employ a model in which values have names or not depends on one's academic upbringing. If your first encounter with a formal model of a problem of induction was in a statistics course, you would probably view the values of the observations as the natural primitives of the model, and the theories, or statistical models, as more involved or derived concepts. Similarly, if you started out with formal languages and computational models, such as Turing machines, you would naturally think of 0s and 1s written on a tape as your starting point. By contrast, if your first formal course was in mathematical logic, you may think in terms of general concepts, or functions, from which specific observations would have to be derived. In this language, "Socrates is a man" is a more natural proposition than "Socrates is a man at time t." And when specific observations are captured by such propositions, you may also ask yourself how you would know that "man," as used in this proposition, looks the same when you consider different t's.

To state this a bit more bluntly, if you use the language of logic, you may find it simpler to have functions as primitives and values as derived concepts. Conversely, if you use the language of Turing machines, values would appear simple and functions, complex. Goodman's basic point is confirmed again: the choice of the language determines your notion of simplicity. This can also be interpreted as suggesting an advantage of Turing machines over logic as the fundamental model of induction: Goodman's paradox appears to be a problem for the latter but not for the former.

4.2.5   Evolutionary Explanations

To conclude this discussion let us take the viewpoint of evolutionary psychology. Thinking about how the human mind has evolved serves descriptive and normative purposes alike. From a descriptive viewpoint, such explanations can help us understand why we tend to make certain inferences and why we tend to select certain languages. From a normative point of view, we can make the arguable assumption that the human mind is a more or less optimal tool for its purposes. Under this assumption, it is worthwhile to ask why we evolved to think the way we did and what are the benefits of such modes of thinking.

We should not assume that the human mind is always an optimal tool for its purpose. But explaining why it works as it does is worth a try. It will never be too late to conclude that we're simply stupid after all.

Green versus Grue

One might try to imagine a process by which a very "low" form of life starts evolving into a smart human. Suppose that the animal in question has eyes, and its eyes reflect the image they see in some neurons. The animal may have a certain neuronal firing configuration when it sees the color green (i.e., receives wavelengths that correspond to what we call green in everyday life) and others, for blue. These neuronal configurations will probably be rather stable, so that a particular configuration would be correlated with particular wavelengths whenever we (as outside observers) perform the experiment. Importantly, such a stable correlation can be established way before the animal has any conception of time, past and future, or any ability to generalize. That is, we know that "for every time t, configuration c is associated with wavelength w," but this knowledge cannot be attributed to the animal. The animal cannot reason about t.

We can go further and endow the animal with the ability to speak and to name the colors, still without allowing it to think about time. That is, our creature observes a wavelength w, has a neuronal reaction c, and may learn to make an utterance u, naming the color as "green" or "blue." Assuming that naming colors is useful (say, for communication and coordination with others), the creature can say the correct color word whenever presented with the color. We can go as far as to say that the creature *knows* what color is presented to it. Thus, at every time t, the creature knows what is the color presented at t. Still, no quantifier over t can be ascribed to our creature, which is still ignorant of time and incapable of generalizations.

At the risk of repeating the obvious, let me stress that the "green" or "blue" uttered by our animal are not the same "green" or "blue" to which Goodman refers. Goodman thinks of "green" as a property that involved generalization and induction. That is, for him "green" means "whenever tested, emanates waves in the green range." Not so for our creature. The latter cannot think in terms of "whenever," not even in terms of "now." We, the outside observers, know that the creature responds, at time t, to the input presented at time t. But there is no clock inside the creature's mind, and there is no consciousness of time.

Assume now that another layer of intelligence is added to our creature, and the notion that it is going to live in the future as well finally dawns on it. Starting to think about time, it may ask itself what is the nature of emeralds. Now the nature of emeralds is indeed a function from time into the two timeless colors, that is, neuronal configurations "green" or "blue." Again, these are not the predicates "whenever tested, appears green" or "whenever tested, appears blue"; these are simply the names that the creature learned to associate with certain neuronal configurations. But if such names already existed in its language, the functions "whenever tested, appears green" or "whenever tested, appears blue" now seem simpler than the functions describing "grue" and "bleen."

Preference for Simplicity

Why do we prefer simpler theories to more complex ones? One obvious explanation would be along the lines of bounded rationality – due to limitations of the human mind, simpler theories are easier to conceive of, recall, communicate, and test. While this explanation is certainly valid, it is worth our while to ask whether there might be an innate advantage in preferring simpler theories. That is, assume that you are programming an organism endowed with unlimited computational power. When the organism compares different theories, would you like to instruct the organism to prefer simpler ones (keeping accuracy and generality constant)? One may attempt an affirmative answer along the following lines.

Our organism is likely to face many phenomena. Some, such as the behavior of simple organisms around it, are simple due to cognitive limitations of these organisms. For concreteness, assume that our organism attempts to hunt animals that can choose route 0 or 1 every day. Because these are simple animals, they would tend to choose simple patterns such as "always 0" or "always 1." Faced with a sequence such as 000, our organism should choose between the predictions 0 and 1. Having no preference for simplicity, the two would look equally plausible. By contrast, preference for simplicity would prefer 0 over 1. Given the simplicity of the prey, this would be a correct prediction, since a simple animal is more likely to generate the sequence 0000 than 0001.

Next consider a phenomenon that may be highly complex, such as the weather. Suppose that Nature selects a sequence of realizations 0 and 1, say, denoting no-rain and rain, respectively. Assume that Nature's choice is completely random. Should Nature choose, by some coincidence, the sequence 000, it is just as likely to be followed by 0 as by 1. In this case, the preference for simplicity does not result in better predictions, but not in worse ones either. Thus, preference for simplicity is beneficial when faced with a simple phenomenon, but not harmful when faced with a complex one. Overall, a preference for simplicity weakly dominates preference for complexity.[13]

This argument supposes that Nature does not attempt to choose complex patterns on purpose.[14] It will have to be qualified if the environment includes other competing organisms, who may try to act strategically, not to be predictable, but perhaps also to coordinate.

---

[13] Gilboa and Samuelson (2008) make this argument more formally and find that the preference for simplicity should also be augmented by preference for stability, namely, for preferring theories that have performed well (in terms of fitting the data) for a long time.

[14] There are more complex patterns than simple ones. Hence, a random selection of a pattern is likely, a priori, to result in a complex pattern. However, given a certain history, a random choice will not exhibit a conditional bias for the more complex pattern.

Another way to state this argument is that the preference for simplicity is a guarantee against overfitting.[15] Assume, to the contrary, that our organism does not have any preference for simplicity. Faced with n data points, it has no reason to choose theories with fewer than n parameters. In fact, attempting to explain the data well and suffering from no shortage of computational power, the organism will come up with a theory that fits all past observations with perfect accuracy. When it comes to prediction, however, our organism will likely do poorly, due to overfitting.

When statisticians prefer theories with fewer variables, fewer parameters, or, in general, lower complexity, they do not do so because of laziness or computational limitations. By analogy, our organism should develop a taste for simplicity in order to better predict the future, even if no cognitive limitations rule out complex theories.

The argument against overfitting relies on the assumption that at least some phenomena around us are simple, that is, simple enough to allow for prediction. As earlier, if all that we wish to predict is completely random, the theory we choose makes no difference, and overfitting involves no loss of predictive power. But it suffices that apart from the random phenomena there be some that are simple, such as the changing of the seasons or the behavior of other species, to make the preference for simplicity adaptive.

4.3 PROBLEMS WITH THE FREQUENTIST APPROACH

The lengthy discussion given previously may convince us that defining probabilities by empirical frequencies shares the fundamental problems of inductive inference that are common to all scientific and everyday reasoning. As such, we can just shrug these problems off and accept (with serenity) the fact that our probabilistic assessments will not enjoy a higher degree of confidence than do scientific conclusions in general. This approach is valid for many problems, as in our Examples (1) and (2) given in Chapter 1. When tossing a coin under similar conditions, one is justified in taking empirical frequencies as a definition of probability. Likewise, when considering the probability that a car will be stolen, taking the average theft rate to be the probability of theft is a reasonable approach. However, I claim that the same cannot be said of Examples (3) and (4) (in Chapter 1).

In Example (3), I ask my physician what is the probability of my survival in an imminent medical procedure. My physician presumably has access to

---

[15] Overfitting is a statistical term, referring to explanation of data by a theory that is potentially very complex, but that explains past observations very well. A well-known phenomenon is that such a theory can perform very well in explaining (fitting) past data, but very poorly in predictions. A classical example is explaining n observations with $(n-1)$ variables in linear regression. If the variables are randomly chosen, they will provide a perfect fit to the data with probability 1, even if they have no relation to the variable explained and therefore no predictive power. Statistical theory offers general approaches to the trade-off between fitting data and simplicity (see Akaike, 1974).

many studies published in the professional press, as well as experience of her own and of other doctors in her clinic. Thus, she knows what is the average survival rate for this procedure. But this average rate contains cases that are not entirely relevant. For instance, very old or frail patients may not have survived the procedure, but their history should not bother me too much if I happen to be generally healthy. On the other hand it is possible that women have a higher survival rate than do men, and in this case I would like to know what is the percentage of survival only among men. There are other variables that are of interest, such as blood pressure and the presence of diabetes. To complicate things further, the survival probability is likely to vary with the hospital in which the procedure is performed and with the surgeon performing it. In short, there are many observable variables that might distinguish my case from others. If I wish to take them all into account, my physician might well tell me, "I only know general statistics. I don't know what is the probability that *you* will survive. Once I operate on you, I'll be able to tell you if you survived or not."

A similar problem will be encountered in Example (4), namely, assessing the probability of war in the Middle East this year. The frequentist approach to this problem would suggest that we go back in time, check for every year whether a war has or has not occurred in that year, and define the probability of war in the Middle East as the relative frequency of war in the past.[16] No two patients were identical in Example (3), and no two years are identical in Example (4). There are years in the database in which the cold war was on and years in which it wasn't; years of economic booms and of recessions; recent years and less recent ones; and so forth.

The preceding discussion suggests that in both Example (3) and Example (4) we do not have an experiment that was conducted "under the same conditions." Reality is too complex for us to assume that two patients are identical or that two years are. In a sense, the same could be said of any two experiments, even in the simple example of tossing a coin. Indeed, no two moments in history are precisely identical. Different tosses of the same coin might have been conducted under slightly different circumstances: constellations of stars that affect the gravitational field, the force exerted on the coin by the person who tosses it, and so forth. Hence, the assumption that there are experiments conducted "under the same conditions" is, generally speaking, a simplification. Conditions that appear to us sufficiently similar are lumped together as "identical." This simplifying assumption seems reasonable in Examples (1) and (2). One may decide to neglect the differences between different tosses, and even between different cars.[17] However, one would be mistaken to neglect the differences between different patients or different years.

---

[16] To simplify matters, assume that we ignore the occurrence of several wars in the same year or the possibility of a war extending over several years.

[17] Observe that in assessing probabilities of theft or other claims, insurance companies do take into account certain variables, such as the type of the car and the zip code, in an attempt to make the experiments discussed as similar to each other as possible.

When using empirical frequencies to assess probabilities in examples such as (3) and (4), we find that there is a great deal of subjective judgment in defining the relevant database. In Example (3), the physician can look at the entire database, focus only on patients of the same gender and age, consider only patients who were operated on in the same hospital, and so on. Insisting that all patients in the sample be identical to me would most likely result in an empty database. Thus, some variables should be taken into account, while others are ignored. The physician's choice of the variables to focus on may greatly affect the probability she ends up with. Similarly, in Example (4) one may consider wars between two particular countries, or between classes of countries (say, "a western power" versus "a local state"), one may consider or ignore concurrent events elsewhere in the world, and so forth. In both examples we find that the frequentist approach, which had a claim to generate objective probabilities, turns out to be rather subjective, due to the choice of the relevant database.

Despite these similarities, there is one important way in which Example (4) is more complicated than Example (3). In the latter, the experiments may be considered causally independent. That is, one can assume that, for the most part, the outcome of one patient's operation does not affect the other's.[18] This is not the case in Example (4). Consecutive wars in the Middle East are anything but causally independent. A particular war might cause parties to be belligerent and seek retribution, or deter parties from further wars and destruction. The causal relationship between consecutive (potential) wars might be quite intricate indeed. The only obvious thing is that causal independence is not a tenable assumption.

The law of large numbers, using the language of probability, requires random variables to be identically and independently distributed. Seeking a definition of the term "probability" we resort to intuitive, nonprobabilistic versions of these conditions. Thus, we apply the frequentist approach when an experiment is repeated "under the same conditions." Informally, we expect two properties to hold, which roughly correspond to "identical and independent distributions": (i) that the experiments be the same, and (ii) that they be causally independent. I will later argue that when (i) fails but (ii) still holds (as in Example (3)), we may still define probabilities based on (a version of) the frequentist approach. I will also attempt to argue that when both assumptions (i) and (ii) are violated (as in Example (4)), it is not at all clear that one can assign probabilities in any rational way.

---

[18] This assumption may not be literally true. If my physician hears that another patient just died on the operating table, she might be more careful, or more tense, and the outcome of my operation might be affected by her attitude. However, such causal relationships may often be neglected.

CHAPTER 5

Subjective Probabilities

A major part of this book is devoted to understanding subjective probabilities and their derivation from axioms on behavior. This chapter deals with the concept in a more direct way. I start with two examples and then discuss the notion of Bayesian statistics, namely, statistical inference relying on subjective probabilities.

5.1 LINDA THE BANK TELLER

The third approach to probability assignments is to treat probabilities as purely subjective. According to this approach, saying that the probability of event A is p does not describe a property of the event. Rather, it reflects one person's beliefs about it. The basic idea is to use the machinery of probability theory as a tool to model beliefs, and perhaps to clarify and sharpen them in the process.

To understand how the probability model can help us sharpen our intuitions, let us consider a famous example of an experiment by Tversky and Kahneman (1974). Participants were asked to fill a questionnaire, in which one of the questions read as follows:

> Linda is 31 years old, single, outspoken, and very bright. She majored in philosophy. As a student, she was deeply concerned with issues of discrimination and social justice, and she participated in antinuclear demonstrations.
>
> Rank order the following eight descriptions in terms of the probability (likelihood) that they describe Linda:
>
> a. Linda is a teacher in an elementary school.
> b. Linda works in a bookstore and takes yoga classes.
> c. Linda is active in a feminist movement.
> d. Linda is a psychiatric social worker.
> e. Linda is a member of the League of Women Voters.
> f. Linda is a bank teller.
> g. Linda is an insurance salesperson.
> h. Linda is a bank teller who is active in a feminist movement.

Many participants rank (h) as more likely than (f), even though (h) is the conjunction of (f) and (c). Almost no one ranks (h) as more likely than (c). Kahneman and Tversky explained this phenomenon as follows: Clearly, the majority of the pairs to be compared in this exercise are descriptions that cannot be ranked by any logical or mathematical criterion. Moreover, they refer to a variety of events about which the participants have only very partial information. In the absence of sufficient information for a reasoned answer, participants attempt to use whatever they can. In particular, they employ a "representativeness heuristic": they ask themselves to what extent each description is representative of Linda. Viewed thus, being a bank teller is not very representative, given Linda's description, but being active in a feminist movement is. Hence, the description that has at least one feature that is representative of Linda ends up being ranked higher.[1]

I have used this example in many classes, and the responses tend to be similar. Some 40–50% of the students rank (h) as more likely than (f). When the point is explained, no one insists on their original choice. (This is precisely my preferred test for rationality. Ranking (f) below (h) is irrational because, having chosen this ranking, people change their minds based solely on an exposure to the analysis of their choice. See the discussion in Section 13.2.) Some students are a bit angry and they claim that by (f) they understood "a bank teller who is not active in a feminist movement." Others admit that they were wrong.

The point of this example is that the beliefs that the students are asked to express are subjective. There is no objective way to rank the statements based on the data provided. And yet, if one were to use subjective probabilities as a model for one's beliefs, one would avoid the mistake of ranking (h) above (f). Subjective probabilities can be viewed as a way to use the mathematical apparatus of probability theory to avoid judgments or decisions that we would consider to be mistaken.

5.2   PASCAL'S WAGER

Subjective probability dates back to the very early days of probability theory. Pascal, who is credited as one of the forefathers of the field, was also the first to use the concept of subjective probability in his famous "wager." He also suggested several important ideas in decision theory in his argument. It is therefore worth going over.

---

[1] Ranking statements by their likelihood is not a very common task that people normally perform. By contrast, judging whether others are telling us the truth is a much more common task we face in everyday life. When we perform the latter task, the more details there are, as long as there are no obvious contradictions among them, the more reliable does the speaker seem to us. This is true even though the probability of the statement they make can only go down the more conjunctions are involved. It is possible that part of what drives the ranking of (h) above (f) is the tendency to put more faith in a speaker who provides more details.

The basic idea of Pascal's wager can be described as follows: consider two states of the world, one in which God exists and one in which he doesn't. Next, consider two possible strategies – to believe or not. In filling up the payoff matrix, allow the payoffs in case God exists to be infinite, but keep them finite if God doesn't exist. Say,[2]

	God exists	God doesn't exist
Believe	∞	$-c$
Not believe	$-\infty$	0

Then, if you admit that the probability that God exists is some $\varepsilon > 0$, no matter how small, you find that "believe" is preferred to "not believe." This is one version of the popular account of the wager. However, reading the account provided by Hacking (1975, pp. 63–67), one finds several subtleties.[3]

First, Pascal was aware of the conceptual difficulty in choosing one's beliefs. But he argued that one can *become* a believer. That is, one need not choose what to believe at present – one may choose a lifestyle that would, most probably, lead one to be a believer on one's death bed (or at least early enough to gain the infinite payoff of the afterlife). Pascal implicitly thought in terms of a multiself model. Importantly, he did not sin in confusing acts with states.

Second, Pascal started out with the argument that one has nothing to lose by believing even if God does not exist ($c = 0$).[4] Only as a second line of defense he admits that there might be a cost to believing (namely, giving up on some pleasurable sins) and resorts to the argument that the infinite payoff, even when multiplied by a small probability, outweighs the finite cost. Moreover, Pascal goes on to say that should one argue that the probability that God does not exist is not known, it suffices that one accepts that this probability is in some interval $(0, \bar{\varepsilon})$, and then one can repeat the argument for every $\varepsilon \in (0, \bar{\varepsilon})$ and establish the result that believing is preferred to not believing.

It is quite astonishing that in his informal discussion, Pascal introduced several key ideas in decision theory:

1. The notion of a decision matrix. The matrix is not described as a mathematical object, but what such a description should be is quite clear from the verbal description. Moreover, Pascal was sensitive to the rational demand that one not choose one's beliefs.
2. The notion of a weakly dominant strategy.
3. The idea of expected utility maximization. Again, expectation is not formally stated, but the argument obviously refers to this mathematical concept. Moreover, expected utility is used in a rather sophisticated

[2] Pascal seems to have meant mostly a positive infinite payoff if God exists. Assigning $-\infty$ to "not believe" in case God exists is not an obvious implication of Pascal's text. Clearly, it is not necessary for the argument either.

[3] See also Connor (2006) for historical and religious background.

[4] In fact, being a believer himself, he describes righteous life as very satisfying in its own right.

way, employing subjective probabilities and involving nonmonetary payoffs.
4. The notion of multiple priors admitting that a single probability may be hard to pin down, but using an argument that holds for all possible probabilities (in Bewley, 2002, see section 18.6).

Pascal's argument has been attacked on many grounds. The most convincing ones are that one may not know whether God really wants us to believe (for all we know, God may exist but reward the nonbelievers for their independent spirit) or that God may exist but turn out to be Muslim, while the Christian and the Muslim Gods want us to have contradictory beliefs. Yet, Pascal's argument is quite sound, especially given the genre. Some of the greatest minds in history performed embarrassing mental acrobatics when it came to justifying faith. By contrast, Pascal's argument makes sense and retains a high degree of clarity of thought despite the delicate topic.[5]

5.3   CLASSICAL VERSUS BAYESIAN STATISTICS

5.3.1   Basic Definitions

"Classical statistics" refers to the statistical inference tools such as confidence intervals and hypotheses tests, developed by Fisher, Neyman, Pearson, and others. It is the statistics that you studied in undergraduate and graduate courses, and it is the bread and butter of all scientific research, including empirical and experimental work in economics. "Bayesian statistics" refers to another approach to the same inference problems, according to which one has subjective probabilities regarding the unknown parameters of the distributions in question.

The Bayesian way of inference is credited to Bayes (1763). The term "Bayesian" is used differently in different disciplines. In statistics and computer science, for instance, anything that updates a prior to a posterior based on evidence is referred to as "Bayesian." In economic theory, by contrast, the term "Bayesian" refers to a more demanding ideological position, according to which anything and everything that is not known should be modeled explicitly in a state-space model and be subject to a prior probability. This extreme position is sometimes referred to as "Bayesianism." It has its roots somewhere in the beginning of the twentieth century, and Bruno de Finetti is probably the person most responsible for the development of this viewpoint.

To consider a simple example from everyday statistical inference, assume that we observe a sequence of i.i.d. (independently and identically distributed) Bernoulli random variables X_i with an unknown parameter p. We are attempting to estimate p. In a classical setup, for every p there is a separate probability model, with states defined by the values of $(X_i)_{i \geq 1}$, and a probability measure

---

[5] Part of the reason might be that Pascal did not try to prove that God existed, only that it was worthwhile to believe in him.

ν defined on this state space, according to which the variables $(X_i)_{i \geq 1}$ are i.i.d. with $\nu(X_i = 1) = p$ for every i. In each such probability model (characterized by a certain p), we know that the law of large numbers holds and that, apart from an event with ν probability of zero, the average of the X_is will converge to p.

By contrast, a Bayesian statistics approach to the same problem would hold that if the parameter p is not known, we should have subjective beliefs about it and treat it as a random variable. Thus, the Bayesian approach would consider a single probability model, whose state space is the product of the values of the unknown parameter and the variables we sample. In other words, rather than a separate probability measure on the values of $(X_i)_{i \geq 1}$, the Bayesian formulation would have a single probability measure λ, stating the joint distribution of p (viewed as a random variable) and $(X_i)_{i \geq 1}$. It is easily seen that should one specify a certain prior distribution f on $p \in [0, 1]$, there is a unique measure λ such that (i) conditional on p, the variables $(X_i)_{i \geq 1}$ are i.i.d. with $\nu(X_i = 1) = p$ for every i; and (ii) the marginal distribution of p is f.

Once the Bayesian model is set, learning from observations becomes a simple task: it reduces to Bayesian updating. Given observations $X_1, \ldots, X_n$, one can compute the posterior probability $\lambda_{|X_1,\ldots,X_n}$ and from its marginal compute the posterior belief about p.[6] And if God were to reveal to us the true value of p, we would similarly update λ and find the conditional distribution of $X_1, \ldots, X_n$ given p. In this approach no distinction is made between the observable variables, which may be "truly" random (whatever that may mean), and the unknown parameter, which is assumed to be fixed. Anything we do not know becomes a random variable, and we have a joint distribution for all of these variables, reflecting our subjective beliefs. All uncertainty is treated in the same way, and all information is used in the same way.

5.3.2   The Gambler Fallacy

Observe, however, that in such a Bayesian setup the law of large numbers does not apply. The reason is that the law of large numbers assumes independence of the random variables, and this independence holds only *conditional* on p.

This is related to Kahneman and Tversky's "gambler fallacy": you sit in a casino and observe the roulette game. Over the past 10 round, the wheel came up on red. You now decide to bet – should you bet on red or black?

Many people think that they should bet on black, because there were 10 red outcomes in a row, and the law of large numbers suggests that in the long run there should be as many "blacks" as "reds." Hence, the intuitive reasoning

---

[6] In this context, there is a special interest in families of distributions on $[0, 1]$ that would be "closed" under Bayesian updating, that is, that have the property that should the prior f belong to the family, so will the posterior. Such a family is called a *conjugate* family of distributions. For example, for the problem discussed here, the beta family (see DeGroot, 1975, pp. 294–296) is such a conjugate family.

goes, "black has to catch up" for the law to hold, and therefore we are more likely to observe black than red in the next trial.

Clearly, this reasoning is flawed. As Kahneman and Tversky put it, when it comes to Nature obeying the law of large numbers, "mistakes are not corrected; they are diluted." More precisely, there are two possibilities, depending on your trust in the fairness of the wheel. If you are confident that the roulette wheel is fair, you have to believe that the probabilities of red and black are equal and that the trials are i.i.d. Under the assumption of independence, there is absolutely nothing to learn from past observations about future ones. Luckily for you, you also know all there is to know about the probability of the different outcomes in the next trial. If, however, you are not quite sure that the wheel is fair, you should engage in some statistical learning. And in this case, having observed "red" 10 times, you may start wondering whether the wheel may not be biased. But in this case it would be biased toward red, not black.[7]

The important lesson from this example is that when we do not know the parameters of the distribution, our sample does not consist of i.i.d. random variables. Independence holds *given* the unknown parameters; that is, we have only conditional independence. Observe that if independence were to hold, there would be no point in taking a sample in the first place, since there would be nothing to learn from some variables about the others.

Classical statistics refers to i.i.d. random variable in this conditional sense. It does not always emphasize that the variables are i.i.d. given the parameter, say p, because it anyway has no probabilistic way to quantify over different p values. Bayesian statistics, by contrast, does have a joint distribution over p and the variables X_i, and even if the variables are i.i.d. given p, they are not i.i.d. when p is not known.

5.3.3   Exchangeability

The preceding discussion suggests that a Bayesian cannot apply the law of large numbers for estimation of unknown parameters. That is, if a Bayesian is to take her beliefs seriously, she should admit that the random variables she samples, as far as her subjective beliefs suggest, are not independent. Again, there would be little point in taking the sample if they were independent. What is therefore the meaning of taking samples and computing their averages?

Luckily for the Bayesian approach, de Finetti (1930) solved this problem by extending the law of large numbers from i.i.d. random variables to what he called *exchangeable* random variables. A sequence of random variables $X_1, \ldots, X_n, \ldots$ is exchangeable if the following is true: for every $n \geq 1$, the joint distribution of $X_1, \ldots, X_n$ is symmetric. This, in particular, implies that the marginal of X_1 equals that of X_n, and hence the variables are identically

---

[7] The gambler fallacy is an interesting example because it originates in a misunderstanding of a mathematical result. People who have never heard of the law of large numbers are unlikely to err in this way.

distributed. Moreover, if the variables are independent and identically distributed, they are clearly exchangeable. But the converse is false: exchangeability generalizes the notion of identical and independent distribution in a nontrivial way.

The simplest way to see an example of random variables that are exchangeable but not i.i.d. is to "mix" two distinct i.i.d distributions. For example, assume that $X_i \sim B(p)$, as given previously, and that conditional on p, they are independent. Assume now that p takes the values $1/3$ and $2/3$ with equal probability. It is easy to see that for every n, the joint distribution of $X_1, \ldots, X_n$ is symmetric. For example, consider $n = 2$. The joint distribution of X_1 and X_2 is given by one of the following matrices, each with probability 50%:

	$X_2 = 0$	$X_2 = 1$	
$X_1 = 0$	4/9	2/9	2/3
$X_1 = 1$	2/9	1/9	1/3
	2/3	1/3	1

$$p = 1/3$$

	$X_2 = 0$	$X_2 = 1$	
$X_1 = 0$	1/9	2/9	1/3
$X_1 = 1$	2/9	4/9	2/3
	1/3	2/3	1

$$p = 2/3$$

And overall we obtain the following distribution of X_1 and X_2:

	$X_2 = 0$	$X_2 = 1$	
$X_1 = 0$	5/18	2/9	1/2
$X_1 = 1$	2/9	5/18	1/2
	1/2	1/2	1

Clearly, X_1 and X_2 are identically but not independently distributed. To see that this is an example of exchangeability, one has to complete the definition of the joint distribution of $X_1, \ldots, X_n$ for all n, which is straightforward.

To consider a more extreme example, assume that $p = 0$ with probability .5 and $p = 1$ with probability .5. Then the joint distribution of X_1 and X_2 is

	$X_2 = 0$	$X_2 = 1$	
$X_1 = 0$	1/2	0	1/2
$X_1 = 1$	0	1/2	1/2
	1/2	1/2	1

This is a very extreme case in which X_1 and X_2 are as dependent as they can be: knowing one of them completely determines the other. Yet, they are exchangeable.

In both examples we generated exchangeable random variables by "mixing" i.i.d random variables: we considered a family of sequences of joint distributions that are i.i.d and depend on a parameter p; we assumed that p is randomly selected according to some distribution μ and that given the selection of p, the random variables are i.i.d. We could also think of p as an unknown "objective" probability that governs the process we observe, and of μ, as our subjective belief about this unknown probability. de Finetti has shown that this is the only way to generate exchangeable distributions. That is, if you start with an exchangeable sequence, $X_1, \ldots, X_n, \ldots$, you can always think of it as a sequence of random variables that are i.i.d *given* some "parameter" p, over which you have subjective beliefs μ.[8] According to this representation of exchangeable variables, all correlations between variables in the sequence are due to the fact that this parameter is not known a priori.

de Finetti also showed that, in this case, if we take $\bar{X}_n$ to be the average of the first n random variables from the exchangeable sequence $X_1, \ldots, X_n, \ldots, \bar{X}_n$ will converge, with probability 1, to the conditional expectation of X_i, that is, to the expectation of X_i given the parameter p. (Note that it is independent of i.) This theorem provided the theoretical basis for Bayesian estimation: one need not assume independence in order to obtain the desired result, namely, that the sample average will converge to the "true" expectation.[9]

5.3.4   Confidence Is Not Probability

To see more clearly the difference between classical and Bayesian statistics, it is useful to remind ourselves of some basic definitions of classical statistics.

Consider a textbook problem. Suppose that we consider a random variable $X \sim N(\mu, 1)$. For simplicity we assume a known standard deviation, $\sigma = 1$, and a single observation, $n = 1$. We know that we can construct a confidence interval for μ, for instance, of length 2 and confidence level 68%:

$$P(\mu \in [X - 1, X + 1]) = 68\%. \tag{5.1}$$

Suppose that we take the sample and observe $X = 3$. The interval is therefore $[2, 4]$. What is the probability that μ is in this interval? That is,

$$P(\mu \in [2, 4]) = ? \tag{5.2}$$

It is very tempting to reply that the probability is 68%, which is what we get by substituting $X = 3$ into (5.1). But this is wrong. The statement (5.1) is a probability statement about the random variable $[X - 1, X + 1]$ or, if you wish, the random variable X, but *not* about μ. In the classical statistics setup, μ is not a random variable, and we don't have probabilistic beliefs about it. This is true before as well as after we observe X.

As this point is important, it is worth repeating it with another example: assume that Y is the outcome of a roll of a fair die. A priori, before rolling the die, we state that

$$P(Y = 3) = 1/6, \tag{5.3}$$

---

[8] The "parameter" need not be a single, real-valued parameter. In general, it is only an abstract index that denotes i.i.d distributions.

[9] If this line is taken seriously, we need to say something about the distribution of the sample average, $\bar{X}_n$, as well. A central limit theorem for exchangeable sequences of random variables was proved by Chernoff and Teicher (1958).

which is a probability statement about the random variable Y. Once we observe Y, we can't plug it into (5.3). Whether we observed $Y = 3$ or, say, $Y = 2$, it will be nonsensical to substitute the value for Y and say $P(3 = 3) = 1/6$ or $P(2 = 3) = 1/6$. The probability statement (5.3) is a statement about the random variable Y when it was still random, as it were. To be precise, $Y = 3$ is a name of an event, containing some states and not others. $P(Y = 3)$ is the probability of this event. Before Y is observed, we use the letter Y to designate a function defined on the state space and thereby to define the event by the condition $Y = 3$. But after Y was observed, we have a realization $Y = y$, but the specific value y cannot substitute for the function Y. Precisely the same logic applies to the previous example, namely, to the substitution of $X = 3$ into (5.1).

What does the 68% probability in (5.1) mean? It means that we are using a certain procedure that generates intervals, and we are guaranteed that no matter what μ really is, this procedure has an a priori probability of 68% to cover μ. Part of the trick (and the beauty) in classical statistics is that we can make this statement uniformly, for every μ. In the problem we started out with, this is simple, because $(X - \mu) \sim N(0, 1)$. But when σ is not known, it's not so obvious that we will indeed be able to say anything about any interesting random variable. Luckily, it turns out that some things can be said – t and F distributions pop up for various expressions, independently of the unknown parameters. This is indeed a miracle, without which we would not have been able to perform classical statistical inference.

In any event, it is important to recall that confidence levels, as well as significance levels for hypotheses tests, are not probabilities in the Bayesian sense. They are probabilities only a priori, before the sample was taken, and they can be uniformly computed, or bounded, regardless of the unknown parameters. But once the sample has been taken, we are left with confidence or significance levels that only reflect the a priori probabilities, and may not incorporate all relevant information. The following example illustrates.

5.3.5   Classical Statistics Can Be Ridiculous

Consider a random variable with a uniform distribution over an interval of length 1.[10] We do not know where the interval is located. Let $\theta \in \mathbb{R}$ denote its midpoint, so that

$$X \sim U(\theta - 0.5, \theta + 0.5).$$

Assume that we take $n = 2$ i.i.d. random variables from this distribution, X_1, X_2, and construct an interval between them, $[\min(X_1, X_2), \max(X_1, X_2)]$. What is its confidence level?

Observe that in order for the interval $[\min(X_1, X_2), \max(X_1, X_2)]$ to "miss" θ you need both X_1, X_2 to be in $[\theta - 0.5, \theta)$ or both to be in $(\theta, , \theta + 0.5]$,

---

[10] This example is taken from DeGroot (1975).

where each of these events has probability .25. Hence we obtained a 50% confidence interval: whatever is θ,

$$P\left(\theta \in [\min(X_1, X_2), \max(X_1, X_2)]\right) = 0.5.$$

Next assume that $X_1 = 0$ and $X_2 = 0.6$. What is the probability that $\theta \in [0, 0.6]$? Indeed, we just agreed that this is a meaningless question. And yet, in this case we know the answer: the probability is 1. This is so because the two cases in which $[\min(X_1, X_2), \max(X_1, X_2)]$ misses θ are such that $|X_1 - X_2| < 0.5$. If we observe $|X_1 - X_2| > 0.5$, we *know* that this is one of those cases in which the sample hit θ. But this knowledge is not reflected in the confidence level, which remains the same 50% it used to be before the sample was taken.

By a similar token, if we observe $X_1 = 0$ and $X_2 = 0.001$, we probably don't really think that we hit θ this time. Conditional on $|X_1 - X_2| \leq 0.001$, we would have to be very lucky to have included θ in our interval. But the language of classical statistics does not allow us to express all these feelings, intuitions, or even knowledge (in the case, $|X_1 - X_2| > 0.5$). We are confined to discuss what the probability of the interval including the parameter *used to be*, being unable to update this probability in light of the evidence in our sample.

5.3.6   Different Methods for Different Goals

So why do we use classical statistics? How can we trust such a flawed set of procedures to conduct our everyday as well as scientific statistical inference?

Indeed, there used to be days in which classical and Bayesian statisticians were engaged in fierce intellectual battles.[11] I maintain, however, that classical and Bayesian statistics are not competing at all, because they have different goals. In bold strokes, classical statistics is a collection of tools for a society to agree on what can be stated as officially established, with the understanding that this society includes different people with different beliefs and different goals. Bayesian statistics is the tool for individual reasoners or decision makers, who attempt to sort out their knowledge, belief, evidence, and intuition. As such, classical statistics aspires to be objective. Bayesian statistics, by contrast, hopes to capture all beliefs and intuition, whether objective or subjective.

Two examples might be useful. Let us start with an analogy used by basic textbooks to explain hypothesis testing, a prominent workhorse of classical statistics. Consider a murder case brought before the court. The default assumption, H_0, is the hypothesis that the defendant is innocent. The alternative, H_1, is that he is guilty. Before collecting the evidence, we define a test – a function from the potential observations to {*accept, reject*}, where "rejecting H_0" is considered to be a "proof" that it is wrong, namely, that the defendant

---

[11] Apparently, over the years each side has been willing to make certain concessions and admit that the other method has some merits.

is guilty, while "accepting H_0" is viewed as not saying much. In particular, the defendant enjoys the benefit of the doubt, and inconclusive evidence would likely result in not rejecting or in "accepting" H_0. Importantly, if we were to switch roles between H_0 and H_1, making guilt the default assumption, it may well be the case that neither H_0 nor H_1 can be rejected, namely, that neither H_1 nor H_0 can be "proved." In selecting the test, we consider the bounds on the probabilities of type I and type II errors, asking ourselves what is the maximal a priori probability we allow for a guilty defendant to be declared innocent and vice versa.

This setup is cumbersome. One has to define tests based on a significance level, which refer only to the a priori probability; one has to treat H_0 and H_1 asymmetrically; and so on. In order to understand why we hold on to this mess, consider the Bayesian alternative. In this alternative, the judge or the jury (depending on the legal system) would have to form a prior probability about the defendant's guilt, update the given evidence, and find a posterior probability of guilt. But where will the judge take the prior from? What happens if the judge assigns prior probability of 100% that the defendant is guilty? No amount of evidence would convince him of the contrary. Alternatively, the judge might happen to be the defendant's mother, who assigns, honestly or strategically, a prior probability of 0 to the defendant's guilt.

Clearly, we prefer to live in a society in which the court system aspires to be objective. We know that there might be cases in which the system, committed to certain rules, will not allow us to prove something in which we tend to believe. In this case there might be a gap between our subjective beliefs and the official declarations made by the court system.

To continue with our example, assume that the defendant is accused of having raped and murdered a woman on their first date. Assume further that the police searches the defendant's house and finds incriminating evidence, including a gun, bloodstained clothes, and so on. In the course of the trial, however, the defense manages to suggest alternative theories explaining this evidence, and guilt cannot be established beyond reasonable doubt.

Now ask yourself two separate questions: (i) do you want to send the defendant to jail and (ii) would you like your sister to date him? It is quite possible that your answer will be "Well, I think that it's important we stick to our laws. Guilt was not established unequivocally, and the defendant should enjoy the benefit of the doubt. At the same time, I will certainly not want to see my sister dating such a character – I'm pretty sure that this guy is a murderer!" The gap between what you think society should officially declare and what you would like to do in your own decision problem is analogous to the difference between classical statistics inference and Bayesian updating.

To consider another example, suppose that a renowned pharmaceutical firm developed a new drug that may slow down a certain type of cancer. I suffer from this disease. The new drug might help me, but it has not yet been approved by the Food and Drug Administration (FDA). Considering my personal decision problem, I want to use all my information in Bayesian reasoning, and I may conclude that I should try the drug if I can. In particular, I know the firm's reputation, I know that it had never introduced a drug that hasn't eventually been approved by the FDA, I realize that the firm has too much to lose from its product being turned down, and I put a very high posterior probability on the drug being effective (given that it has been submitted by this firm). At the same time, I will probably not want the FDA to automatically approve drugs by this firm, just because it has a good reputation. Again, we have to distinguish between two questions: (i) do I want the FDA to approve the drug without testing it and (ii) do I want to use the drug before FDA approval? It is perfectly consistent to answer (i) in the negative and (ii) in the affirmative. Declaration by official bodies should be held to a standard of objectivity. Decisions of individuals should allow subjective input as well.

Observe that scientific research is another field in which individual intuition and societal declarations often diverge. Scientists might have various hunches and intuitions. But we can't allow them to say, "Based on my prior belief that A is true, I took a sample, updated the prior, and found that it is indeed true with very high probability." We realize that scientists have very different intuitions. Moreover, they have many incentives to publish various results. We therefore hold scientific research to high standards of objectivity. In particular, all branches of science use classical statistics and test hypotheses. Prior beliefs can guide individual scientists in developing research conjectures, but they cannot enter the protocol of scientific proofs.

It should be emphasized that the preceding discussion deals with what classical and Bayesian statistics *attempt* to do, not their degrees of success in achieving their goals. Classical statistics aspires to objectivity, but it faces many difficulties and pitfalls in attaining this goal. By contrast, Bayesian statistics should incorporate all our intuition, but one may find that it is too demanding in that it requires prior beliefs about many issues on which one has no well-defined beliefs. The main point, however, is that each of these methods has a completely different goal.

PART II

BEHAVIORAL DEFINITIONS

Let us take stock. We considered four probability assignment problems and three definitions of probability. The first, the principle of indifference, was so flawed that we struggled to find justifications for it even in the few examples in which it seems to make sense to a certain degree. The second, the frequentist approach, seemed fine for certain problems, but unable to cope with questions such as the occurrence of war or a stock market crash, or even the success of medical procedures. Unfortunately, some of the more important problems in our personal and professional lives are of the tricky types – those that cannot be assumed to be repeated in the same way, and maybe even not in a causally independent fashion. Lastly, we considered the subjective approach, which appears to be a powerful conceptual tool, dealing in the same way with coins as with wars.

But what exactly is this subjective probability? How do we determine it? Are there more or less rational ways to assign such probabilities? And are we sure that the probability apparatus is the right one to capture our intuition?

All of these questions call for an axiomatic approach. Such an approach can simultaneously explain to us what subjective probabilities mean exactly, how we can calibrate and measure them, why (and when) we should use them, and so forth. To understand the approach better, let us more carefully analyze the case study of maximization of utility.[1]

---

[1] This "case study" actually deals with the meaning of the utility function. As this issue is also quite fundamental to decision theory under uncertainty, I allow myself to discuss it at length.

CHAPTER 6

A Case Study

6.1 A CHARACTERIZATION THEOREM FOR MAXIMIZATION OF UTILITY

The theorem I present here dates back to Cantor (1915), and it is given in Kreps (1988, pp. 25–26). Cantor had no interest (as far as I know) in economics or decision theory. He was fascinated, however, by the real numbers, and he attempted to understand them from various points of view. In particular, he was interested in understanding the order ("greater than") on the real numbers. What does it take to think of elements of a set with a binary relation on it as the real line and the relation $\geq$? In answering this question, Cantor provided a theorem, which can be interpreted as a characterization of a preference relation that can be thought of as maximizing utility.

For our purposes, we will consider a set of alternatives X, and a binary relation on it, $\succsim \subset X \times X$, interpreted as "preferred at least as." Our main interest is in the question, when can we represent $\succsim$ by maximization of a function $u : X \to \mathbb{R}$, namely, when does there exist a real-valued function u that satisfies

$$x \succsim y \quad \text{iff} \quad u(x) \geq u(y) \qquad \forall\, x, y \in X \tag{6.1}$$

in which case we will say that u *represents* $\succsim$?

Define the asymmetric ($\succ$) and symmetric ($\sim$) parts of $\succsim$ as usual, and consider the following three axioms:

- C1. **Completeness:** For every $x, y \in X$, $x \succsim y$ or $y \succsim x$.
- C2. **Transitivity:** For every $x, y, z \in X$, $x \succsim y$ and $y \succsim z$ imply $x \succsim z$.
- C3. **Separability:** There exists a countable set $Z \subset X$ such that for every $x, y \in X \backslash Z$, if $x \succ y$, then there exists $z \in Z$ such that $x \succsim z \succsim y$.

Axioms C1 and C2 are quite familiar from consumer theory. Yet, for the sake of comparison with the same axioms in other context, it is worthwhile to remind ourselves how they are typically justified. If we take a descriptive interpretation, completeness is almost a matter of definition: the choice that we observe is defined to be the preferred one. Since a decision maker faced with the choice set $\{x, y\}$ will have to make some choice, we will be able to say that x was chosen in the presence of y ($x \succsim y$) or vice versa.

This account is a little misleading, because completeness is taken to mean some regularity as well. More precisely, given the same choice set $\{x, y\}$, we expect the decision maker to always choose from the same nonempty subset $C(\{x, y\}) \subset \{x, y\}$. Thus completeness rules out random choices.[1]

Transitivity has an obvious descriptive interpretation. In the following subsections we discuss two families of situations in which it is often violated. For the time being, we can satisfy ourselves with following its basic logic.

Taking a normative interpretation, the completeness axiom is quite compelling. It suggests that a certain choice has to be made.[2] The axiom implicitly calls upon us to make this choice explicit. One may argue that one does not have well-defined preferences. The decision theorist would respond, "do you then prefer to sweep your choice under the rug, simply decide not to look at it?" The completeness axiom is therefore viewed as a call to face reality and explicitly model choices.

The transitivity axiom is probably easier to defend. The intuition behind it is clear and, indeed, compelling.

Let us now briefly understand the mathematical content of C3. Separability says, roughly speaking, that countably many elements (those of Z) tell the entire story. If I want to know how an alternative x ranks, it suffices that I know how it ranks relative to all elements of Z. Observe that, if X is countable, C3 vacuously holds, since one may choose $Z = X$.

Separability is obviously a condition that is needed for the mathematics to work. It is not terribly compelling from a descriptive or a normative point of view. At the same time, it is not particularly bothersome. In fact, it has no obvious observational meaning. Since our observations are always finite, we cannot imagine an experiment that would refute C3. This suggests that the axiom has no empirical content and therefore does not restrict our theory, whether interpreted descriptively or normatively. Rather, the axiom is a price we have to pay if we want to use a certain mathematical model. We will get used to the existence of such axioms in practically all the axiomatizations we will see in this book. Such axioms will often be referred to as "technical," and while I do not like this disparaging term, I may use it as well for lack of a better one. However we refer to them, axioms that are devoid of a scientific content are differently treated than others. We will not bother to justify them; nor will we find them very objectionable – they will be justified by mathematical necessity.

To see that the separability axiom has some mathematical power and that it may give us hope for utility representation, let us see why it rules out Debreu's famous example (Debreu, 1959; see also Mas-Colell et al., 1995).

---

[1] Both Kreps (1988) and Mas-Colell et al. (1995) start the theory with choice functions and present theorems that guarantee that a choice function be summarized by a binary relation.

[2] Of course, a satisfactory model would have "doing nothing" specified as one of the alternatives.

In this example, $X = [0, 1]^2$ and $(x_1, x_2) \succsim (y_1, y_2)$ if and only if $x_1 > y_1$ or $(x_1 = y_1$ and $x_2 \geq y_2)$. As you may recall from your first microeconomics class, this example does not satisfy continuity: the sets defined by strict preference are not open in the standard topology on $\mathbb{R}^2$. Hence, it has no continuous numerical representation. Moreover, it does not satisfy separability: assume that $Z \subset X$ is a countable set. Consider its projection on the first coordinate; that is,

$$Z_1 = \{x_1 \in [0, 1] \mid \exists x_2 \in [0, 1] \quad s.t.(x_1, x_2) \in Z\}.$$

Clearly, Z_1 is also countable. Consider $x_1 \in [0, 1] \backslash Z_1$ and note that $(x_1, 1) \succ (x_1, 0)$. However, no element of Z can be between these two in terms of preference, since it cannot have x_1 as its first coordinate.

The theorem, as you must have guessed, is as follows.

Theorem 6.1 *(Cantor) A binary relation $\succsim$ can be represented by a real-valued function u if and only if it satisfies C1–C3.*

Under these conditions, the function u is unique up to increasing transformations.

As opposed to the more familiar theorem of Debreu (1959), the present one does not assume a topology on X. Hence, it is meaningless to ask whether the utility obtained is continuous. However, if X happens to be endowed with a topology, Cantor's theorem still does not guarantee continuity. This can be a limitation, for instance, if you are interested in continuity and you wonder what does it take, in terms of observed preferences, to assume continuity. This can also be an advantage if you are be interested in utility functions that are not everywhere continuous.[3]

6.2 PROOF

The discussion is simplified if we assume, without loss of generality, that there are no equivalences. Formally speaking, we consider $\sim$-equivalence classes, that is, $X/\sim$. It is easy to verify that a numerical representation of $\succsim$ between representatives of the equivalence classes is necessary and sufficient for a numerical representation of $\succsim$ on all of X.

To understand the proof of Theorem 6.1, it might be useful to first assume that X is finite. In this case completeness and transitivity suffice for representation by a utility function u. There are several ways to prove that. For instance, you may take one element x_1 and assign it an arbitrary number $u(x_1)$. Then you take another element x_2 and assign it a value higher/lower than $u(x_1)$ depending on whether x_2 is preferred to/less preferred than x_1. And you continue this way. One may prove by induction that if u is defined on $\{x_1, \ldots, x_k\}$ and it represents

---

[3] The discussion of the various interpretations of the theorem, however, can be done in the context of Debreu's theorem as well.

$\succsim$ on this set, then it can be extended to a function u defined on $\{x_1, \dots, x_{k+1}\}$ and it represents $\succsim$ on this larger set. The point in the extension is that one need not change values of u assigned to points in $\{x_1, \dots, x_k\}$. There is enough space on the line to place the utility of any new point.

Another way to prove the theorem for a finite X is to first order the elements so that $x_i \prec x_{i+1}$ for all i and then set $u(x_i) = i$. This definition is equivalent to setting

$$u(x) = \#\{y \in X | x \succsim y\};\qquad(6.2)$$

that is, every x is assigned a number, which is the number of elements it is at least as good as. This might remind you of a chess tournament or a soccer league, in which any two contestants compete and each collects a certain number of points for every victory.

This latter idea does not work when the set is infinite – one may find that there are infinitely many elements y such that $x \succsim y$, and then $u(x)$ will not be a real number. Moreover, adding infinity to the range of u will not be sufficient, since many elements that are not equivalent will be mapped to the same value, ∞. It so happens, however, that for countable sets X the first proof still works. Since any element of a countable set can be reached by induction, at any stage (k) we can add an element (x_{k+1}), while the set of predecessors contains only finitely many elements $(\{x_1, \dots, x_k\})$ to which u-values were assigned.

But what should we do if X is uncountable? We can go over it by transfinite induction, but in this case it will no longer be the case that for every x, as we look back at the values already assigned, we have a finite set of predecessors. And if the set of predecessors is infinite, we might be in trouble – we may find, for instance, that $x \succ y$ and $x_n \succ x$ for every $n \geq 1$, while we already assigned $u(y) = 0$ and $u(x_n) = 1/n$.

Surprisingly, the second proof technique, given by (6.2), can be used in this case, provided that we make two modifications. Our problem with (6.2), even in the countable case, was that the set discussed may be infinite. But this difficulty can be solved if we allow the elements to have weights that generate a convergent series. But convergent series are defined for countably many elements, you say. Indeed, we know that separability will have to be used at some point. And this is the time to put it all together: let $Z = \{z_1, z_2, \dots\}$ and define

$$u(x) = \sum_{\{z_i \in Z | x \succsim z_i\}} \frac{1}{2^i} - \sum_{\{z_i \in Z | z_i \succsim x\}} \frac{1}{2^i}.\qquad(6.3)$$

The main point is that $u(x) \in \mathbb{R}$ for all x. It is easy to see that $x \succsim y$ implies $u(x) \geq u(y)$. To see the converse, assume that $x \succ y$. If one of $\{x, y\}$ is in Z, $u(x) > u(y)$ follows from the definition (6.3). Otherwise, invoke separability to find $z \in Z$ such that $x \succsim z \succsim y$ and then use (6.3).

Another little surprise in this theorem, somewhat less pleasant, is how messy is the proof of the converse direction. Normally we expect axiomatizations to have sufficiency, which is a challenge to prove, and necessity, which is simple. If it is obvious that the axioms are necessary, they are probably quite transparent and compelling. (If, by contrast, sufficiency is hard to prove, the theorem is surprising in a good sense: the axioms take us a long way.) Yet, we should be ready to work harder sometimes to prove the necessity of conditions such as continuity, separability, and others that bridge the gap between the finite and the infinite.

In our case, if we have a representation by a function u and if the range of u were the entire line $\mathbb{R}$, we would know what to do: in order to select a set Z that satisfies C3, take the rational numbers $\mathbb{Q} = \{q_1, q_2, \ldots\}$, for each such number q_i select z_i such that $u(z_i) = q_i$, and then show that Z separates X. The problem is that we may not find such a z_i for each q_i. In fact, it is even possible that $range(u) \cap \mathbb{Q} = \varnothing$.

We need not worry too much if a certain q_i is not in the range of u. In fact, life is a little easier: if no element will have this value, we will not be asked to separate between x and y whose utility is this value. However, what happens if we have values of u very close to q_i on both sides, but q_i is missing? In this case, if we fail to choose elements with u-values close to q_i, we may later be confronted with $x \succ y$ such that $u(x) \in (q_i, q_i + \varepsilon)$ and $u(y) \in (q_i - \varepsilon, q_i)$, and we will not have an element of z with $x \succsim z \succsim y$.

Now that we see what the problem is, we can also find a solution: for each q_i, find a countable nonincreasing sequence $\{z_i^k\}_k$ such that

$$\left\{u\left(z_i^k\right)\right\}_k \searrow \inf\{u(x)|u(x) > q_i\}$$

and a countable nondecreasing sequence $\{w_i^k\}_k$ such that

$$\left\{u\left(w_i^k\right)\right\}_k \nearrow \sup\{u(x)|u(x) < q_i\},$$

assuming that the sets on the right-hand sides are nonempty. The (countable) union of these countable sets will do the job.

6.3 INTERPRETATIONS

There are several different interpretations of the preceding theorem, as there will be of practically all the other axiomatizations discussed here. It is worth going over them in this case study in detail. Two interpretations relate to standard roles of theories, namely, normative and descriptive. The other one is meta-theoretic, as it relates to theoretical questions regarding what theories are or what theories should be. Observe that there are normative and descriptive questions here, but these are normative and descriptive questions of philosophy of science, rather than economics. A few digressions are in order here.

6.3.1   A Few Definitions

What Is Meant by "Normative"?

In economics we usually distinguish between descriptive and normative theories. Descriptive theories deal with the "is," while normative, with the "ought." The former attempt to provide an accurate description of reality, while the latter, to tell us what reality should be like.[4] It is important to recall that the distinction between normative and descriptive theories is very often in the interpretation, rather than in the mathematical model. When you consider the theorem given previously, it is not clear whether, say, transitivity is suggested as a claim about how real people actually make decisions or as a recommendation to decision makers. Loosely speaking, whether a paper suggests a normative or a descriptive theory will be judged by its introduction, not by its formal model.

We have a rather clear understanding of what it means for a theory to be accurate. We can contrast a theory's predictions with observed data, compute various measures of goodness of fit, and so on. Accuracy is not the only criterion for judging theories, and we are interested in generality and in simplicity as well.[5] Overall, there can be quite a bit of disagreement over the appropriate measure of simplicity, generality, and accuracy, and certainly over the appropriate way to trade them off. And yet, we more or less understand what we are after and hope to recognize it when we see it.

By contrast, what is meant by "normative"? Is any recommendation a normative theory? And how do we judge normative theories? If I were to walk around with a sign "Repent!," will I be engaging in normative science? Will I be a good normative scientist? And will your answer change if my sign read, "Repent, Doomsday is Near!"?

I think that "Repent!" hardly qualifies as a normative theory of the type that we want to see academics do in universities, especially if they spend taxpayers' money on these academic activities. Most of us do not think that religious preachers should be in universities, allegedly doing "normative science."

On the other hand, someone who comes with a reasoned argument such as "Observe, my friends: I have found out that doomsday is approaching. Given that, those of you who do not want to burn in hell may want to consider repentance" – which is a more polite way to say, "Repent, Doomsday is Near!" – is

---

[4] A word of warning: fellow social scientists tend to think that "normative" is a poor choice of a term. In psychology and related fields, the term means "complies with existing norms." As such, it can be a recommendation for individual behavior, but it is obviously quite different from the common usage in economics. The term "prescriptive" is sometimes used for a theory that provides recommendations, but it seems less popular these days.

[5] We often judge theories also on a scale of "intuitiveness." One can make the claim that this criterion is reducible to simplicity: intuitive theories are those that are part of a simple explanation of a wider array of phenomena, including everyday experiences. In fact, generality may also be reduced to simplicity: a theory that is less general would have to be complemented by another theory for the cases it does not apply to, resulting in a union of theories that is typically more complex.

hardly engaging in normative claims at all. She will only be making statements about reality: an unconditional statement about the timing of doomsday, and a conditional one about the relationship between repentance and burning in hell. Both statements can be considered purely descriptive, and they become recommendations for courses of action only if we couple them with our goals (presumably, to avoid burning in hell if possible).

The way I will use "normative" here[6] is a little different. A normative theory will be a descriptive theory, but not about observed reality, rather about the reality that people *would like* to observe. Thus, if we think of transitivity as a normative axiom, we will not just tell people that they should be transitive because we told them so. We will suggest transitivity as a mode of behavior that people would like to see themselves following. Similarly, an axiom such as anonymity in social choice theory can be interpreted as "wouldn't you like to live in a society where people's names do not affect the outcome of social interaction, namely, where the axiom of anonymity holds?"

It follows that the success of a normative theory, paralleling that of a descriptive theory, is in fitting observations. But the observations are not of people's behavior, rather, of their expressed wishes. A normative scientist can therefore be thought of as trying to market her theories to her audience. Should most of her listeners like the theory and decide to follow it (whether as individuals or as a group), we will crown the theory a success. If her listeners object, or just yawn and shrug their shoulders, we will have to admit that the theory failed as a normative one.[7]

What Is Meant by "What Is Meant"?

A side comment may be due here: when we ask earlier, "what is meant by . . . ," we try to find definitions that are, more or less, in accordance with common usage. In this sense, finding the definition for a term – such as "normative" and "rational" – is a bit like fitting a function to data. The data are positive and negative examples – phenomena that we agree do and do not fit the term – and the function is an attempt to find a simple characterization of the cases in which the term is considered appropriate. So described, defining terms is a task of a purely descriptive nature. In fact, it is completely equivalent to the task known as "classification problem" in computer science/machine learning: faced with positive and negative examples, one looks for a general rule, or at least an algorithm, that may be of help in classifying future instances.

However, sometimes the act of definition may take a more normative flavor: observing the usage of a certain term, one might conclude that some of it is confusing and that simple definitions would be more accurate if we decide to use the term a little differently. This is what happens when someone suggests

---

[6] This definition also appears in Gilboa and Schmeidler (2001).

[7] In fact, a theory in the social sciences has two souls: it can start as a descriptive theory of behavior, and if it fails, we can also try to repackage it and market it as a normative theory.

that we stop referring to tomatoes as "vegetables." This will also happen in this course when I ask you to use the word "rational" a little differently than some of my colleagues do.

It is important to recall that definitions are up to us to choose. We are free to define terms any way we wish. We should be clear on the definitions to avoid unnecessary confusion. And we can ask ourselves which definitions are the most useful for our discussion, but definitions do not designate any innate properties that entities might or might not have. For instance, there is no need to argue whether economics (or decision theory, or sociology) is a science. We may define "science" in a way that includes economics or in a way that doesn't, depending on which generalizations will be easier to state using the definition.[8]

Another comment that may be useful to bear in mind is that the classification of entities to those that satisfy a definition and those that don't is often blurred. For almost any dichotomous definition in real life one may find examples that are a little unclear. This does not mean that the distinction suggested by the definition is useless. It is sometimes hard to tell good from evil, and yet this is not a useless definition. Even the distinction between black and white has its gray areas.

Philosophy as a Social Science

I'll make one more personal comment and then we'll get back to business. I use the terms "descriptive" and "normative" theories in the context of the philosophy of science, namely, discussing what scientific theories are and what they should be like. This may raise the question, is philosophy of science similar to a social science, having a descriptive and a normative interpretation?

My view is that much of philosophy is indeed a social science. This is not only a minority view – most people I have mentioned this to think that I'm completely out of my mind, and have no idea what philosophy is about. Needless to say, it is also considered a major offence by philosophers. I will nevertheless try to defend this definition.

First, I refer only to those parts of philosophy that I can understand. Apparently, these are quite limited. If you excuse the personal confession, I'll admit that I suffer from a certain learning disability that makes me completely incapable of understanding metaphysics. As in the discussion of the grue-bleen paradox given in Chapter 5, I need to make things very concrete, preferably modeled by sequences of 0s and 1s, to feel that I understood them. For this reason, philosophers I talk to tell me that I systematically confound ontology

---

[8] This example is chosen to highlight the implicit assumption that the discussion is conducted in good faith. If we are vying for resources of the National Science Foundation, for instance, calling a field a "science" might have important political implications. We assume here that we are among friends and can ignore such considerations.

with epistemology – when they are trying to discuss what exists, I reformulate the discussion in terms of what I can know or grasp.[9]

But when I restrict attention to those philosophical discussions I can understand, I find that they deal with phenomena related to the human mind – how we think and how we should be thinking. This applies to philosophy of mind and language, to aesthetics and ethics, to philosophy of science and religion, and so on. Viewed as a collection of models of the way we think, reason, believe, and so forth, philosophy gets, perhaps expectedly, very close to psychology, which is typically viewed as a social science. Admittedly, psychology is much more descriptive than is philosophy. The latter deals much more with normative questions such as what should we believe, how should we reason, how should we use language, and how should we do science. But these normative discussions may well be part of social science. More importantly, these discussions are not divorced from descriptive ones. For instance, when dealing with questions such as the problem of induction or free will, our use of language or our moral judgment, our intuition provides the data for the discussion. Free will would not be a problem if we didn't have a sensation of free will. Goodman's paradox would not be puzzling if we didn't have a sense of what is a reasonable way to perform induction. Moral questions would have no bite if we didn't have a sense of right and wrong in at least some situations of choice. In short, philosophy often resorts to data, namely, to our intuition and to common practice in our way of reasoning, forming beliefs, talking, and so forth.

Even if you find my views quite outrageous, I would suggest that you consider the distinction between descriptive and normative philosophy, a distinction which I find useful for organizing our discussion.

6.3.2 A Meta-Scientific Interpretation

At the end of the nineteenth century and the beginning of the twentieth century there were several philosophers of science – most of them physicists – who devoted a lot of thinking to what science should look like. Physics was making tremendous progress at the time, but it had a long history that did not all seem very fruitful from a scientific point of view. In parallel, there were other fields that were making claims to the status of a science, but that seemed quite different from physics. Most notably, Freud appeared on the stage, revolutionizing psychology, but, at the same time, making claims that seemed very hard to judge on a scientific basis. The question then arose, how should science be conducted? What tells apart science from nonscience?

The body of thought that I refer to is known as *logical positivism*. It started in the writings of thinkers such as Mach, Duhem, Bohr, Einstein, and others,

---

[9] I think that my fascination with axiomatizations goes back to the same problem: translating potentially vague concepts such as "probability" and "utility" to observations makes me feel that I understand these concepts better. Others feel that I miss something deeper in this translation.

and culminated in what has become to be called the *Received View*, formulated by Carnap (1923). The principle of the *Received View* that affected economics mostly was the notion that any theoretical concept that is used in a theory should be related to observables. In the context of physics, this meant that even something as intuitive as mass should be related to the way in which it is measured. One can describe the procedure by which mass is measured, say, weighing objects on a scale, and then when the concept is used in physical laws, one knows how the laws translate to observations. Taking this view very seriously, some writers wondered whether one can theorize about the mass of the sun, since the sun cannot be put on a scale to be weighed. While this concern may seem a bit extreme, it gives us a sense of how seriously these physicists were taking their notion of observability.[10]

Popper (1934) took the logical positivist approach a step further and insisted that theories should be falsifiable. As is well known, Popper argued that theories can never be proved and that they can only be refuted or falsified. Emphasizing falsifiability, Popper argued that theories should state what cannot happen. Ideally, he argued, theories should have only universal quantifiers, for which it is easy to imagine a falsifying observation, and not involve existential quantifiers, which cannot be falsified by a single observation.

The notion of revealed preference in economics of the twentieth century is evidently an intellectual descendant of logical positivism. Whereas economists in the eighteenth and nineteenth centuries felt at ease theorizing about such concepts as utility, probability, or well-being, the discipline brought about by the logical positivist approach demanded that such concepts be defined in terms of observables.[11]

Theorem 6.1 can be viewed as a definition of "utility" along the lines suggested by logical positivism: we consider binary choices as direct observations. Observing the decision maker choosing x where y was also available, we claim that we observed $x \succsim y$. The axioms of completeness and transitivity have direct observable meaning. Completeness implies that some choice will be made and, in fact, also that the same choice will be made in repeated experiments. Transitivity also has a clear observational meaning. Separability, by contrast, is not as obvious. We should be a bit suspicious as soon as we notice that it involves an existential quantifier, and we know that Popper didn't like these. How would we know if the axiom is violated, namely, if there does not exist

[10] Quantum mechanics is considered to be the only field of science that was developed in light of the *Received View*. Indeed, it puts a great emphasis on what can be measured. In particular, Heisenberg's principle of uncertainty discusses the fact that the world is not deterministic *insomuch as we can measure it*. At the same time, modern developments in physics are often criticized for being observable only in theory, while in practice one can never get the energy levels required to test them.

[11] A similar development occurred in psychology. The rise of "behaviorist" psychology in the mid-twentieth century in the United States was an attempt to base psychology on observable phenomena, veering away from psychoanalysis, which was one of Popper's famous examples of a nonscientific enterprise.

a countable set Z such that so and so happens? Moreover, since all the data we can hope ever to observe are finite, what is the meaning of separability then?

As mentioned earlier, here, and in other axiomatizations later on, we should expect to have some axioms that are needed for the mathematics to work, but do not have a clear observable meaning. Axioms such as separability, continuity, and Archimedeanity will be there because we need them. They are stated in the language of the observable phenomena, but we do not seriously think that they can be directly tested in experiments.[12]

Having made this concession, we go back to the interpretation of the theorem as a definition of utility: the theorem suggests that the observable meaning of utility maximization is completeness and transitivity. Moreover, it tells us something not only about the existence of the function u but also about its uniqueness. Here it turns out to be the case that the function is far from being unique. Any monotone transformation thereof would do as a utility function representing preferences.

This is a very important lesson that we learn from playing the logical positivist game. Without the axioms, one may ask, for instance, whether the utility function from money, $u : \mathbb{R} \to \mathbb{R}$, is concave or convex. One may have some intuition for concavity based on the notion of decreasing marginal utility. But one can also challenge this notion and argue that u is convex. Which is a more plausible claim? The exercise of axiomatization tells us that this is a meaningless debate. One function u may be concave, and a monotone transformation thereof may be convex. In this case, the argument goes, the concavity/convexity debate is devoid of empirical content. The two theories are *observationally equivalent*. We should better save our time and efforts and concentrate on other questions, which do have some empirical meaning and which can possibly be determined by observations. The exercise of an axiomatization, asking what is the empirical import of a theoretical question, can thus save us a lot of time. It tells us what are scientific questions that are worth asking and what are metaphysical questions that will never be determined by evidence.

I often wish I could leave this lesson at that. The fact that the utility function is only ordinal (rather than cardinal) is perhaps the most obvious contribution of the axiomatic approach when interpreted meta-scientifically. Unfortunately, I do not believe in this claim. In Section 6.4 I try to convince you that the utility function is, in reality, much more unique than the theorem would have us believe.

The meta-scientific interpretation, being so closely related to measurement, can also be used to elicit the utility function. This application is not very

---

[12] Sometimes we can test the implications of these axioms in conjunction with other axioms. But this amounts to a test of a theory, rather than of each of its axioms. Axioms can also be tested for plausibility by "thought experiments," but these are not actual observations and may, among other difficulties, be subject to various framing effects.

obvious in this example, partly because the axioms are very simple and partly because they result in a class of functions that leaves a large degree of freedom. However, in other axiomatizations in this book, we will see that the axioms can often suggest ways to measure or calibrate theoretical concepts. These measurement procedures may be useful for an experimentalist who wishes to find a person's utility function or for the person herself, if she wishes to ask herself simple preference questions, pinpoint her utility function, and then use it in more complicated problems. We will comment on this type of application in many of the following axiomatizations.

6.3.3   A Normative Interpretation

The normative interpretation of Theorem 6.1 is perhaps the most straightforward. Consider an imaginary exchange with a decision maker (DM), who needs to make a choice. Assume that this is a choice about where to live or whom to marry. The analyst (A), who wants to engage in normative science, attempts to tell the decision maker how she should make decisions:

A: I suggest that you attach a utility index to each alternative and choose the alternative with the highest utility.

DM: Obviously, you studied math.

A: A bit, so what?

DM: You've been brainwashed. You think only in terms of functions. But this is an important decision, there are people involved, emotions, these are not functions! You obviously understand nothing about the human soul!

A: Let's do it slowly. You will make a decision in the end, won't you?

DM: And suppose I don't?

A: Well, we can call that a decision, too. If this is included, you will make a decision?

DM: OK, suppose I will.

A: Would you feel comfortable with cycling among three possible options?

DM: What do you mean?

A: Preferring x to y, and then y to z, but then again z to x.

DM: No, this is very silly and counterproductive. I told you that there are people involved, and I don't want to play with their feelings.

A: Good. So now let me tell you a secret: if you follow these two conditions – making decisions and avoid cycling – then you can be described as if you are maximizing a utility function. Wouldn't you like to bring it forth and see explicitly what function you will end up maximizing? Is it more rational to ignore it? Moreover, choosing a function and maximizing it may be the only known algorithm to avoid indecision or incoherent decisions – isn't this another reason to specify your function?

This is supposed to be the way that the axioms are used normatively – they are used as rhetorical devices, as a way to convince the decision maker that the theoretical procedure of utility maximization, which may otherwise appear arbitrary and perhaps inappropriate, actually makes sense. Observe that the way the analyst used the axioms previously is consistent with our notion of a normative theory – the decision maker is the ultimate judge. If she rejects the axioms, the analysts will have to go back to the drawing board. Suggesting the axioms as normative criteria is an attempt to model the decision maker's preferences – not over the actual choice, but over the type of procedure she would like to follow or the type of decision maker she would like to be.[13]

6.3.4 A Descriptive Interpretation

Suppose that we are interested in descriptive theories only. What purpose do the axioms serve? If the axiomatization, as Theorem 6.1, is a characterization theorem, it provides two equivalent descriptions of the same theory. The theory does not become more or less accurate as a result of having an equivalent description thereof.

Yet, axiomatizations are useful for descriptive purposes as well. First, the axioms define the exact scope of phenomena that are consistent with the theory. In particular, they clarify when (if at all) the theory may be refuted. Second, the axioms can help us test different ingredients of the theory separately. Especially if the theory does not perform very well and we wish to amend it, it may be useful to test each axiom separately and see which one should be modified to obtain better predictions. Third, and perhaps most importantly, the axioms are needed when theories are not expected to be accurate descriptions of reality. This point calls for elaboration.

If an economic theory is tested directly in terms of the accuracy of its predictions, it should not matter which description, out of several equivalent ones, is used for the test. But we often view economic theories only as metaphors, illustrations, or some other notion of the kind. That is, the theories are tools that help us think about problems, but they need not be taken literally. As such, theories are used as rhetorical devices also when interpreted descriptively.

Consider an example. Suppose that A and B engage in a heated debate about the merits and woes of globalization. A brings the first welfare theorem as a reason to allow free trade and support globalization. B counters that the

---

[13] Gilboa *et al.* (2008) focus on another normative interpretation of axioms, which is their application in concrete cases. According to this interpretation, the decision maker need not be aware of universal statements (such as the axioms) or theorems (such as the representation theorem discussed), but only of instances of the axioms. Thus, the decision maker may agree that since she preferred a to b and b to c, she should better prefer a to c, and she may even agree with this statement for any specific a, b, c that are brought before her. But she need not be aware, let alone agree with the statement "For every $x, y, z,$ if . . . , then. . . ." In this interpretation, this general statement, as well as the theorem using it, is part of the knowledge of the analyst, but not necessarily of the decision maker.

theorem discusses Pareto optimality, which is defined in terms of maximization of utility functions, and therefore has limited applicability. "No one walks around maximizing utility functions. Only sick minds can view human beings this way. The welfare theorems refer to non-existent entities that should better never come into existence."

In response, A can patiently go through a dialog (similar to that given earlier), getting B to admit that most human beings, no matter how free their souls are and how unique they are in human history, can be thought of as making decisions and making them in a transitive way. Then A can say "Ah-ha! If you admit that this is how people behave, for the most part, you have just admitted that people maximize a utility function, for the most part."

Precisely because economic theories are not accurate and are not expected to be accurate, their representation matters. A theory can appear more or less plausible given a different mathematical formulation. If accuracy is directly tested, different representations would lead to the same results. But when accuracy is only roughly and informally assessed, representation can make a difference.

In this context, mathematical results, in particular, characterization theorems, can be viewed as "framing effects" (Tversky and Kahneman, 1981): equivalent representations should be just as compelling. And yet, they are not. In our example, the same theory is much more compelling when framed in the language of completeness and transitivity than in the language of utility maximization.

Mathematical economics is often associated with a modernist view of the profession, believing in a clear and testable objective reality that, presumably, mathematical machinery may help us decipher. By contrast, postmodern theories suggest that objective reality does not exist and that the scientific arena is a battlefield in which different groups in society compete for power by constructing "reality" and "evidence," which are but rhetorical devices. This view is typically not associated with formal mathematical analysis. We find, however, that mathematics may be useful in a postmodern view of the profession even more than in a modern one. Precisely because theories are rhetorical devices, their representation matters. Indeed, if it's all about rhetoric, what better rhetorical device can one suggest than a surprising mathematical proof?

6.4 LIMITATIONS

As mentioned previously, the meta-scientific interpretation of the result was supposed to tell us to what extent the utility function u is observable. Specifically, we are told that since the only observable data are binary choices, the function is only ordinal, given up to an arbitrary monotone transformation. This is one of the most basic, as well as most prominent, examples in which the axiomatic approach teaches us something new and even counterintuitive. As a person who makes a living out of axiomatizations, it is therefore painful to admit that this lesson is misleading. The fact is that in real preferences there is much more information than in binary relations. So much more information that the utility function, to the extent that we can observe it, is probably cardinal after all.

6.4.1 Semiorders

Psychophysics

It might have happened to you that you were carrying a pile of papers, or clothes, and didn't notice that you dropped a few. The decrease in the total weight you were carrying was probably not large enough for you to notice. Two objects may be too close in terms of weight for us to notice the difference between them.

This problem is common to perception in all our senses. If I ask you whether two rods are of the same length or not, there are differences that will be too small for you to notice. The same would apply to your perception of sound (volume and pitch), light, temperature, and so forth. The fact that our perceptive capabilities are limited has long been recognized. It has also been observed that our perception obeys certain laws.

Weber (1834) noticed the following regularity: consider a certain measurable stimulus S (to a given person under given conditions). Consider the minimal increase in S that is needed for the person to notice the difference, namely, the *just noticeable difference* (jnd), ΔS. Next, consider varying the initial stimulus S. For every initial level S, we may find a different jnd, $\Delta S = \Delta S(S)$. Weber's law[14] states that the two are proportional. That is, there exists a constant $k > 0$ such that

$$\frac{\Delta S}{S} = k.$$

For example, suppose that I show you two rods, one of length of 1 foot, and the other, 1.1 feet. Suppose you can tell that the latter is longer than the former, but that this is the minimal length for which you can discern the difference. Next, assume that I show you a rod of 2 feet and compare it to an even longer rod. The law states that the minimal length at which you would notice the difference is 2.2 feet.

The constant k may naturally depend on the person and the experimental conditions, such as the amount of light in the room and the distance from the rods. But if we hold all these fixed, the law says that k does not change with S. As any law in the social (or even medical) sciences, the accuracy of Weber's

---

[14] The literature often refers to the "Weber–Fechner law." Daniel Algom has pointed out to me that Fechner's (1860) contribution is quite different from Weber's (1834). Weber dealt only with just-noticeable differences on the stimulus scale, whereas Fechner was also interested in a quantitative theory of subjective sensation (see Marks and Algom, 1998). Since our focus here is only on the ability to discern differences, rather than on modeling subjective sensation, Weber's law is the appropriate reference.

law should not be expected to be perfect. But it is apparently a rather good approximation.[15]

It is important to emphasize that the definition of "discerning the difference" is probabilistic. If we ask a participant in an experiment to tell us which of two rods is longer, we do not expect the success rate (in identifying the longer rod) to switch from 50% (chance level) to 100% as ΔS crosses the threshold kS. The transition in the probability of detection is bound to be continuous, and the operational definition of "discern the difference" is "identifies the larger stimulus with probability at least p," where $p = 75\%$ is a popular value in experiments.

Intransitive Indifference

Motivated by Weber's law, Luce (1956) suggested to apply the same logic to the measurement of utility. His starting point was that due to our imperfect perception ability, our preferences cannot possibly be transitive. Luce provided the following example: suppose that I offer you two cups of coffee, one without any sugar and another in which I put one grain of sugar. Do you think you will be able to tell the difference? If your answer is positive, cut the grain in half. At some point you will have to concede that your palate is not so refined as to tell one cup from the other. In this case, you will also have to admit that you are indifferent between them. Indeed, how can you strictly prefer one to the other if you won't even be able to tell which is which?

To state the obvious, one may be indifferent between two alternatives that are very different from each other. You can find a price of, say, a vacation package that would make me precisely indifferent between taking the vacation or foregoing it and keeping my money. Thus the inability to perceive differences is sufficient, but not necessary for indifference.

Let us now consider two cups of coffee, one with a single grain of sugar and one with two. If we denote by c_i a cup with i grains of sugar, it seems likely that we will observe $c_i \sim c_{i+1}$ for every $i \geq 0$, simply because a single grain is never observable. However, if $\succsim$ were transitive (as Theorem 6.1 assumes), $\sim$ would also be transitive, and one would find that $c_i \sim c_j$ for every $i, j \geq 0$; that is, two cups of coffee with any amounts of sugar in them are equivalent in the eyes of the decision maker. This is clearly unrealistic.

It seems natural to relax the assumption that the indifference relation is transitive. Proximity is typically not a transitive relation. "Sitting next to," "bordering on," and "being in an ε-neighborhood of" are all intransitive binary relations. "Being closer than the just noticeable difference" belongs to this class of relations.

---

[15] Fechner's law, stating that subjective sensation is a logarithmic function of physical stimulus, has often been challenged (see Marks and Algom, 1998; Stevens, 1957). Weber's law, restricted to the notion of discernability, is still considered a robust finding. (My source here is, again, Daniel Algom.)

Refining Preference Theory

Luce (1956) went on to redefine observable preference. He considered a binary relation P on a set of alternatives X. The relation P is interpreted as strict preference, where $I = (P \cup P^{-1})^c$, as absence of preference in either direction or "indifference."[16] Suppose that, in the spirit of Weber's law, we are interested in a utility representation of the following type: we say that $u : X \to \mathbb{R}$ *L-represents* P if for all $x, y \in X$,

$$x P y \quad \text{iff} \quad u(x) - u(y) > 1. \tag{6.4}$$

Luce formulated three axioms, which are readily seen to be necessary for an L-representation. He defined a relation P to be a semiorder if it satisfied these three axioms and analyzed its properties.

To state the axioms, it will be useful to have a notion of concatenation of relations. Given two binary relations, $B_1, B_2 \subset X \times X$, let $B_1 B_2 \subset X \times X$ be defined as follows: for all $x, y \in X$,

$$x B_1 B_2 y \quad \text{iff} \quad \exists z \in X, \ x B_1 z, \ z B_1 y.$$

We say that P (or (P, I)) is a *semiorder* if:

L1. P is irreflexive (i.e., $x P x$ for no $x \in X$).
L2. $P I P \subset P$.
L3. $P P I \subset P$.

The meaning of L2 is, therefore, as follows: assume that $x, z, w, y \in X$ are such that $x P z I w P y$. Then it has to be the case that $x P y$. Similarly, L3 requires that $x P y$ hold whenever there are $z, w \in X$ such that $x P z P w I y$.

Since I is reflexive, each of L2 and L3 implies transitivity of P (but not of I!). But L2 and L3 require something beyond transitivity of P. For example, if $X = \mathbb{R}^2$ and P is defined by Pareto domination, P is transitive but you can verify that it satisfies neither L2 nor L3.

Conditions L2 and L3 restrict the indifference relation I. For the Pareto relation P, the absence of preference, I, means intrinsic incomparability. Hence we can have, say, $x P z P w I y$ without being able to say much on the comparison between x and y. It is possible that y is incomparable to any of x, z, w because one of y's coordinates is higher than the corresponding coordinate for all of x, z, w. This is not the case if I reflects only the inability to discern small differences. Thus, L2 and L3 can be viewed as saying that the incomparability of alternatives, reflected in I, can only be attributed to issues of discernability and not to fundamental problems as in the case of Pareto dominance.

It is an easy exercise to show that L2 and L3 are necessary conditions for an L-representation to exist. It takes more work to prove the following.[17]

---

[16] For a relation $P \subset X \times X$, define P^{-1} to be the inverse; that is, $P^{-1} = \{(x, y) | (y, x) \in P\}$. Thus, $I = (P \cup P^{-1})^c$ is equivalent to, say, $x I y$ if and only if neither $x P y$ nor $y P x$.
[17] The existence result is not explicit in Luce (1956).

Theorem 6.2 *(Luce) Let X be finite. $P \subset X \times X$ is a semiorder if and only if there exists $u : X \to \mathbb{R}$ that L-represents it.*

We will not prove this theorem here,[18] but we will make several comments about it.

1. You might wonder what happened to a third natural condition, namely:

L4. $IPP \subset P$.

It turns out that it is implied by L2 and L3, as is L3 by L2 and L4.

2. If you drop L3 (but do not add L4), you get a family of relations that Fishburn (1970*b*, 1985) defined as *interval relations*. Fishburn proved that if X is finite, a relation is an interval relation if and only if it can be represented as follows: for every $x \in X$, we have an interval, $[b(x), e(x)]$, with $b(x) \le e(x)$, such that

$$x P y \quad \text{iff} \quad b(x) > e(y),$$

that is, $x P y$ if and only if the entire range of values associated with x, $[b(x), e(x)]$, is higher than the range of values associated with y, $[b(y), e(y)]$.

Given such a representation, you can define $u(x) = b(x)$ and $\delta(x) = e(x) - b(x)$ to get an equivalent representation

$$x P y \quad \text{iff} \quad u(x) - u(y) > \delta(y). \tag{6.5}$$

Comparing (6.5) to (6.4), you can think of (6.5) as a representation with a variable just noticeable difference, whereas (6.4) has a constant jnd, which is normalized to 1.

3. If P is a semiorder, one can define from it a relation $Q = PI \cup IP$, that is, $x Q y$ if there exists a z such that $(x P z$ and $z I y)$ or $(x I z$ and $z P y)$. This is an indirectly revealed preference: suppose that $x I y$ but $x P z$ and $z I y$. This means that a direct comparison of x and y does not reveal a noticeable difference and therefore no preference either. But, when comparing x and y to another alternative z, it turns out that x is different enough from z to be preferred to it, while y isn't. Indirectly, we find evidence that x is actually better than y for our decision maker, even though the decision maker herself cannot discern the difference when the two are presented to her. (Similar logic applies if $x I P y$.)

If P is a semiorder, Q turns out to be the strict part of a weak order. Moreover, one can get an L-representation of P by a function u that simultaneously also satisfies

$$x Q y \quad \text{iff} \quad u(x) - u(y) > 0.$$

4. When X is infinite, there are two types of difficulties. The first has to do with numerical representations in general, as in the case of Theorem 6.1, and calls for appropriate separability conditions. The second has to do with the

---

[18] The proof can be found in Beja and Gilboa (1992).

fact that we want a fixed just noticeable difference, which we normalized to 1. Suppose, for instance, that we have an infinite but bounded sequence of strict preferences, say, $x_1 P x_2 P \ldots P x_*$. As the sequence is infinite, we will not be able to find a real number that is low enough to be the u-value of x_*. Necessary and sufficient conditions on P that would allow an L-representation in general are provided in Beja and Gilboa (1992).

Uniqueness of the Utility Function

We finally get back to the question of uniqueness. How unique is a utility function that L-represents a semiorder P? In general the answer may be very messy. Let us therefore suppose that we are dealing with a large X and that there are two functions $u, v : X \to \mathbb{R}$, such that for all $x, y \in X$,

$$x P y \Leftrightarrow u(x) - u(y) > 1 \Leftrightarrow v(x) - v(y) > 1$$
$$x Q y \Leftrightarrow u(x) - u(y) > 0 \Leftrightarrow v(x) - v(y) > 0$$

and that $range(u) = range(v) = \mathbb{R}$. Assume without loss of generality that $u(0) = v(0) = 0$. The functions u and v can be quite different on $[0, 1]$. But if x is such that $u(x) = 1$, we will also have to have $v(x) = 1$. To see this, imagine that $v(x) > 1$. Then there are alternatives y with $v(y) \in (1, v(x))$. This would mean that according to v, $y P 0$, while according to u, $y I 0$, a contradiction.

The same logic applies to any point we start out with. That is, for every x, y,

$$u(x) - u(y) = 1 \Leftrightarrow v(x) - v(y) = 1$$

and this obviously generalizes to $(u(x) - u(y) = k \Leftrightarrow v(x) - v(y) = k)$ for every $k \in \mathbb{Z}$. Moreover, we obtain

$$|u(x) - v(x)| < 1 \qquad \forall x.$$

In other words, the just noticeable difference, which we here normalized to 1, has an observable meaning. Every function that L-represents P has to have the same jnd. Similarly, if we consider any two alternatives x and y and find that

$$3 < u(x) - u(y) < 4,$$

we know that these inequalities will also hold for any other utility function v. And the reason is, again, that utility differences became observable to a certain degree: we have an observable distinction between "greater than the jnd" and "smaller than (or equal to) the jnd." This distinction, however coarse, gives us some observable anchor by which we can measure distances along the utility scale: we can count how many integer jnd steps exist between alternatives.

One can make a stronger claim if one recalls that the semiorders were defined for a given probability threshold, say, $p = 75\%$. If one varies the probability, one can obtain a different semiorder. Thus we have a family of semiorders

$\{P_p\}_{p>.5}$. Under certain assumptions, all these semiorders can be represented simultaneously by the same utility function u and a corresponding family of jnd's, $\{\delta_p\}_{p>.5}$, such that

$$x P_p y \iff u(x) - u(y) > \delta_p$$
$$x Q y \iff u(x) - u(y) > 0.$$

In this case, it is easy to see that the utility u will be unique to a larger degree than before. We may even find that as $p \to .5, \delta_p \to 0$, that is, if we are willing to make do with very low probabilities of detection, we will get very low jnd's, and correspondingly, any two functions u and v that L-represent the semiorders $\{P_p\}_{p>.5}$ will be identical.

Observe that the uniqueness result depends discontinuously on the jnd δ: the smaller is δ, the less freedom we have in choosing the function u, since $\sup |u(x) - v(x)| \leq \delta$. But when we consider the case $\delta = 0$, we are back with a weak order, for which u is only ordinal.

One can argue that the jnd steps on the utility scale are psychologically meaningful. I may ask you if you prefer to be able to consume a worth of $100 to $0 a day, and whether you prefer to consume a worth of $200 to $100 a day. I trust that in both cases the answer will be in the affirmative. Perhaps I can also ask you what would make a bigger difference in your utility level – the increase from $0 to $100 or from the latter to $200. You may or may not be willing to respond to such questions.[19] Even if you are, your microeconomics teacher may come to haunt you at night, asking in a menacing tone, "but what does it mean?" Indeed, in the absence of additional structure (such as lotteries, states of the world, or additional goods that can be traded off with money), you will be hard-pressed to give a decision situation in which these comparisons correspond to different choices. But you will be able to say, "Let's count how many jnd's are there between $0 and $100, and then do the same for $100 and $200." When you start with $0, you are probably hungry and homeless. The first $5 a day buy you a meal, which is a huge difference in your well-being. In fact, a fraction of a meal is very noticeable if you are starving. But the next $5 are less meaningful, and the difference between $100 and $105 a day may not be noticeable. Thus, in the range $100–$200 there will be fewer just noticeable differences than in the range $0–$100.

The intuition of this example is precisely the ancient intuition for which economists used to believe that the utility function exhibits decreasing marginal utility. When Daniel Bernoulli (1738) suggested the expected utility resolution to his St. Petersburg's paradox, he argued that the marginal utility of money is inversely proportional to the amount of money one already has.[20] We therefore find that the intuitive discussions of the behavior of the marginal utility in

---

[19] Alt (1936) derived a cardinal utility based on comparisons of this nature.

[20] Obviously, from $u'(x) \propto 1/x$, we obtain the logarithmic function that solved Bernoulli's problem.

the eighteenth and nineteenth centuries were not as meaningless as modern economics would have us believe.[21]

6.4.2 Other Ways to Measure Utility

The previous discussion suggests that real preferences have much more information in them than a simple weak order $\succsim$. When we observe the choices of real people, we find that choices have a random component to them. Indeed, discrete choice theory, which is widely used in marketing, attempts to explain consumer behavior by assuming that choice is probabilistic and by asking what factors affect the distribution of choice. Using probabilities of choice as additional data, we have argued that these additional data suffice to pin down a utility function with much less degrees of freedom than do deterministic choice models.

The probability of choice is not the only additional source of information we may have on consumer preferences. We may measure response times, speculating that larger differences in utility might be reflected in shorter response times. And we may also use neurological studies, using brain activity to identify strength of preferences.

It turns out that the notion of an ordinal utility function and the belief that it is meaningless to discuss utility differences are artifacts of a mathematical model. Deciding to model preferences by a weak order is a modeling choice. It greatly simplifies our lives as we do not need to deal with messy objects such as probabilities of choice. Economic theory opted for a model that ignores some of the data in favor of analytical ease. This is a perfectly legitimate choice to make. But it is not perfectly legitimate to decide to ignore some observable data and then declare as meaningless questions that could be answered using the data we chose to ignore.

---

[21] One may try to push this line of thought a little further and ask whether just noticeable differences may help us solve problems of interpersonal comparisons of utility. Gilboa and Lapson (1995) contains results that can be interpreted as derivation of utilitarianism based on this idea. (This interpretation does not appear in the paper because, to be honest, the editor was unconvinced that it adds much to the paper.)

CHAPTER 7

The Role of Theories

7.1 THEORIES ARE ALWAYS WRONG

In the heat of the debate regarding the uniqueness of the utility function we may have failed to highlight some observations regarding the way we think about theories. We have to discuss it at some point, and this seems as good as any.

Transitivity of preferences implies transitivity of indifference, and we convinced ourselves that this is a highly idealized assumption. We even concluded that transitivity is the main culprit in obtaining the wrong conclusion that the utility function is only ordinal. At the same time, we argued that it might be a "legitimate" assumption. How can an assumption that is violated by all people almost all the time be legitimate? What is meant by a "legitimate" or "reasonable" assumption?

Let us consider an example. Suppose that A and B debate the issue of globalization, as in Section 6.3.4. A mentions the welfare theorems, and B counters that they rely on the assumption of transitive indifference, which is totally and absolutely false. What would you say?

You may wonder whether competitive equilibria exist and whether they are optimal when weak orders are replaced by semiorders.[1] But you may also feel that the argument is besides the point. We are mature enough to understand that our theories are not perfect descriptions of reality and that they are simplifications, abstractions, illustrations, caricatures,[2] metaphors, or any other term that you may use to downplay the theorist's aspirations. Theories are never correct, and in the case of the social sciences they tend to be almost always wrong. The question is, therefore, not whether they are right or wrong, but whether they are wrong in a way that invalidates the conclusions drawn from them. In other ways, theories are tools for reasoning and rhetorical devices.[3] In

---

[1] For an existence result, see Jamison and Lau (1977).

[2] A term used by Gibbard and Varian (1978).

[3] The term "rhetorical device" need not be understood as a negative term, suggesting manipulability and dishonesty. It may well refer to a sound argument that convinces us of a certain conclusion.

the context of the preceding debate, there appears to be no reason to question the intuition behind the welfare theorems due to the issue of just noticeable differences.

Contrast imperfect perception with another problem. Suppose that transitivity is violated because of the existence of cycles of strict preferences. For example, consider a bowl of peanuts, where you strictly prefer to consume $(i + 1)$ peanuts to i for every $i \geq 0$, but you also strictly prefer to consume 0 peanuts to 100. This is typical of self-discipline problems: there is a temptation to obtain a short-run payoff, and it competes with a long-run goal. The long-run goal is, overall, much more important than the short-run payoff. But in a sequence of pairwise comparisons, the short-run payoff is clear and palpable, while the long-run goal is not affected in a significant way. Moreover, there is a temporal dimension that allows this sequence of comparisons to lead to a sequence of often-irreversible decisions. The decision maker ends up with an alternative that she judges to be much worse than the one with which she has started out. Thus, people find themselves smoking and drinking more than they would have liked to, staying in bed in the morning longer than they can afford to, and incurring debt more than they think they should.

Faced with such violations of transitivity, in particular in a classical economic context such as debt, one may ask whether the conclusions of the welfare theorems are indeed valid. For example, suppose that B were suggesting to limit people's ability to use credit cards. A insists that consumers are sovereign decision makers, and if they decide to incur debt, so they should. Any intervention in the credit market, says A, will result in a Pareto-dominated outcome. But then B counters that decision makers who have cyclical preferences often regret their past choices, something that does not happen to the agents in the competitive equilibrium model of Arrow and Debreu.

You may or may not agree with B's claim, but I think that it seems much more relevant than the just noticeable difference claim. Both claims are based on violations of the same axiom, namely, transitivity. The just noticeable difference (jnd) violation of transitivity is rather universal and ubiquitous – all people, practically in all problems, are prone to exhibit imperfect perception abilities. Yet, we feel that jnd's are irrelevant to our views on competitive equilibria. Violations of transitivity due to a lack of self-control, by contrast, are relevant only to some people in some decision problems. Many people do not have self-control problems, and there are many economic decisions that do not pose temptations and do not require self-control in the first place. And yet, despite the more limited scope of violations of transitivity in the second example, we may find that these violations undermine certain results of transitivity more than do the violations in the first example.

It follows that the degree to which we are willing to accept an assumption does not need to be a monotone function of its degree of accuracy. The assumption is tested based not only on its direct implications, but also on its indirect implications, which may involve nontrivial theorems. That is, we wish to test the validity of an assumption in the context of a theory, based on the accuracy of all the conclusions drawn from the theory, and not just by those drawn from the assumption in isolation.

The preceding discussion brings to mind Friedman's celebrated argument that theories should not be judged based on the validity of their assumptions, but on that of their conclusions. This argument is a bit extreme, and I would be careful to accept it. First, if a "theory" may also be an assumption, such as transitivity, the assumption is also a conclusion of the theory (in a trivial sense). It is generally hard to draw a sharp distinction between assumptions and conclusions, completely ignoring the veracity of the former and testing only the latter. Second, Friedman's argument has been used for many years by economists to fend off various attacks, especially from psychologists. Justifiably or not, it has become a bit of an excuse not to question the theory.

However, if we refine the argument a bit, it may make more sense. Consider a given theory and imagine a "grade sheet" for it, in which there are many instances where its predictions are tested and compared to data. Some of these predictions are very concrete, such as "If A chose x over y and y over z, A will choose x over z," and some predictions are more involved, such as "Equilibria will be Pareto optimal." Different scientists may put different weights on these predictions. Marketing researchers may focus on the prediction of choices made by individual consumers, whereas economic theorists will find that the welfare theorems are the most important conclusions. Depending on the goal for which a theory is developed, it may be viewed as more or less accurate. And it is possible that certain assumptions jointly lead to conclusions that are more accurate than any of the assumptions when tested in isolation.

7.2   THEORIES AND CONCEPTUAL FRAMEWORKS

The logical positivist heritage (coupled with Popper's contribution) suggests that our theories should be falsifiable. The axiomatization we saw earlier is formulated in terms of conditions that can be violated. However, a theory such as utility maximization is not always easy to falsify. Any empirical phenomenon we observe can be explained in many ways, and often can also be made to conform to the theory, where the latter is appropriately interpreted, recast, and reformulated. Only in carefully designed controlled experiments can one hope to unambiguously refute a theory, but then one faces questions of external validity: the fact that a theory fails in artificial experimental environment may not be an indication that it will also fail in natural environments, to which it was presumably intended in the first place.

Not all theories in economics or in social science, in general, seem to have such flexibility. There are theories whose predictions are very concrete, such as, say, the relation between money supply and inflation. However, this does not seem to be the case with utility maximization, expected utility maximization, Nash equilibrium, and so forth.

In Gilboa and Schmeidler (2001) we referred to such structures as "conceptual frameworks." A conceptual framework has a language to describe phenomena and a subset of predictions (or recommendations, if we adopt a normative interpretation). But it does not specify a mapping from the theoretical concepts to real-life ones. For example, the framework of utility maximization deals with alternatives and choices, and it makes some predictions about the latter. But it does not commit to a particular set of alternatives. These may be consumption bundles, Arrow securities, consumption plans, and so forth. Moreover, an apparent violation of the predictions in one mapping may be explained away under another mapping, embedding the observations in a richer context.

Similarly, expected utility theory has both a language and a set of predictions, but it can be applied to a variety of states of the world and outcomes. Game theory, coupled with the prediction of (say) Nash equilibrium (Nash, 1951), provides precise predictions if we know who the players are, what are their strategies, and so forth. But a given observation that may be at odds with the prediction can be explained away by embedding the game in a larger context, involving more players, more time periods, additional sources of uncertainty, and so forth.

This description may suggest that conceptual frameworks are an evasive tool designed by theorists to avoid refutations. Moreover, it appears that theories in economics are not very clear about their status: they pretend to have observable meaning and to be falsifiable, but then when falsification is a real danger, they are not committed to any prediction. Can we take economic theories seriously?

The argument is that we can, and, in fact, that the dual status of economic "theories" – as conceptual frameworks and as specific theories – can actually be beneficial. Recall that we are not hoping to obtain theories that are very accurate. We use the theories more often as reasoning aids. As such, it is important to know that the theories have some empirical content and that given a particular mapping from theoretical objects to actual ones, a theory is not vacuous. At the same time, we would needlessly limit ourselves if we commit to a particular mapping and do not allow ourselves, for example, to apply lessons from consumer theory to decision under uncertainty, from one-shot to repeated games, and so forth. Precisely because we take a humble point of view, according to which theories are never correct, we can be justified in reinterpreting the theoretical terms, hoping to gain insight where precise prediction may be beyond our aspirations. At the same time, we do and should use the guidelines of logical positivism. This is not because we pretend to construct theories that are as valid as theories in physics. Rather, it is because some of the lessons regarding how physics should not be done apply to our field as well.

Having said that, it is always a good idea to keep in mind that one has a choice among conceptual frameworks and that their scope of applicability is not universal. A conceptual framework will seldom be refuted by empirical evidence. However, its language may appear less appropriate to describe certain phenomena and its predictions may seem to require too much adaptation in order to be valid. We should not wait for a conceptual framework to be refuted in order to replace it. It suffices that the framework be inconvenient for us to look for alternatives.

7.3 LOGICAL POSITIVISM AS A METAPHOR

The Received View was considered to be the dominant view of the way science should be conducted for about three decades. In the 1950s there were two directions of attacks on the Received View (and on logical positivism). One direction was, as it were, internal, and challenged the theory on its own grounds. Quine (1953) called into question the distinction between analytic and synthetic propositions, namely, propositions whose truthfulness follows from definitions versus propositions with an external empirical content. Hanson (1958) went further to challenge the distinction between theories and observations, arguing that the latter were always theory laden.

The other direction was quite different from the Received View itself, and it is often described as a switch from the philosophy of science to the sociology of science. It started with Kuhn (1962), who asked questions about scientific paradigms and the way they changed. Kuhn described scientific evolution as a social phenomenon that need not converge to any objective truth. Rather, it was a process involving many factors, including accumulating evidence on the one hand, but also personal interests and tastes on the other. This postmodern line of thought has been brought to extremities by Foucault, Latour, and other writers who deny the existence of any objective truth and conceptualize all scientific activity as a struggle for power, influence, and other resources.

Between the two lines of attacks, logical positivism lost much of its luster. It is to a large extent discredited. As an outside observer who is certainly not a professional philosopher, I may not be qualified to comment on this state of affairs. But you realize that I'm going to anyway. So the truth is that I can't help feeling that some lessons from the social sciences might be useful for philosophy (which, you may recall, I view as a social science).

Let us start with the analytic critique of logical positivism. The fact that one may not always be able to draw the line between analytic and synthetic propositions, or between theory and evidence, does not make these distinctions useless. In economic theory we are accustomed to discuss imprecise theories, or rather too precise theories that are at odds with a messy reality. If we take the view that philosophy of science is a social science, and if we consider logical positivism as a model of how science should be done, it is not such a bad model. It can serve as a rather good approximation and as a guideline, not to mention as a mental toolbox to carry with us when we face specific problems.

The postmodern critique sometimes appears to confound descriptive and normative claims. It may well be true that science will never be able to be completely objective. But this does not mean that it shouldn't try. It is probably right that every scientist will forever be influenced by the social milieu in which he was brought up, his financial incentives, and his never-ending conflict with his father. But this is a far cry from accepting these forces and legitimizing them. There are instances of postmodern critique that sound to me similar to the argument, "We know that wars are inevitable. Hence, let's start shooting people."

To conclude, I find that, at least for the purposes of economic theory, logical positivism is alive and well. We have to understand it as a normative theory of the philosophy of science, as it was originally intended to be. The sociology of science, much more descriptive by nature, might indicate what is the scope of expectations we can reasonably entertain about the theories we can develop. As is usually the case, descriptive theories inform us about the practicality of normative ones. But we should not confuse the descriptive with the normative. We should bear in mind that logical positivism itself, as a theory, is but an illustration, or a metaphor, but we should not dismiss it as wrong.

CHAPTER 8

Von Neumann–Morgenstern's Theorem

8.1 BACKGROUND

The idea of maximization of expected utility first appeared explicitly in Daniel Bernoulli's St. Petersburg paradox (Bernoulli, 1738), which goes as follows:[1] you are faced with a sequence of tosses of a fair coin. Every toss has a probability of 50% to come up on head and on tail, and the game will end the first time the coin comes up head. If this happens on the nth trial, you get 2^n dollars. The "paradox" is that most people are willing to pay only a finite (and rather small) amount of money to play this game, despite the fact that the expected value is infinite. As a resolution, Bernoulli suggested that people maximize the expectation of a utility function, rather than of monetary value. If the function is logarithmic, the expected utility is finite and the paradox is resolved.[2]

As an aside, it may be worthwhile to wonder what is meant by a "paradox." For many people, there is nothing paradoxical about the fact that people do not necessarily maximize expected value. It is possible that an example showing this was deemed "paradoxical" to Bernoulli's audience in 1738 but not to graduate students in economics in the twenty-first century. Indeed, the notion of a "paradox" is a subjective and quantitative matter. A contradiction between assumptions (implicit or explicit) is paradoxical to the extent that it makes you feel uncomfortable and it depends on how strongly you are attached to the assumptions. A paradox that leaves one sleepless may be shrugged off by another. Similarly, a "resolution" to a paradox is any attempt to avoid the contradiction, and it may be convincing to some, while not to others.

Whether we think of Bernoulli's example as a "paradox" or not, it motivated expected utility theory, as a descriptive theory of choice under risk. Following its introduction by Bernoulli, expected utility theory was rather dormant for about 200 years. In 1928 von Neumann proved the maxmin theorem, stating

---

[1] As discussed in Section 5.2, expected utility was already used implicitly by Pascal.
[2] Clearly, one can generate similar paradoxes for any utility function that is unbounded. However, unbounded sums of money anyway do not exist and so it's doubtful that it is worth the trouble fine-tuning the utility function to avoid any such possible "paradoxes."

that for finite two-person zero-sum games the maxmin equals the minmax in mixed strategies. This common value is called the "value" of the game.

It is hard to exaggerate the importance of this theorem to game theory (and to mathematics). Maxmin strategies constitute a Nash equilibrium in two-person zero-sum games. In fact, the two concepts coincide for such games, and the general definition of a Nash equilibrium was considered by some a natural extension of the maxmin. There is even a claim that von Neumann viewed Nash's contribution as a minor generalization of the value (regarding both the concept and its proof of existence). It is a more or less established historical fact (i.e., pure gossip) that von Neumann and Morgenstern were left cold by Nash's definition of equilibrium (and proof of existence), since they believed that the key to understanding non–zero-sum games was cooperative, rather than noncooperative, game theory.

Gossip aside, there is no denying that von Neumann and Morgenstern and many game theorists after them believed that two-person zero-sum games were solved by the notion of maxmin strategies and the value. The power of the maxmin solution resides in the equality between the security levels that the two players can guarantee themselves. If player I can choose a strategy that guarantees her a payoff of v or more, while player II can guarantee that he won't pay player I more than v, the argument goes, why would they choose any other strategies? Playing something else would be betting on your opponent being less smart than you are, or betting on him betting on you being less smart than he is, or.... Well, I suppose that nowadays the maxmin solution appears much less compelling than it did at the time, but this is a separate issue. The main point is that this beautiful theorem works only if we use mixed strategies. And it relies on the assumption that when players choose among mixed strategies, they select a strategy that has the highest expected payoff.

But why would players choose mixed strategies that maximize expected payoff, as opposed to, say, evaluate strategies by some combination of expectation and variance, or of higher moments, or by the median payoff? This is where the von Neumann–Morgenstern (vNM) theorem comes into play.

Observe that the theorem is about decisions under "risk," that is, in circumstances with known probabilities, as opposed to situations of "uncertainty," where probabilities are not known.[3] As such, the vNM theorem does not help us understand the concept of probability, though it may shed light on the meaning of utility.

8.2 THE THEOREM

vNM's original formulation involved decision trees in which compound lotteries were explicitly modeled. We use here the more compact formulation of Jensen (1967) and Fishburn (1970a), which implicitly assumes that compound lotteries are simplified according to Bayes's formula. Thus, lotteries are defined

---

[3] This distinction goes back to Knight (1921). See also Keynes (1921).

by their distributions, and the notion of "mixture" implicitly supposes that the decision maker exhibits sophistication in terms of her probability calculations.

Let X be a set of alternatives. There is no additional structure imposed on it. As in Theorem 6.1, X can be a familiar topological and linear space, but it can also be anything you wish. In particular, X need not be restricted to a space of product bundles such as $\mathbb{R}^l_+$ and it may include outcomes such as, God forbid, death.

The objects of choice are lotteries with finite support. Formally, define

$$L = \left\{ P : X \rightarrow [0, 1] \;\middle|\; \begin{array}{c} \#\{x \mid P(x) > 0\} < \infty, \\ \sum_{x \in X} P(x) = 1 \end{array} \right\}.$$

Observe that the expression $\sum_{x \in X} P(x) = 1$ is well defined, thanks to the finite support condition that precedes it.

A mixing operation is performed on L, defined for every $P, Q \in L$ and every $\alpha \in [0, 1]$ as follows: $\alpha P + (1 - \alpha)Q \in L$ is given by

$$(\alpha P + (1 - \alpha)Q)(x) = \alpha P(x) + (1 - \alpha)Q(x)$$

for every $x \in X$. The intuition behind this operation is of conditional probabilities: assume that I offer you a compound lottery that will give you the lottery P with probability α and the lottery Q with probability $(1 - \alpha)$. You can ask yourself what is the probability to obtain a given outcome x, and observe that it is, indeed, α times the conditional probability of x if you get P plus $(1 - \alpha)$ times the conditional probability of x if you get Q.

Since the objects of choice are lotteries, the observable choices are modeled by a binary relation on L, $\succsim \subset L \times L$. The vNM axioms are as follows:

V1. **Weak order**: $\succsim$ is complete and transitive.
V2. **Continuity**: For every $P, Q, R \in L$, if $P \succ Q \succ R$, there exist α, $\beta \in (0, 1)$ such that

$$\alpha P + (1 - \alpha)R \succ Q \succ \beta P + (1 - \beta)R.$$

V3. **Independence**: For every $P, Q, R \in L$, and every $\alpha \in (0, 1)$,[4]

$$P \succsim Q \quad \text{iff} \quad \alpha P + (1 - \alpha)R \succsim \alpha Q + (1 - \alpha)R.$$

The weak-order axiom is not very different from the same assumption in consumer theory or in choice under certainty, as in Theorem 6.1. It has the same strengths and weaknesses as in the context of choice under certainty, and will not be dwelt on here.

Continuity may be viewed as a "technical" condition needed for the mathematical representation and for the proof to work. Indeed, one cannot design a real-life experiment in which it could be directly violated, since its violation

---

[4] It is sufficient, in fact, to require one direction of the following equivalence. But it seems to me that it is hard to be convinced of one direction without being convinced of the other.

would require infinitely many observations.[5,6] But continuity can be hypo-
thetically "tested" by some thought experiments (Gedankenexperiments). For
instance, you can imagine very small, but positive, probabilities, and try to
speculate what your preferences would be between lotteries involving such
probabilities.

If you're willing to engage in such an exercise, consider the following
example, supposedly challenging continuity: assume that P guarantees \$1; Q,
\$0; and R, death. You are likely to prefer \$1 to nothing, and both, to death, that
is, to exhibit preferences $P \succ Q \succ R$. The axiom then demands that for a high
enough $\alpha < 1$, you will also exhibit the preference

$$\alpha P + (1 - \alpha)R \succ Q,$$

namely, that you will be willing to risk your life with probability $(1 - \alpha)$ in
order to gain \$1. The point of the example is that you're supposed to say that
no matter how small is the probability of death $(1 - \alpha)$, you will not risk your
life for a dollar.

A counterargument to this example (suggested by Raiffa) was that we often
do indeed take such risks. For instance, suppose that you are about to buy a
newspaper, which costs \$1. But you notice that it is distributed at no cost on
the other side of the street. Would you cross the street to get it for free? If you
answer yes, you are willing to accept a certain risk, albeit very small, of losing
your life in order to save \$1.

This counterargument can be challenged in several ways. For instance, you
may argue that even if you don't cross the street your life is not guaranteed with
probability 1. Indeed, a truck driver who falls asleep may hit you anyway. In this
case, we are not comparing death with probability 0 to death with probability
$(1 - \alpha)$. And, the argument goes, it is possible that if you had true certainty on
your side of the street, you would have not crossed the street, thereby violating
the axiom.

It appears that framing also matters in this example: I may be about to cross
the street in order to get the free copy of the paper, but if you stop me and say,
"What are you doing? Are you nuts, to risk your life this way? Think of what
could happen! Think of your family!," I will cave in and give up the free paper.
It is not obvious which behavior is more relevant, namely, the decision making
without the guilt-inducing speech or with it. Presumably, this may depend on
the application.

In any event, we understand the continuity axiom, and I also think that we
are willing to accept it as a reasonable assumption for most applications.

---

[5] Observe that our emphasis here is on direct observable tests of each axiom, as opposed to tests
of an axiom in the context of others, namely, tests of sets of axioms or of a theory. This is in line
with the basic idea that the axioms should tell us what the precise observable implications of the
theory are.

[6] As you may recall, Popper didn't like axioms that involve existential quantifiers. He would have
said here, "I told you you should avoid these. Now how will you be able to refute continuity?
What observations will prove that there *are no* $\alpha, \beta \in (0, 1)$ such that so-and-so?!"

The independence axiom is related to dynamic consistency. However, it involves several steps, each of which could be and indeed has been challenged in the literature (see Karni and Schmeidler, 1991*a*). Consider the following four choice situations:

1. You are asked to make a choice between P and Q.
2. Nature will first decide whether, with probability $(1 - \alpha)$, you get R and then you have no choice to make. Alternatively, with probability α, Nature will let you choose between P and Q.
3. The choices are as in (2), but you have to commit to making your choice before you observe Nature's move.
4. You have to choose between two branches. In one, Nature will first decide whether, with probability $(1 - \alpha)$, you get R, or, with probability α, you get P. The second branch is identical, with Q replacing P.

Clearly, (4) is the choice between $\alpha P + (1 - \alpha)R$ and $\alpha Q + (1 - \alpha)R$. To relate the choice in (1) to that in (4), we can use (2) and (3) as intermediary steps, as follows: compare (1) and (2). In (2), *if* you are called on to act, you are choosing between P and Q. At that point R will be a counterfactual world. Why would it be relevant? Hence, it is argued that you can ignore the possibility that did not happen, R, in your choice and make your decision in (2) identical to that in (1).

The distinction between (2) and (3) has to do only with the timing of your decision. Should you make different choices in these scenarios, you would not be dynamically consistent: it is as if you plan (in (3)) to make a given choice, but then, when you get the chance to make it, you do (or would like to do) something else (in (2)). Observe that when you make a choice in problem (3) you know that this choice is conditional on getting to the decision node. Hence, the additional information you have should not change this conditional choice.

Finally, the alleged equivalence between (3) and (4) relies on changing the order of your move (to which you already committed) and Nature's move. As such, this is an axiom of reduction of compound lotteries, assuming that the order of the draws does not matter, as long as the distributions on outcomes, induced by your choices, are the same.

Whether you find the independence axiom compelling or not, I suppose that its meaning is clear. We can finally state the theorem.

Theorem 8.1 *(vNM)* $\succsim \subset L \times L$ *satisfies V1–V3 if and only if there exists* $u : X \to \mathbb{R}$ *such that, for every* $P, Q \in L$,

$$P \succsim Q \quad \textit{iff} \quad \sum_{x \in X} P(x)u(x) \geq \sum_{x \in X} Q(x)u(x).$$

Moreover, in this case, u is unique up to a positive linear transformation (plt).

8.3 PROOFS

Necessity of the axioms and the uniqueness of u in case the representation holds are rather straightforward. The main part is the proof that the axioms are sufficient for the representation. There are several ways to prove it. Naturally, there is quite a bit of overlap between different proofs, and if you go through each of them carefully you'll find many familiar lemmas. In particular, it is useful to prove that preferences along "segments" between two lotteries are monotonic: for every P, Q,

(i) if $P \succ Q$, then for every $\alpha, \beta \in [0, 1]$,[7]

$$\alpha P + (1 - \alpha)Q \succsim \beta P + (1 - \beta)Q \quad \Leftrightarrow \quad \alpha \geq \beta; \tag{8.1}$$

(ii) if $P \sim Q$, then for every $\alpha \in [0, 1]$,

$$\alpha P + (1 - \alpha)Q \sim P. \tag{8.2}$$

Equipped with these, we may proceed.

8.3.1   The Algebraic Approach

This approach to the proof is used in Kreps (1988, pp. 49–57) and in Mas-Colell *et al.* (1995, pp. 176–178). One of its merits is that it suggests a way of elicitation of the decision maker's utility function. It goes roughly as follows: first assume that there are a best and a worst outcomes, x^* and x_*, respectively. Without loss of generality, assume that $x^* \succ x_*$. (Otherwise you can show that $\sim = L \times L$, and a constant u does the job.)

We first wish to show that for every x, there exists a unique $\alpha_x \in [0, 1]$ such that

$$x \sim \alpha_x x^* + (1 - \alpha_x)x_*,$$

where x^* and x_* denote the lotteries that guarantee the outcomes x^* and x_* with probability 1. (Here and in the sequel we abuse notation shamelessly.)

To see this, consider the sets

$$\left\{\alpha \in [0, 1] \mid \alpha x^* + (1 - \alpha)x_* \succ x\right\}$$

and

$$\left\{\alpha \in [0, 1] \mid x \succ \alpha x^* + (1 - \alpha)x_*\right\}.$$

You observe that they are nonempty, open (due to the continuity axiom), and disjoint. Hence, they cannot cover $[0, 1]$. This implies that there exists $\alpha_x \in [0, 1]$ for which equivalence $x \sim \alpha_x x^* + (1 - \alpha_x)x_*$ holds. Fact (8.1) implies that α_x is unique.

Now we consider a lottery P, say $(p_1, x_1; p_2, x_2; \ldots; p_n, x_n)$ (i.e., $P(x_i) = p_i > 0$), and you find a sequence of lotteries P_i such that (i) $P_0 = P$; (ii)

---

[7] This requires two consecutive applications of the independence axiom. See lemma 5.6 in Kreps (1988, pp. 46–48).

$P_i \sim P_{i-1}$; and (iii) the support of P_i is contained in $\{x_*\ x^*, x_{i+1}, \ldots, x_n\}$. That is, at each stage we are going to eliminate one x_i from the support of P, replacing it by a combination of x_* and x^*. To see that this can be done, observe that

$$P = p_1 x_1 + (1 - p_1) \left(\frac{p_2}{1 - p_1}, x_2; \ldots; \frac{p_n}{1 - p_1}, x_n \right).$$

Thus, P can be thought of as a mixture of x_1 and a lottery $P_1 = (p_2/(1 - p_1), x_2; \ldots; p_n/(1 - p_1), x_n)$ involving only $x_2, \ldots, x_n$. When you do this inductively, you find that

$$P \sim P_n = \left(\sum_i p_i \alpha_{x_i} \right) x^* + \left(1 - \sum_i p_i \alpha_{x_i} \right) x_*,$$

and all that is left, in view of (8.1), is to define $u(x) = \alpha_x$.

If there are no best or worst outcomes, we can take an arbitrary pair $x^* \succ x_*$ and follow the reasoning given previously to obtain an expected utility representation for all lotteries whose support is between x_* and x^* (preference-wise). We then consider an x that is outside of this range, say, $x \succ x^*$, and repeat the construction for the pair $x \succ x_*$. Because the preference "interval" $[x_*, x]$ contains $[x_*, x^*]$, the utility function we get for the former has to agree (up to a plt) with the one we first constructed for the latter. Repeating this exercise for every x defines u over all of X, so that expected utility maximization represents $\succsim$.

8.3.2   A Geometric Approach

To understand the geometry of the independence axiom, it is useful to consider the case in which X contains only three pairwise nonequivalent outcomes. Say, $X = \{x_1, x_2, x_3\}$, where $x_1 \succ x_2 \succ x_3$. Every lottery in L is a vector (p_1, p_2, p_3) such that $p_i \geq 0$ and $p_1 + p_2 + p_3 = 1$. For visualization, let us focus on the probabilities of the best and worst outcomes. Formally, consider the $p_1 p_3$ plane: draw a graph in which the x axis corresponds to p_1 and the y axis to p_3. The *Marschak–Machina triangle* is

$$\Delta = \{(p_1, p_3) \,|\, p_1, p_3 \geq 0, \ p_1 + p_3 \leq 1\}.$$

Thus, the point $(1, 0)$ corresponds to the best lottery x_1 (with probability 1); $(0, 0)$, to x_2; and $(0, 1)$, to the worst lottery x_3. Every lottery P corresponds to a unique point (p_1, p_3) in the triangle and vice versa. We will refer to the point (p_1, p_3) by P as well.

Consider the point $(0, 0)$. By reasoning as in the previous proof, we conclude that along the segment connecting $(1, 0)$ with $(0, 1)$, there exists a unique point that is equivalent to $(0, 0)$. Such a unique point will exist along the segment connecting $(1, 0)$ with $(0, c)$ for every $c \in [0, 1]$. The continuity axiom implies (in the presence of the independence axiom) that these points generate a continuous curve, which is the indifference curve of x_2.

Fact (8.2) means that the indifference curves are linear. (Otherwise, they will have to be "thick," and for some c, we will obtain intervals of indifference on the segment connecting $(1, 0)$ with $(0, c)$.) We want to show that they are also parallel.[8]

Consider two lotteries $P \sim Q$. Consider another lottery R such that $S = R + (Q - P)$ is also in the triangle. (In this equation, the points are considered as vectors in Δ.) We claim that $R \sim S$. Indeed, if, say, $R \succ S$, the independence axiom would have implied $(1/2)R + (1/2)Q \succ (1/2)S + (1/2)Q$, and by $P \sim Q$, also $(1/2)S + (1/2)Q \sim (1/2)S + (1/2)P$. We would have obtained $(1/2)R + (1/2)Q \succ (1/2)S + (1/2)P$ while we know that these two lotteries are identical (not only equivalent, simply equal, because $S + P = R + Q$). Similarly $S \succ R$ is impossible. That is, the line segment connecting R and S is also an indifference curve. However, by $P - Q = R - S$, we realize that the indifference curve going through R and S is parallel to the one going through P and Q. This argument can be repeated for practically every R if Q is sufficiently close to P. (Some care is needed near the boundaries.) Thus all indifference curves are linear and parallel.

But this is what we need: linear and parallel lines can be described by a single linear function. That is, you can choose two numbers a_1 and a_3 such that all the indifference curves are of the form $a_1 p_1 + a_3 p_3 = c$ (varying the constant c from one curve to the other). Setting $u(x_1) = a_1$, $u(x_2) = 0$, and $u(x_3) = a_3$, this is an expected utility representation.

This argument can be repeated for any finite set of outcomes X. "Patching" together the representations for all the finite subsets is done in the same way as in the algebraic approach.

8.3.3   A Separation Argument

Finally, it is worth noticing that the vNM theorem is basically a separating hyperplane theorem. To see the gist of the argument, assume that X is finite, though the same idea applies more generally. Embed L in $\mathbb{R}^X$, so that we have a linear space, and we can discuss, for $P, Q \in L \subset \mathbb{R}^X$, also the difference $P - Q \in \mathbb{R}^X$.

Consider the sets

$$A = \left\{ P - Q \in \mathbb{R}^X \,|\, P \succsim Q \right\}$$

and

$$B = \left\{ P - Q \in \mathbb{R}^X \,|\, Q \succ P \right\}.$$

---

[8] You may suggest that linear indifference curves that are not parallel would intersect, contradicting transitivity. But if the intersection is outside the triangle, such preferences may well be transitive. See Chew (1983) and Dekel (1986).

We first show that $R \succsim S$ if and only if $(R - S) \in A$. This is true because if $R - S = P - Q$, we find, by reasoning similar to that used earlier, that $P \succsim Q$ iff $R \succsim S$. Similarly, $S \succ R$ if and only if $(R - S) \in B$.

Next we show that both A and B are convex. This is again an implication of the independence axiom: suppose, say, $(P - Q), (R - S) \in A$ and consider

$$\alpha(P - Q) + (1 - \alpha)(R - S) = (\alpha P + (1 - \alpha)R) - (\alpha Q + (1 - \alpha)S).$$

$P \succsim Q$ and $R \succsim S$ imply (by two applications of the independence axiom)

$$\alpha P + (1 - \alpha)R \succsim \alpha Q + (1 - \alpha)R \succsim \alpha Q + (1 - \alpha)S,$$

which means that $(\alpha P + (1 - \alpha)R) - (\alpha Q + (1 - \alpha)S) \in A$. The same reasoning applies to B.

Finally, we need to show that A is closed and B is open. The topology in which such claims would be true is precisely the topology in which the continuity axiom guarantees continuity of preferences: an open neighborhood of a point P is defined by

$$\cup_{R \in L} \{\alpha P + (1 - \alpha)R \mid \alpha \in (0, \varepsilon_R)\},$$

where, for every $R \in L$, $\varepsilon_R > 0$. You may verify that this topology renders vector operations continuous. (Observe that this is not the standard topology on $\mathbb{R}^X$, even if X is finite, because ε_R need not be bounded away from 0. That is, as we change the "target" R, the length of the interval coming out of P in the direction of R, still inside the neighborhood, changes and may converge to zero. Still, in each given direction $R - P$, there is an open segment, leading from P toward R, which is in the neighborhood.)

When you separate A from B by a linear functional, we can refer to the functional as the utility function u. Linearity of the utility with respect to the probability values guarantees affinity; that is,

$$u(\alpha P + (1 - \alpha)R) = \alpha u(P) + (1 - \alpha)u(R).$$

Since every P has a finite support, using this property inductively results in the expected utility formula.[9]

8.4 THE THREE INTERPRETATIONS

The various interpretations of the vNM theorem mirror those of Cantor's theorem. From a meta-scientific viewpoint, the theorem provides a definition of a utility function, which is unique up to plt's, that is, "cardinal." Since this is the degree to which the measurement of temperature is unique, we feel that this is a rather concrete measure. The uniqueness of the utility on the set X

---

[9] Herstein and Milnor (1953) generalized the vNM theorem to general mixture spaces, in which a mixture operation is defined abstractly. Their result guarantees representation by an affine utility as given earlier.

was obtained at the cost of more observations – we assume that preferences are observable not only over X, but also over lotteries over X, namely, L.

From a normative viewpoint, one may read the axioms and become convinced that expected utility is the right way to make decisions. For the appropriate choice of the utility function u, there is no need to take higher-order moments. There is also a good reason to prefer the expectation of the utility to, say, its median as the index to be maximized.

Finally, adopting a descriptive viewpoint, the axiomatization may greatly enhance one's confidence in models that assume that all traders in the stock market are expected utility maximizers or that so are economic agents who consider insuring their property.

It is worthwhile to emphasize the possibility of elicitation of utility.[10] The preceding analysis, in particular, the first proof of the theorem, suggests simple questions that can identify the utility function of a given decision maker. For instance, we may ask the decision maker for which probability p will a bet $(p, \$1,000; (1 - p), \$0)$ be equivalent to $\$500$ with certainty. Suppose that the answer is $p = .6$. We can then choose a normalization of the utility function, say, $u(\$0) = 0$ and $u(\$1,000) = 1$, and find that we have to have $u(\$500) = .6$. Continuing in this way, we can map the entire utility function by using only lotteries involving at most two outcomes each (in fact, two outcomes on the one hand versus a single, certain outcome on the other).

Such an elicitation of the utility function may be useful for descriptive and normative purposes alike. Starting with a descriptive example, suppose that we wish to predict an individual's behavior in a complex environment such as trading in the stock market. Measuring one's utility in such an environment may be a difficult task, and it may also involve significant errors of measurement. It might make sense to measure the utility in simple laboratory experiments and then use it for predictions in more complicated ones as well. This program may fail if the experiment has no external validity, say, if it is very artificial. Yet, it holds some promise, based on simplification of the problem.

Considering a normative interpretation, assume that the decision maker is faced with a choice between two complicated lotteries. She is a bit at a loss, looking at all the numbers involved. She may try to find some anchor, perhaps a dominance argument, perhaps some form of cancellation of identical elements, but the problem remains stubbornly complex. If we were to ask the decision maker which lottery she prefers, she may well say that she doesn't yet know.

But if the decision maker likes the vNM axioms and would like to see herself satisfying them, we can suggest to her to calibrate her utility as given earlier, considering only very simple problems, for which she probably has a better intuition, namely, better-defined preferences. From these choices we can map the utility function and use it for complicated decisions. We can go back to the decision maker and explain to her that the choice we computed in the

---

[10] This point was not very obvious in Cantor's theorem because the utility there is only ordinal.

complicated case is the only one that is consistent with the axioms and with her choices in the simple situations.

The procedure for elicitation of the utility function does not logically necessitate the axioms. One may come up with simple preference problems that would uniquely identify the utility function based on the mathematical formula alone. Yet, the language of the axioms, which is concrete and observable, and the quest for simple axioms often facilitate the elicitation/calibration problem significantly.

CHAPTER 9

De Finetti's Theorem

9.1 MOTIVATION

We are finally back to discussing probabilities. To remind you where we left off, we had three definitions of probabilities. One, based on the principle of indifference, didn't bring us very far. The second, based on frequentism, was also limited. Subjective probabilities, by contrast, seemed very general and very flexible. But they are so general and so flexible that one might wonder if they can perhaps explain everything, accommodate everything, and eventually become useless.

In order for the concept to be useful, subjective probabilities need a bit more discipline. Some rules that would tell us when our subjective probabilities are given by a probability measure p and when, by q. What is the difference, indeed, between such subjective probabilities? Is it possible that the difference between two such measures is not observable? And is it the case that everything can be explained by subjective probabilities? If so, what will the logical positivists say?

Driven by such concerns, Ramsey (1931) suggested that subjective probabilities be derived from observable choice behavior. If subjective probabilities are computed from one's willingness to bet, they will have an observable meaning. Hopefully, we will be able to prove that two different probability measures are reflected in different modes of behavior, and can thus be told apart based on observations. Similarly, one should hope that certain modes of behavior will not be consistent with subjective probabilities, rendering the concept meaningful.

In order to relate subjective probabilities to observable data that go beyond mere declaration of such probabilities, one needs to think how are subjective probabilities used. This is a basic lesson that we have learned from logical positivism (and from Wittgenstein): concepts acquire meaning from the way we use them. If we know the answer to *how* (we use a concept), we know the answer to *what* (it is), and probably this is the only meaningful answer we can hope for in terms of essence.

How should subjective probabilities be used then? One possible way is via maximization of expected payoff. It is not a very satisfactory approach from an economic point of view, because we already decided that maximization of expected utility is a much more reasonable objective function than is the maximization of expected monetary payoff. Yet, one has to start somewhere. The contributions of de Finetti date back to the 1930s; that is, they predated von-Neumann and Morgenstern. He was not primarily an economist and he satisfied himself with maximization of expected *value* (rather than expected utility) with a subjective prior. This next step of subjective expected utility maximization had to await Savage.

For the time being, let us accept the idea that we are going to maximize expected payoff with respect to this yet-undefined subjective probability. With this type of usage in mind, what is probability?

9.2 THE THEOREM

de Finetti considered monetary bets on states of nature. Assume that we are about to watch a horse race, and there are n states, $1, \ldots, n$, each corresponding to a particular horse winning the race. (We are going to state and prove the theorem for finitely many states, though the extension to infinite spaces is straightforward.)

A *bet* is a function from states to monetary outcomes; that is, $x \in X = \mathbb{R}^n$, with x_i denoting the gain in case horse i wins. A negative value x_i indicates that we need to make a net payment if i wins. Thus, the bet $(1, -1, 0, 0, \ldots, 0)$ indicates a bet, at even odds, on the fact that horse 1 will win rather than horse 2, where the bet is off if neither horse wins.

de Finetti divided bets into acceptable versus unacceptable, and he required that these sets be convex (see de Finetti, 1937, and the translation in Kyburg and Smokler, 1964). I present here a slightly different formulation, which is in line with the binary preferences approach taken in the other chapters.

Assume that the decision maker has a preference order over bets, $\succsim \subset X \times X$. Consider the following axioms:

D1. **Weak order**: $\succsim$ is complete and transitive.
D2. **Continuity**: For every $x \in X$, the sets $\{y | x \succ y\}, \{y | y \succ x\}$ are open.[1]
D3. **Additivity**: For every $x, y, z \in X$, $x \succsim y$ iff $x + z \succsim y + z$.
D4. **Monotonicity**: For every $x, y \in X$, $x_i \geq y_i$ for all $i \leq n$ implies $x \succsim y$.
D5. **Nontriviality**: There exist $x, y \in X$ such that $x \succ y$.

Axioms D1 and D2 are familiar from consumer theory. Additivity, D3, is evidently a key axiom here, and it is, unfortunately, not very compelling. Knowing the end of the story, that is, the theorem that's coming up, we can't expect it to be any more compelling, in any concrete example, than is expected value maximization, because the latter will be shown equivalent to axioms

---

[1] Here we refer to the standard topology on $\mathbb{R}^n$. The condition is therefore identical to the continuity of consumer preferences in Debreu (1959).

D1–D5. Axiom D3 would make sense if we assumed neutrality to risk. For example, assume that $n = 2$ and that $(1, -1) \sim (-1, 1)$. (Intuitively, you find the two horses just as likely to win.) Then, by setting $x = z = (1, -1)$ and $y = (-1, 1)$, we obtain that D3 implies $(2, -2) \sim (0, 0)$. Observe that the equivalence $(1, -1) \sim (-1, 1)$ is compatible with various attitudes toward risk. This equivalence would hold for any expected utility maximizer who considers the two states equally likely. Yet, in the presence of D3, the indifference to permutation of the states also implies that the random variable is equivalent to its expectation.

The monotonicity axiom, D4, is more palatable and, in fact, hardly objectionable. Since the outcomes are all monetary payoffs, D4 only requires that the decision maker prefer (weakly) more to less, no matter at which states the higher payoffs are offered.

Finally, the nontriviality axiom is needed for the sole purpose of finding a (subjective) probability measure. Without it the representation would still hold, but the vector p would be the zero vector, and we won't be able to interpret it as a probability.

The theorem states

Theorem 9.1 *(de Finetti)* $\succsim \subset X \times X$ *satisfies D1–D5 if and only if there exists a probability vector* $p \in \Delta^{n-1}$ *such that, for every* $x, y \in X$,

$$x \succsim y \quad \textit{iff} \quad px \geq py.$$

Moreover, in this case, p is unique.

As a reminder, Δ^{n-1} is the set of probability vectors on $\{1, \ldots, n\}$. The notation px refers to the inner product, that is, $\sum_i p_i x_i$, which is the expected payoff of x relative to the probability p.

9.3 A PROOF

Let us first show that D1–D3 are equivalent to the existence of $p \in \mathbb{R}^n$ such that

$$x \succsim y \quad \text{iff} \quad px \geq py$$

for every $x, y \in X$. The proof is very similar to the last proof of the von Neumann–Morgenstern (vNM) theorem.

Necessity of the axioms is immediate. To prove sufficiency, observe first that, for every $x, y \in X$,

$$x \succsim y \quad \text{iff} \quad x - y \succsim 0.$$

Define

$$A = \left\{ x \in X \mid x \succsim 0 \right\}$$

and

$$B = \{ x \in X \mid 0 \succ x \}.$$

Clearly, $A \cap B = \varnothing$ and $A \cup B = X$. Also, A is closed and B is open. If $B = \varnothing$, $p = 0$ is the vector we need. Otherwise, both A and B are nonempty.

We wish to show that they are convex. To this end, we start by observing that if $x \succsim y$, then $x \succsim z \succsim y$, where $z = (x + y)/2$. This is true because, defining $d = (y - x)/2$, we have $x + d = z$ and $z + d = y$. D3 implies that $x \succsim z \Leftrightarrow x + d \succsim z + d$; that is, $x \succsim z \Leftrightarrow z \succsim y$. Hence, $z \succ x$ would imply $y \succ z$ and $y \succ x$, a contradiction. Hence, $x \succsim z$, and $z \succsim y$ follows from $x \succsim z$.

Next, we wish to show that if $x \succsim y$, then $x \succsim z \succsim y$ for any $z = \lambda x + (1 - \lambda)y$ with $\lambda \in [0, 1]$. If λ is a binary rational (i.e., of the form $k/2^i$ for some $k, i \geq 1$), the conclusion follows from an inductive application of the previous claim (for $\lambda = 1/2$). As for other values of λ, $z \succ x$ ($y \succ z$) would imply, by continuity, the same preference in an open neighborhood of z, including binary rationals.

It follows that one can separate A from B by a linear function. That is, there exists a linear $f : X \to \mathbb{R}$ and a number $c \in \mathbb{R}$ such that

$$x \in A \quad \text{iff} \quad f(x) \geq c$$

(and $x \in B$ iff $f(x) < c$). Since $0 \in A$, $c \leq 0$. If $c < 0$, consider x with $f(x) = 3c/4$. Then $x \in A$ but $2x \in B$. That is, $x \succsim 0$ but $0 \succ 2x$, in contradiction to D3 (coupled with transitivity). This implies that $c = 0$. Denoting $p_i = f(e_i)$ (where e_i is the ith unit vector), we obtain

$$x \succsim y$$
$$\text{iff} \quad x - y \succsim 0$$
$$\text{iff} \quad x - y \in A$$
$$\text{iff} \quad f(x - y) \geq 0$$
$$\text{iff} \quad px \geq py.$$

It is easily verifiable that, given the preceding conditions, D4 is equivalent to $p_i \geq 0$, and D5 to the claim that $p \neq 0$, or $\sum_i p_i > 0$. Under this condition, p can be normalized to be a probability vector, and it is the unique probability vector representing preference as given earlier.

9.4   THE THREE INTERPRETATIONS

As in the previous two axiomatizations, three types of interpretations are possible. At the meta-scientific level, we now have a definition of subjective probabilities. These are the probabilities that, when used for maximization of expected value, predict betting behavior. We know precisely under what conditions people cannot be assumed to have subjective probabilities of this nature, namely, when they violate the axioms. Thus, there is no danger that expected value maximization will be a vacuous theory. It is surely a refutable one. Alas, it may be too easily refuted, and we will need to seek a more general definition of subjective probabilities.

Normatively, if the axioms are compelling, they convince us that expected value maximization, relative to our own subjective probability, is how we wish to make decisions. Descriptively, they may convince us that such a model captures more than one would have believed based on the mathematical formulation alone.

The axioms can also inspire elicitation procedures in order to measure subjective probability.[2] In particular, monotonicity and continuity (coupled with the weak order assumption) suggest that preferences between simple bets may suffice to identify specific parameters. We may, for instance, ask the decision maker at what odds she is willing to bet between horses 1 and 2. If we find that she expresses indifference between $(\alpha, -1, 0, \ldots, 0)$ and $(0, 0, 0, \ldots, 0)$, we should conclude that $p_2 = \alpha p_1$. Alternatively, we can ask her what amount of money β is the certainty equivalent of a gain of \$1 in case horse 1 wins, that is, what β solves $(1, 0, 0, \ldots, 0)$ and $(\beta, \beta, \beta, \ldots, \beta)$, and conclude that $p_1 = \beta$.

Again, the idea behind such elicitation would be that the decision maker may be able to provide answers that she is comfortable with and that involve little noise, for simple preference questions, and then the theory can help us (or the decision maker herself) infer from the answers to the simple questions what should be the answers to complicated questions if the theory is to be followed.

Finally, let us mention possible defenses of the additivity axioms D3. Some are rather lame, but they make points that may be important in other contexts. First, one may restrict attention to small amounts of money, for which risk neutrality may not be a bad approximation. (Admittedly, one may then obtain responses that are very noisy.) Second, one may assume that the utility function was somehow independently measured and that the payoffs are given in terms of its unit, in "utils," as it were. (This interpretation would require that the additivity axiom be construed as adding utils.) Third, one may imagine that the payoffs are given in terms of objective probabilities. This requires that such objective probabilities be given and agreed on as in the case of a fair roulette wheel. If such a wheel exists, you can interpret a vector x as specifying the number of slots on the roulette wheel in which you win. In other words, the vector x guarantees you a fixed payoff, say \$100, with probability $x_i/37$ if horse i wins the race. In this case, even if you think in terms of expected utility (rather than expected value), you should find the additivity axiom acceptable.[3]

---

[2] Admittedly, as in the case of the vNM theorem, one could come up with the elicitation procedure independently of the axioms.

[3] This is basically the idea of Anscombe–Aumann's model (see Chapter 14).

CHAPTER 10

Savage's Theorem

10.1 BACKGROUND

de Finetti's theorem provides a definition of subjective probability, but it assumes additivity. This axiom is defensible if someone is risk neutral, expected utility maximizer whose payoff is measured in probabilities, or if, more generally, we know the utility function of the decision maker. In other words, if we have a utility function as a measurement tool, we can use it to measure subjective probabilities, as in the elicitation procedures described in Chapter 8. Mathematically, de Finetti's theorem was no more than a separating hyperplane argument – if we have a linear structure of payoffs, we use a duality theorem to obtain a measure on states.

The von Neumann–Morgenstern (vNM) theorem is almost completely symmetric. vNM assumed that probabilities are well defined and measured utility in terms of probability. Again, this is evident both in the elicitation procedures sketched in Chapter 8 and in the mathematical proof. The last proof of the theorem described in Section 8.3.3 was intended to highlight the fact that the vNM theorem is again a separating hyperplane argument. This time, a linear structure is given on the probability measures and the duality theorem helps us obtain numbers on the outcomes.

The two theorems are very elegant and powerful, but, taken together, they do not tell a complete story. von Neumann and Morgenstern tell us how to obtain utilities given probabilities, and de Finetti does the opposite – shows how to obtain probabilities given utilities. But where do we start?

One may try certain hybrid approaches. For instance, assume that we do understand what probabilities mean when we discuss games of chance, such as roulette wheel, dice, and coins. We can use these as an input to a vNM model and measure the decision maker's utility function. We can then use that utility to measure the subjective probabilities of other events in de Finetti's model.

Such a procedure will suffer, however, from the difficulty that it presumes that the same utility function applies in both setups; that is, the utility function measured in the context of games of chance will be the one used when other events are involved. This is not a trivial assumption due to possible interactions of an "outcome" and the circumstances in which it was obtained. For instance, when playing the roulette wheel I may have a utility that is defined solely on money, whereas in a real-life situation my utility would depend on other factors, such as fairness, equality, and so forth. Even if we restrict attention to monetary payoffs, it is possible that the very setup of the chance game makes me much more risk loving than I am in real life. That is, various problems that fall under the category of external validity may make the utility function measured in chance games different from the one appropriate to analyze other situations.

Another approach to measure subjective probabilities based on objective ones is more direct. Rather than measuring the utility function, we can devise experiments in which it is "cancelled out." For instance, I can ask you whether you prefer to get $100 in case of a stock market crash or in case the roulette wheel, once vigorously spun, will stop on an even number. By changing the number of outcomes on the wheel, I will be able to calibrate your subjective probability irrespective of your utility function. To be precise, I do need to know that you prefer $100 to $0, so as not to obtain responses of complete indifference. But I need not worry about ratios of utility differences such as $[u(\$100) - u(\$0)]/[u(\$50) - u(\$0)]$.

This idea seems sound. Indeed, it was the motivation of Anscombe and Aumann (1963), who believed that people understand subjective probabilities by first understanding objective ones. According to their view, it is actually an advantage of a theory to have the two types of probabilities – objective ones, as in games of chance, and subjective ones – and explicitly show how these can be compared by the decision maker.

However, it would seem conceptually more elegant to be able to derive probability and utility in tandem, without assuming any of these concepts as a primitive of the model. This is what Savage (1954) did. He started with a model that assumed only abstract states of the world and outcomes. No numbers are to be seen in the model's primitives, neither as measures of plausibility of events nor as measures of desirability of outcomes. Savage's axioms are stated in this very primitive language, involving no numbers, multiplications, additions, or similar mathematical machinery. And the theorem shows that the axioms are equivalent to the existence of *both* a utility function and a probability measure, such that decisions are being made as if to maximize the expectation of the utility relative to the probability measure.

Conceptually, Savage's theorem is therefore much more satisfactory than those of de Finetti or vNM. Moreover, Savage's conceptual austerity is also reflected in mathematical frugality: since Savage does not assume numbers as part of the input, nor any linear operations, he has much less mathematical apparatus to rely on. He cannot involve separating hyperplane theorems. Instead, he is constructing the numbers with his bare hands. As a result, Savage's theorem is also an impressive mathematical achievement. The combination of a profound mathematical result with a towering conceptual achievement is awe inducing. As Kreps (1988) puts it, Savage's theorem is the "crowning glory" of decision theory.

I start by describing the axioms and explaining the basic logic behind each. I then describe the theorem and say a few words on the proof. The following section deals with the definition of states of the world in Savage's model. It attempts to define the informal user manual for Savage's model, showing how the model does great, conceptually speaking, when properly applied. Yet, some word of criticism will be unavoidable at that point. The main critiques of the model will be described later on in a separate chapter.

10.2   STATES, OUTCOMES, AND ACTS

Savage's model includes two primitive concepts: states and outcomes. The set of *states*, S, should be thought of as an exhaustive list of all scenarios that might unfold. A state, in Savage's words, "resolves all uncertainty": it should specify the answer to any question you might be interested in. The answer should be deterministic. If, for instance, in a given state an act leads to a toss of a coin, you should further split the state into two possible states, each consistent with the original one, but also resolving the additional uncertainty about the toss of the coin. The following chapter elaborates on this notion.

Observe that Savage considers a one-shot decision problem. If the real problem extends over many periods, the decision problem considered should be thought of as a choice of a strategy in a game. The game can be long or even infinite. You think of yourself as choosing a strategy a priori, and assuming that you will stick to it with no difficulties of dynamic consistency, unforeseen contingencies, and so forth. This is symmetric to the conception of a state as Nature's strategy in this game. It specifies all the choices that Nature might have to make as the game unfolds.

An *event* is any subset $A \subset S$. There are no measurability constraints, and S is not endowed with an algebra of measurable events. If you wish to be more formal about it, you can define the set of events to be the maximal σ-algebra, $\Sigma = 2^S$, with respect to which all subsets are measurable.

The set of *outcomes* will be denoted by X. An outcome x is assumed to specify all that is relevant to your well-being, insomuch as it may be relevant to your decision. In this sense, Savage's model does not differ from utility maximization under certainty (as in consumer theory) or from vNM's model. In all of these we may obtain rather counterintuitive results if certain determinants of utility are left outside of the description of the outcomes.

The objects of choice are acts, which are defined as functions from states to outcomes, and denoted by F. That is,

$$F = X^S = \{f \mid f : S \to X\}.$$

Choosing an act f, you typically do not know the outcome you will experience. But if you do know both your choice f and the state s, you know that the outcome will be $x = f(s)$. The reason is that a state s should resolve all uncertainty, including what is the outcome of the act f. In particular, a state s should tell you whether the statement "act f results in outcome x" is true or false.

Acts whose payoffs do not depend on the state of the world s are constant functions in F. We will abuse notation and denote them by the outcome in which they result. Thus, $x \in X$ is also understood as $x \in F$ with $x(s) = x$. There are many confusing things in the world, but this is not one of them.

Since the objects of choice are acts, Savage assumes a binary relation $\succsim \subset F \times F$. The relation will have its symmetric and asymmetric parts, $\sim$ and $\succ$, defined as usual. It will also be extended to X with the natural convention. Specifically, for two outcomes $x, y \in X$, we say that $x \succsim y$ if and only if the constant function that always yields x is related by $\succsim$ to the constant function that always yields y.

Before we go on, it is worthwhile to note what does *not* appear in the model. If you're taking notes, and you know that you're going to see a theorem resulting in integrals of real-valued functions with respect to probability measures, you might be prepared to leave some space for the mathematical apparatus. You may be ready now for a page of some measure theory, describing the σ-algebra of events. You can leave half a page blank for the details of the linear structure on X, and maybe a few lines for the topology on X, or maybe a page or so to discuss the topology on F. But none of it is needed. Savage does not assume any such linear, measure-theoretic, or topological structures. If you go back to the beginning of this subsection, you will find that it only says,

There are two sets, S and X, and a relation $\succsim$ on X^S.

10.3 AXIOMS

The axioms are given here in their original names, P1–P7. They do have nicknames, but these are sometimes subject to debate and open to different interpretations, and they therefore appear in the discussion but not in the titles. The axioms are stated again in a more succinct form before the statement of Savage's theorems.

10.3.1 P1

P1 states that $\succsim$ is a weak order. The basic idea is very familiar, as are the descriptive and normative justifications. At the same time, completeness is a demanding axiom. We will discuss it at length later on (see Section 12.3). For the time being, observe that *all* functions in F are assumed to be comparable. Implicitly, this suggests that choices between every pair of such functions can indeed be observed or at least meaningfully imagined. We return to this point in Section 11.1.

10.3.2 P2

Axiom P2 says that the preference between two acts, f and g, should depend only on the values of f and g when they differ. Assume that f and g differ only on an event A (or even a subset thereof). That is, if A does not occur, f

and g result in the same outcomes exactly. Then, when comparing them, we can focus on this event, A, and ignore A^c. Observe that we do not need to know that f and g are constants outside of A. It suffices that they are equal to each other; that is, $f(s) = g(s)$ when $s \notin A$.

For example, assume that you may be going out with some friends to a concert. One of your friends is trying to get tickets to the concert, and tickets may or may not be available, in which case everyone stays home. While waiting to hear whether your friend got tickets, you wonder whether you should take a raincoat with you, in case you do go out. Obviously, a coat may be very useful if it rains, but it will be a pain to carry it around if it doesn't.

A priori you have to choose between f, "taking the coat if I go out, leaving the coat in the closet if I stay home," and g, "not taking the coat if I go out, leaving the coat in the closet if I stay home." P2 says that when comparing f and g, you can ignore the outcomes they yield if there are no tickets, because in this case they yield identical outcomes.

Thus, P2 is akin to requiring that you have conditional preferences, namely, preferences between f and g *conditional* on A occurring, and that these conditional preferences determine your choice between f and g if they are equal in case A does not occur. Some models assume such conditional preferences as primitive (see Ghirardato, 2002; Luce and Krantz, 1971). Savage chose a different way to model conditional preferences: to express the idea that the values of f and g do not matter where they are equal, he demanded that it not matter what they are equal to. That is, assume that you alter f and g only on A^c, to get f' and g', respectively, such that

$$f(s) = f'(s) \quad \text{and} \quad g(s) = g'(s) \quad s \in A.$$

Assume that you make sure that these altered acts, f' and g', are still equal off A (though not necessarily equal to f and to g). That is,

$$f(s) = g(s) \quad \text{and} \quad f'(s) = g'(s) \quad s \notin A$$

– then you want it to be the case that $f \succsim g$ iff $f' \succsim g'$. In this case, Savage defined f to be at least as preferred as g *given* A, denoted $f \succsim_A g$.

Axiom P2 is often referred to as the "sure-thing principle" (STP). To see why, let us complicate the story a bit. Suppose that if there are no tickets to the concert, you and your friends will be going for a walk. You may, again, take a coat or not. Suppose that you decide that you're better off with a coat if you end up going to the concert, that is, $f \succsim_A g$. You also decide that you should take the coat if you know that you're going for a walk, that is, $f \succsim_{A^c} g$. Unfortunately, before leaving home you still do not know whether tickets were available or not. That is, you have to decide whether to take the coat not knowing whether A or A^c occurs. However, it is not hard to see that if you satisfy P2 (and P1), you can say, "I prefer f to g in case A occurs, as well as in case A doesn't occur, and therefore I should prefer f to g."[1]

---

[1] To see this, apply P2 twice, comparing f to the act h that is equal to g on A and to f on A^c, and then comparing h to g.

Some writers use the name "sure-thing principle" to denote other axioms. Peter Wakker pointed out that in Savage's original usage the term referred to P2 in conjunction with P3 and P7. (Indeed, Kreps (1988) uses the term to denote P7.) But the most common usage identifies the term with P2.

10.3.3 Notation

Before we continue, it will be useful to have a bit more notation. As mentioned earlier, the objects of choice are simply functions from S to X. What operations can we perform on $F = X^S$ if we have no additional structure on X?

The operation we used in the statement of P2 involves "splicing" functions, that is, taking two functions and generating a third one from them, by using one function on a certain subdomain and the other on the complement. Formally, for two acts $f, g \in F$ and an event $A \subset S$, define an act f_A^g by

$$f_A^g(s) = \begin{cases} g(s) & s \in A \\ f(s) & s \in A^c \end{cases}$$

Think of f_A^g as "f, where on A we replaced it by g."

Observe that with this notation, P2 states that for every $f, g, h, h' \in F$, and every $A \subset S$,

$$f_{A^c}^h \succsim g_{A^c}^h \quad \text{iff} \quad f_{A^c}^{h'} \succsim g_{A^c}^{h'}.$$

A common notation for such a function is also $(g, A; f, A^c)$. It has the advantage that it is symmetric, namely, that it is more obvious that $(g, A; f, A^c) = (f, A^c; g, A)$ than that $f_A^g = g_{A^c}^f$. Also, the notation $(g, A; f, A^c)$ can easily be extended to partitions of S into more than two events. However, some of the axioms are easier to read with the current notation.

10.3.4 Null Events

It is also useful to have a definition that captures the intuitive notion that an event is considered a practical impossibility, roughly, what we mean by a zero-probability event when a probability is given. How can we define such an event? That is, what would be the behavioral manifestation of the fact that you believe an event A cannot occur?

One natural definition is to say that an event A is *null* if for every $f, g \in F$, $f \sim_A g$. That is, if you know that f and g yield the same outcomes if A does not occur, you consider them equivalent.

For example, assume that I want to know if you truly believe that little green people from outer space may be on their way here. Define the event A to be "Little green people from outer space are about to enter the room within the next five minutes." Assume that f denotes your life as you know it, and g, the same as f, but you also get a $100 if A occurs. These two acts are identical off A. If you nevertheless strictly prefer g to f, I would have to assume that you think that there is some chance that green people will indeed open the door. Conversely, if I observe that $f \sim_A g$, I can conclude that even though A is not a logical impossibility, you don't assign any weight to it in your decisions. I will say that A is null for you.

Some people object to the idea that such events might exist. The point is that, however unlikely the invasion by little green people is, why would you turn down the $100 conditional on their arrival? There are several responses to this claim. First, one may extend the model to deal with lexicographic probabilities or probabilities that employ nonstandard numbers. Blume et al. (1991) provide an axiomatic derivation of a Savage-like model that allows such probabilities. In this model, an event A may be sufficiently unlikely so that you will reject any bet on it with finite odds, but you will still not be indifferent to the payoffs on A. Second, the interpretation of "zero-probability events" in probability, or, correspondingly, of null events here, is troublesome because we use models with infinitely many states. Using such models is often very convenient. For example, they allow us to use continuous distributions in probability and statistics. But these models also incur some cost, and, in particular, they do not allow us to equate "zero probability" with "logical impossibility." Recalling that the world is finite and that infinite models are supposed to be only a mathematical convenience, one may decide to learn to live with such interpretational problems, as long as the infinite model in question makes our lives easier in other ways.

10.3.5 P3

Axiom P3 states, roughly, the following: if you take an act, that guarantees an outcome x on an event A, and you change it, on A, from x to another outcome y, the preference between the two acts should follow the preference between the two outcomes x and y (when understood as constant acts).

More formally, consider an act $f \in F$, an event A, and two outcomes $x, y \in X$. Compare f_A^x to f_A^y, namely, two acts that are identical off A, one yielding x on A, and the other, y. If $x \succsim y$, it is natural to require that $f_A^x \succsim f_A^y$, that is, weakly improving the outcome you get if A occurs should also weakly improve the act. We want this to be a two-way implication; that is, $x \succ y$ will also imply $f_A^x \succ f_A^y$. But this last implication is not necessarily convincing if A is null. For example, increasing my payoff in case a coin tossed falls and stands on its side may not strictly improve the act in my eyes. Thus the formulation of P3 is

For every $f \in F$, nonnull event $A \subset S$, and $x, y \in X$,

$$x \succsim y \quad \text{iff} \quad f_A^x \succsim f_A^y.$$

There are two main interpretations of P3. One, which appears less demanding, holds that P3 is simply an axiom of monotonicity. Indeed, suppose that you are trying to argue that preferences should be monotonic. In de Finetti's model, we could increase the monetary payoff in a given state and require that the resulting vector be at least as highly evaluated as the original one. What would be the equivalent condition here? We can't increase a monetary payoff, because all that we have are abstract outcomes such as $x, y \in X$. But if the decision maker prefers getting x for sure to getting y for sure, it seems that x is "better" than y, and changing y to x over some event should result in improvement for monotone preferences.

The interpretation of P3 as monotonicity is quite convincing when the outcomes are monetary payoffs. However, when other outcomes are concerned, we may find that the desirability of the outcome depends on the state at which it is experienced. To quote a classical example, assume that I do not know whether the weather is going to be rainy or sunny. You ask me to choose between an umbrella, x (at every state s), and a swimsuit, y (also at every state s). Considering the possible outcomes, and being the nerdy risk-averse individual that I am, I prefer the umbrella, $x \succ y$. But if you consider the act $f = y$, and the event A in which the weather is sunny, you will not be surprised to find that I prefer to keep y, rather than substitute it for x, over A, that is, $y = y_A^y \succ y_A^x$, in violation of P3. We discuss this type of violations of P3 (and P4) in Section 12.2. At this point we wish to observe that P3 requires a bit more than simple monotonicity.[2]

The other interpretation of P3, which highlights this issue, is the following: the game we play is to try to derive utility and probability from observed behavior. That is, we can think of utility and probability as intentional[3] concepts related to desires and wants on the one hand and to knowledge and belief on the other. These concepts are measured by observed choices. In particular, if I wish to find out whether the decision maker prefers x to y, I can ask her whether she prefers to get x or y when an event A occurs, that is, to compare f_A^x to f_A^y. If she says that she prefers f_A^x, I'll conclude that she values x more than y.

But what would happen if you come to the same decision maker, offer her the choice between f_B^x and f_B^y for another event B, and find out that she actually prefers the latter? By the same method of measurement, you'll find that y is preferred to x. In this case, there will be no clear preference over the outcomes – preferences will depend on the associated event.

If I view this exercise as an attempt to measure the decision maker's ranking (let alone her cardinal utility function), I will prefer that the observations not depend on the measurement device. Here the function f and the events A, B are but measurement tools. We would therefore like it to be the case that for every f and every nonnull A, B,

$$f_A^x \succsim f_A^y \quad \text{iff} \quad f_B^x \succsim f_B^y.$$

Clearly, it suffices to fix one nonnull event, B, and to require that the ranking for B be the same as the ranking for every A. If you set $B = S$, you get P3. According to this interpretation, P3 requires that the ordinal ranking of outcomes be independent of the events with which they are associated.

---

[2] Still, I would stress that if one were trying to assume monotonicity and nothing more, P3 has no obvious simple alternative.

[3] "Intentional" is a term used to refer to mental phenomena that humans experience, such as desires and beliefs.

10.3.6   P4

P4 is the counterpart of P3 under the second interpretation. Let us continue with the same line of reasoning. We wish to measure not only the ranking of outcomes, but also the ranking of events. Specifically, suppose that I wish to find out whether you think that event A is more likely than event B. Let me take two outcomes x, y such that $x \succ y$. For example, x will denote $100 and y, $0. I now intend to ask you whether you prefer to get the better outcome x if A occurs (and otherwise, y) or to get the better outcome if B occurs (again, with y being the alternative).

Suppose that you prefer the first, namely,

$$y_A^x \succ y_B^x.$$

It seems reasonable to conclude that A is more likely in your eyes than is B. But imagine now that another decision theorist approaches you and conducts the same experiment, with one minor change: the other decision theorist promises you $400 ($z$) as the better outcome and $200 ($w$) as the worst. Suppose that you say that in this case you prefer to bet on B; that is,

$$w_B^z \succ w_A^z.$$

What are we to make of it? Using the measurement tool (x, y) we find that you think that A is more likely than B. Given the measurement tool (z, w) we find the converse conclusion. Thus, the alleged measurement tools change the outcome of the experiment. In fact, we can't say which of the two events, A and B, is more likely in your eyes.

P4 demands that this not be the case. Formally, for every $A, B \subset S$ and every $x, y, z, w \in X$ with $x \succ y$ and $z \succ w$,

$$y_A^x \succsim y_B^x \quad \text{iff} \quad w_A^z \succsim w_B^z.$$

10.3.7   P5

P5 states that there are $f, g \in F$ such that $f \succ g$.

If it does not hold, we get $f \sim g$ for every $f, g \in F$; that is, $\succsim = F \times F$. This relation is representable by expected utility maximization: you can choose any probability measure and any constant utility function. Moreover, the utility function will be unique up to a positive linear transformation, which boils down to an additive shift by a constant. But the probability measure will be very far from unique.

In other words, Savage could have used six instead of seven axioms to state that there exist a utility function and a probability measure such that $\succsim$ is represented by expected utility maximization. He could have added that apart from the trivial case $\succsim = F \times F$, the measure is also unique. But since a major goal of the axiomatization is to define subjective probability, and we want to pinpoint a unique probability measure, which will be "*the* subjective probability of the decision maker," P5 appears as an explicit axiom.

Once we understand what P5 rules out, we realize that it is a necessary axiom. Not only in the mathematical sense, namely, that P5 follows from the representation (as long as u is not constant), but in the sense that P5 is necessary for the elicitation program to succeed. As mentioned earlier, the idea is to observe choices and, using "reverse engineering," to ask what preferences over outcomes and what beliefs over events could give rise to such choices. It is absolutely necessary that the decision maker make choices or express some preferences. Someone who is incapable of expressing preferences cannot be ascribed subjective probabilities by the reverse engineering program of Ramsey–de Finetti–Savage.

10.3.8 P6

We are left with two "technical" axioms, namely, assumptions that are needed for the mathematical proof to work, but are not necessarily justified on conceptual grounds. The first one, P6, has a flavor of continuity, but it also has an Archimedean twist.[4]

Let us assume that we start with strict preferences between two acts, $f \succ g$, and we wish to state some notion of continuity. We cannot require that, say, $f' \succ g$ whenever $|f(s) - f'(s)| < \varepsilon$, because we have no metric over X. We also can't say that $f' \succ g$ whenever $P(\{s \mid f(s) \neq f'(s)\}) < \varepsilon$, because we have no measure P on S. How can we say that f' is "close" to f?

One attempt to state closeness in the absence of a measure P is the following: assume that we had such a measure P and that we could split the state space into events $A_1, \ldots, A_n$ such that $P(A_i) < \varepsilon$ for every $i \leq n$. Not every measure P allows such a partition, but let's assume we found one. Then we can say that if f' and f differ only on one of the events $A_1, \ldots, A_n$, then f' is close enough to f and therefore $f' \succ g$. This last condition can be stated without reference to the measure P. And this is roughly what P6 requires. More precisely, P6 requires this both for $f \succ g$ (implying $f' \succ g$) and for $g \succ f$ (implying $g \succ f'$). On the other hand, P6 will make a weaker requirement, allowing the partition to depend on the values of f'.

Formally, P6 requires that for every $f, g, h \in F$ with $f \succ g$, there exists a partition of S, $\{A_1, \ldots, A_n\}$,[5] such that for every $i \leq n$,

$$f^h_{A_i} \succ g \quad \text{and} \quad f \succ g^h_{A_i}.$$

Observe that when you are choosing the partition $\{A_1, \ldots, A_n\}$, you may condition it on f, g, h. That is, you know which f and g are involved, as well as how wild h could be.

---

[4] Archimedes stated the axiom: for every positive integers n and m, there exists another, k, such that $kn > m$. That is, if your step size n is positive, you will be able to get as far as you wish if you repeat it sufficiently many times. There are many axioms of this nature in decision theory, and they are called "Archimedean."

[5] A partition of S is a collection of pairwise disjoint events whose union is S.

Still, P6 is a restrictive axiom. In particular, it rules out the possibility of a finite state space S. In fact, P6 implies that every state $s \in S$ is null. To see this, observe that if s were not null, there would be $x, y \in X$ and $f \in F$ such that $f^x_{\{s\}} \succ f^y_{\{s\}}$. Choosing $f = f^x_{\{s\}}$, $g = h = f^y_{\{s\}}$, P6 would be violated, because any partition would have one i such that $s \in A_i$, and changing f to h on this A_i would result in g. Next, observe that P2 implies that the union of null events is a null event, which means that if S were finite, S itself would be null, in violation of P5.

The precise implications of P6 will become clearer later. For the time being, observe that it combines two types of constraints: first, it has a flavor of continuity: changing f (or g) on a "small enough" event does not change strict preferences. Second, it has an Archimedean ingredient, because the way to formalize the notion of a "small enough" event is captured by saying "any of finitely many events in a partition." P6 thus requires that the entire state space not be too large; we have to be able to partition it into finitely many events, each of which is not too significant.

The fact that we need infinitely many states and that, moreover, the probability measure Savage derives has no atoms[6] is certainly a constraint. The standard way to defend this requirement is to say that given any state space S, we can always add to it another source of uncertainty, say, infinitely many tosses of a coin. Let S_1 be an auxiliary state space, describing the infinite tosses of the coin. We can now expand the state space to be the product $S' = S \times S_1$, describing both the original source of uncertainty and the coin tosses. Even if S had atoms, the product space need not have atoms: every atom of S is now an event that can be further split according to the auxiliary space.

Importantly, observe that we do not need to assume that the coin is a fair one, nor even that the tosses are independent. Indeed, if we made any of these assumptions, we would be assuming that there are some events for which we have objective probabilities or at least conditional probabilities.[7] We only need to assume that subjective beliefs, as reflected in preferences over acts in $X^{S'}$, are nonatomic. Having said that, let us admit that the very fact that preferences that are defined only on X^S can be extended to preferences over all of $X^{S'}$ in such a way that all the other axioms still hold is a nontrivial requirement.

10.3.9   P7

If there is a "technical" axiom, this is it. Formally, it is easy to state what it says. But it is hard to explain what it does or what it rules out. It is, in fact,

---

[6] See later for precise definitions.

[7] If you know that the coin is fair, you know that $P(Head) = 0.5$. If you do not know the distribution of the coin, but you know that consecutive tosses are i.i.d. (independently and identically distributed), you could divide tosses to consecutive pairs and ask what will be observed first – the sequence (*Head, Tail*) or a sequence (*Tail, Head*). These two sequences have unknown, but equal, probabilities. Hence you can generate a conditional probability that is known to be 50%, and it is conditioned on an event that will occur with probability 1.

very surprising that Savage needs it, especially if you were already told that he doesn't need it for the case of a finite X. But Savage does prove that the axiom is necessary. That is, he provides an example, in which axioms P1–P6 hold, X is infinite, but there is no representation of $\succsim$ by an expected utility formula.[8]

P7 states the following: consider acts $f, g \in F$ and an event $A \subset S$. If it is the case that for every $s \in A$, $f \succsim_A g(s)$, then $f \succsim_A g$, and if for every $s \in A$, $g(s) \succsim_A f$, then $g \succsim_A f$.

Let us first assume that we only discuss $A = S$. P7 requires that if f is weakly preferred to any particular outcome that g may obtain, then f should be weakly preferred to g itself. This is puzzling. If we didn't have the axioms P1–P6, one can generate weird preferences that do not satisfy this condition. But we have P1–P6. Moreover, restricting attention to finitely many outcomes, we already hinted that there is a representation of preferences by an expected utility formula. How wild can preferences be, so as to violate P7 nevertheless?

The answer has to do with finitely additive measures, which we discuss shortly. You may wish to ignore technicalities and skip to Section 10.4.3. In any event, P7 is another type of continuity condition, one imposed on the outcome space.

10.4 THE RESULT FOR A FINITE OUTCOME SET

Before stating Savage's theorem(s), a few definitions may be useful.

10.4.1 Finitely Additive Measures

Normally, when you study probability, you define a measure μ to be a probability on a measurable space (Ω, Σ) if it is a function $\mu : \Sigma \to \mathbb{R}_+$ such that

$$\mu \left(\cup_i^\infty A_i \right) = \sum_i^\infty \mu(A_i) \tag{10.1}$$

whenever $i \neq j \Rightarrow A_i \cap A_j = \varnothing$ and $\mu(\Omega) = 1$. Condition (10.1) is referred to as σ-additivity.

Finite additivity is the condition known as $\mu(A \cup B) = \mu(A) + \mu(B)$ whenever $A \cap B = \varnothing$, which is clearly equivalent to (10.1) if you replace ∞ by any finite n:

$$\mu \left(\cup_i^n A_i \right) = \sum_i^n \mu(A_i) \tag{10.2}$$

whenever $i \neq j \Rightarrow A_i \cap A_j = \varnothing$

---

[8] See p. 78 of the 1972 edition.

If you already have a finitely additive measure, σ-additivity is an additional constraint of continuity: define $B_n = \cup_i^n A_i$ and $B = \cup_i^\infty A_i$. Then $B_n \nearrow B$ and (10.1) means

$$\mu \left(\lim_{n \to \infty} B_n \right) = \mu \left(\cup_i^\infty A_i \right) = \sum_i^\infty \mu (A_i) = \lim_{n \to \infty} \mu (B_n) ;$$

that is, σ-additivity of μ is equivalent to saying that the measure of the limit is the limit of the measure, when increasing sequences of events are concerned.

As such, σ-additivity is a desirable constraint. At the same time, it can sometimes be too demanding. Lebesgue, who pioneered measure theory, observed that there is no σ-additive measure that is defined for all the subsets of the real line (or of [0, 1]), equals the length when applied to intervals, and is invariant to shifts.[9] His solution was to distinguish between sets that are "measurable" and sets that aren't. That is, he defined measurable sets, proved that they generate a σ-algebra, and restricted attention to sets in this σ-algebra. Importantly, he showed that one can extend the notion of length to a σ-additive measure on this σ-algebra; that is, one need not forego the notion of continuity of the measure with respect to increasing sequences of events.

One may argue, however, that the definition of a σ-algebra of events, of which one may speak, and the exclusion of other events from the discussion is a little artificial. Allowing us to consider only measurable events, the argument goes, is tantamount to sweeping the continuity problem under the rug.

An alternative approach is to relax the continuity assumption and allow measures to be only finitely additive. If we do that, we can bring back to light more subsets. In fact, one can define finitely additive measures on all subsets of, say, [0, 1] that would still coincide with Lebesgue measure on (Lebesgue)-measurable subsets.

The definition of an integral with respect to a finitely additive measure is similar to the usual one, and many nice properties of integration are retained in the finitely additive case. However, some nice theorems do not hold for finitely additive measures, such as Fubini's theorem, which allows us to change the order of integration when multiple integrals are involved.

de Finetti, Savage, and other probabilists in the twentieth century (such as Lester Dubins) had a penchant or, perhaps, an ideological bias for finitely additive probability measures.[10] If probability is to capture our subjective intuition, it does indeed seem much more natural to require finite additivity, namely, that $\mu (A \cup B) = \mu (A) + \mu (B)$ for disjoint A and B, rather than a sophisticated mathematical condition such as (10.1). Given this background, it should come

---

[9] That is, if we wish it to be the case that $\mu([a, b]) = b - a$ for every $b \geq a$ and $\mu(A + x) = \mu(A)$ for every set $A \subset \mathbb{R}$ and $x \in \mathbb{R}$, we can't demand that μ be σ-additive.

[10] de Finetti was probably the first probabilist to promote this idea, and he did so with religious zeal. The literature includes nice stories on the arguments de Finetti had with probabilists such as Cantelli and Frechet over this issue.

as no surprise to us that Savage's theorem yields a measure that is (only) finitely additive. As we have seen, foregoing continuity allows us to consider all the subsets of the state space as events, and we do not need to use algebras to restrict the language used to describe events and acts.

Having said that, two comments are in order. First, if one is willing to restrict attention to measurable sets, Savage's theorem can be proved for measurable acts (see Wakker, 1993b). Further, one may add conditions that imply σ-additivity of the measure obtained (Villegas, 1964).

Second, restricting certain subsets of S from being "events" may appear very artificial if you start with the state space S. But if you go back to ask where the state space originated from, you may find that not all subsets of S are equally natural. Specifically, assume that we start with a syntactic model, listing countably many propositions, and define a state of the world as a consistent truth assignment to these propositions. Every atomic proposition is mapped to an event, namely, all the states that assign a truth value of 1 to this proposition. We can now consider the σ-algebra generated by these events, and observe that events in this σ-algebra correspond to (countable) conjunctions, disjunctions, and negations of the original propositions. Yet, not all subsets of the state space correspond to such compound propositions, and therefore not all such subsets can be at all referred to. In fact, one may well argue that we can refer only to finite conjunctions, disjunctions, and negations, namely, only to the algebra generated by the original propositions. Taking this point of view, restricting attention to measurable events in the state space need not be as arbitrary as it might seem if the state space is the primitive of the model.

10.4.2   Nonatomic Measures

The discussion of P6 given earlier made references to "atoms" of measures, but we have not defined the term precisely.

You may have seen a definition in the standard case of a σ-additive measure: an event A is an atom of μ if

(i) $\mu(A) > 0$;
(ii) for every event $B \subset A$, $\mu(B) = 0$ or $\mu(B) = \mu(A)$.

That is, an atom cannot split, in terms of its probability. When you try to split it into B and $A \backslash B$, you find either that all the probability is on B or that all of it is on $A \backslash B$. A measure that has no atoms is called *nonatomic*.

There are two other possible definitions of nonatomicity, trying to capture the same intuition: you may require, for every event A with $\mu(A) > 0$, that there be an event $B \subset A$ such that $\mu(B)$ is not too close to 0 or to $\mu(A)$. For instance, you may require that

$$\frac{1}{3}\mu(A) \leq \mu(B) \leq \frac{2}{3}\mu(A).$$

Finally, you may consider an even more demanding requirement: that for every event A with $\mu(A) > 0$ and for every $r \in [0, 1]$, there be an event $B \subset A$ such that $\mu(B) = r\mu(A)$.

In the case of a σ-additive μ, all three definitions coincide. But this is not true for finite additivity. Moreover, the condition that Savage needs, and the condition that turns out to follow from P6, is the strongest.

Hence, we will define a finitely additive measure μ to be *nonatomic* if for every event A with $\mu(A) > 0$ and for every $r \in [0, 1]$, there is an event $B \subset A$ such that $\mu(B) = r\mu(A)$.

10.4.3   The Theorem

It may be worthwhile to restate the axioms:

P1. $\succsim$ is a weak order.
P2. For every $f, g, h, h' \in F$, and every $A \subset S$,

$$f_{A^c}^h \succsim g_{A^c}^h \quad \text{iff} \quad f_{A^c}^{h'} \succsim g_{A^c}^{h'}.$$

P3. For every $f \in F$, nonnull event $A \subset S$, and $x, y \in X$,

$$x \succsim y \quad \text{iff} \quad f_A^x \succsim f_A^y.$$

P4. For every $A, B \subset S$ and every $x, y, z, w \in X$ with $x \succ y$ and $z \succ w$,

$$y_A^x \succsim y_B^x \quad \text{iff} \quad w_A^z \succsim w_B^z.$$

P5. There are $f, g \in F$ such that $f \succ g$.
P6. For every $f, g, h \in F$ with $f \succ g$, there exists a partition of S, $\{A_1, \ldots, A_n\}$, such that for every $i \leq n$,

$$f_{A_i}^h \succ g \quad \text{and} \quad f \succ g_{A_i}^h.$$

P7. For every $f, g \in F$ and event $A \subset S$, if for every $s \in A$, $f \succsim_A g(s)$, then $f \succsim_A g$, and if for every $s \in A$, $g(s) \succsim_A f$, then $g \succsim_A f$.

Theorem 10.1 *(Savage) Assume that X is finite. Then $\succsim$ satisfies P1–P6 if and only if there exist a nonatomic finitely additive probability measure μ on S ($= (S, 2^S)$) and a nonconstant function $u : X \to \mathbb{R}$ such that for every $f, g \in F$,*

$$f \succsim g \quad \text{iff} \quad \int_S u(f(s))d\mu(s) \geq \int_S u(g(s))d\mu(s).$$

Furthermore, in this case, μ is unique and u is unique up to positive linear transformations.

10.5   THE CASE OF A GENERAL OUTCOME SET

Theorem 10.2 *(Savage) $\succsim$ satisfies P1–P7 if and only if there exist a nonatomic finitely additive probability measure μ on S ($= (S, 2^S)$) and a nonconstant* *bounded function $u : X \to \mathbb{R}$ such that for every $f, g \in F$,*

$$f \succsim g \quad \textit{iff} \quad \int_S u(f(s))d\mu(s) \geq \int_S u(g(s))d\mu(s). \tag{10.3}$$

Furthermore, in this case, μ is unique and u is unique up to positive linear transformations.

Observe that this theorem restricts u to be bounded. (Of course, this was not stated in Theorem 10.1 because when X is finite, u is bounded.) The boundedness of u follows from P3. Indeed, if u is not bounded one can generate acts whose expected utility is infinite (following the logic of the St. Petersburg paradox). This, in and of itself, is not an insurmountable difficulty, but P3 will not hold for such acts: you may strictly improve f from, say, x to y on a nonnull event A, and yet the resulting act will be equivalent to the first one, both having infinite expected utility. Hence, as stated, P3 implies that u is bounded. An extension of Savage's theorem to unbounded utilities is provided in Wakker (1993a).[11]

A corollary of the theorem is that an event A is null if and only if $\mu(A) = 0$. In Savage's formulation, this fact is stated on par with the integral representation (10.3).

10.6   INTERPRETATIONS

This is the fifth characterization theorem we see in this course. The three interpretations should now be very routine. You should feel like filling a form. Yet, it is important for me to highlight that all three interpretations are valid.

In fact, because Savage's theorem is conceptually much more satisfactory than the previous ones, the normative and descriptive interpretations are more compelling than before. For example, suppose that you're trying to convince me that decision makers maximize expected utility. On the basis of the vNM theorem, you'll be restricted to situations in which probabilities are given. But you'll also be restricted to decision makers who can understand numbers, compound lotteries, and Bayes's rule. Using Savage's theorem, you can tell a story about decision makers who have much less structured information and who need not reason in terms of probabilities.

It is important to recall that the utility and probability obtained in Savage's model get their meaning from the way we use them; that is, when we consider maximization of expected utility using both the probability and the utility provided by the theorem. A decision maker who does not satisfy the axioms may still have a different notion of utility or probability. Machina and Schmeidler (1992) defined a decision maker to be "probabilistically sophisticated" if there exists a probability measure, μ, such that the decision maker's choice between

---

[11] In 1954 Savage was apparently unaware that the boundedness of u follows from P3. Fishburn reports that this became obvious during a discussion they had later on.

any pair of acts depends solely on the distributions over the outcomes induced by these acts and the measure μ. Machina and Schmeidler also provided an axiomatic derivation of probabilistic sophistication. That is, they characterized the decision makers to whom a subjective probability can be ascribed, without restricting the decision rule that is used in conjunction with this probability.

Rostek (2006) provided a Savage-style derivation of maximization of a certain quantile of the utility, say, the median. The quantile is defined relative to a subjective probability measure, and she obtains this measure from the axiomatization in a way that parallels Savage's. Her decision makers are probabilistically sophisticated (in the sense of Machina and Schmeidler), and they use their subjective probability for quantile (rather than expected) utility maximization. Thus, a decision maker may not be an expected utility maximizer, and still have a well-defined subjective probability.

10.7   THE PROOF AND QUALITATIVE PROBABILITIES

Savage's proof is too long and involved to be covered here. Savage (1954) develops the proof step by step, alongside conceptual discussions of the axioms. Fishburn (1970) provides a more concise proof, which may be a bit laconic, and Kreps (1988, pp. 115–136) provides more details. Here I will say only a few words about the strategy of the proof and introduce another concept in this context.

Savage first deals with the case $|X| = 2$. That is, there are two outcomes, say, 1 and 0, with $1 \succ 0$. Thus every $f \in F$ is characterized by an event A; that is, $f = 1_A$. Correspondingly, $\succsim \subset F \times F$ can be thought of as a relation $\succsim \subset \Sigma \times \Sigma$ with $\Sigma = 2^S$.

In this setup P4 has no bite. Let us translate P1–P3 and P5 to the language of events. P1 would mean, again, that $\succsim$ (understood as a relation on events) is a weak order. P2 is equivalent to the condition:

Cancellation: For every $A, B, C \in \Sigma$, if $(A \cup B) \cap C = \varnothing$, then

$$A \succsim B \quad \text{iff} \quad A \cup C \succsim B \cup C.$$

Taken together, P1–P5 are equivalent to

(i) $\succsim$ is a weak order;
(ii) $\succsim$ satisfies cancellation;
(iii) for every A, $A \succsim \varnothing$;
(iv) $S \succ \varnothing$.

A binary relation on an algebra of events that satisfies these conditions was defined by de Finetti to be a *qualitative probability*. The idea was that subjective judgments of "at least as likely as" on events that satisfied certain regularities might be representable by a probability measure; that is, a probability measure μ would satisfy

$$A \succsim B \quad \text{iff} \quad \mu(A) \geq \mu(B). \tag{10.4}$$

If such a measure existed, and if it were unique, one could use the likelihood comparisons $\succsim$ as a basis for the definition of subjective probability. Observe that such a definition would qualify as a definition by observable data if you are willing to accept judgments such as "I find A at least as likely as B" as valid data.[12]

de Finetti conjectured that every qualitative probability has a (quantitative) probability measure that represents it. It turns out that this is true if $|S| \leq 4$, but a counterexample can be constructed for $|S| = 5$. Such a counterexample was found by Kraft *et al.* (1959), who also provided a necessary and sufficient condition for the existence of a representing measure.

You can easily convince yourself that even if such a measure exists, it will typically not be unique when S is finite. The set of measures that represent a given qualitative probability is defined by finitely many inequalities. Generically, one can expect that the set will not be a singleton.

However, Savage found that for $|X| = 2$, his relation was a qualitative probability defined on an infinite space, which also satisfied P6. This turned out to be a powerful tool. With P6 one can show that every event A can be split into two, $B \subset A$ and $A \setminus B$, such that $B \sim A \setminus B$.[13] Equipped with such a lemma, one can go on to find, for every $n \geq 1$, a partition S into 2^n equivalent events, $\Pi_n = \{A_1^n, \ldots, A_{2^n}^n\}$. Moreover, using P2 we can show that the union of every k events from Π_n is equivalent to the union of any other k events from the same partition. Should there be a probability measure μ that represents $\succsim$, it has to satisfy $\mu(A_i^n) = 1/2^n$ and $\mu(\cup_{i=1}^k A_i^n) = k/2^n$.

Given an event B such that $S \succ B$, one may ask, for every n, what is the number k such that

$$\cup_{i=1}^{k+1} A_i^n \succ B \succsim \cup_{i=1}^k A_i^n.$$

Any candidate for a probability μ will have to satisfy

$$\frac{k+1}{2^n} > \mu(B) \geq \frac{k}{2^n}.$$

With a little bit of work one can convince oneself that there is a unique $\mu(B)$ that satisfies the preceding condition for all n. Moreover, it is easy to see that

$$B \succsim C \quad \text{implies} \quad \mu(B) \geq \mu(C). \tag{10.5}$$

The problem then is that the converse is not trivial. In fact, Savage provides beautiful examples of qualitative probability relations, for which there exists a unique μ satisfying (10.5) but not the converse direction.

Here P6 is used again. Savage shows that P6 implies that $\succsim$ (applied to events) satisfies two additional conditions, which he calls fineness and tightness. (Fineness has an Archimedean flavor, while tightness can be viewed as a

---

[12] We will discuss such cognitive data in Part IV.
[13] Kopylov (2007) provides a different proof, which also generalizes Savage's theorem.

continuity of sorts.) With these conditions, it can be shown that the only μ satisfying (10.5) satisfies also

$$B \succ C \quad \text{implies} \quad \mu(B) > \mu(B).$$

and thus represents $\succsim$ as in (10.4).[14]

Having established a representation of $\succsim$ by a measure, Savage's proof loses some of its dramatic effect. First, we, the audience, know that he's going to make it. In fact, he already has: restricting attention to two outcomes, and yet defining a subjective probability measure in a unique and observable way is quite a feat. Second, the rest of the proof is less exciting, though by no means trivial. Savage chose to use the vNM theorem, though this is not the only way to proceed. He first shows that if two acts have the same distribution (with finite support), according to μ, they are equivalent. This means that for a finite X, one can deal with equivalence classes defined by distributions over outcomes. Then Savage proves that the preference relation over these classes satisfies the vNM axioms, and finally he extends the representation to an infinite X.

---

[14] The examples provided by Savage also show that fineness and tightness are independent conditions. He shows a qualitative probability relation that has a unique μ satisfying (10.5), which is fine but not tight, and one which is tight but not fine, and neither of these has a probability that represents it as in (10.4).

CHAPTER 11

The Definition of States

At several points we have touched on the definition of states, and you probably have a rather good idea of what I have to say about it now. Still, this is an important issue and it is worth being stated clearly. Besides, we'll get to see (and resolve) a few more "paradoxes," which should be fun.

11.1 CAUSALITY

11.1.1 Newcomb's Paradox

Consider the following "paradox," attributed to Newcomb and related by Nozick (1969). You are presented with two boxes. One is opaque, and may or may not contain $1M. The other is transparent, and it contains $1,000. You are asked to choose between taking the content of the opaque and of both.

Yes, both, there is no typo here. Indeed, it sounds like a dominant choice to take both. However, there is a twist. In the original version, the person who presents you with the boxes is an omniscient predictor, who can predict your choice with perfect accuracy. Further, she remunerates modesty and penalizes greediness. If she predicted that you'd choose both, she put no money in the opaque box, and vice versa. What is your choice?

Since I find it hard to comprehend what is an omniscient predictor, and how I can know that such a predictor exists while still have a notion of free will, let's change the story a bit. This time no omniscience is involved, but you are told of past observations. It turns out that about 1,000 people made the same choice before you. Roughly 500 chose both boxes and walked away with $1,000. The rest chose only the opaque box and they are now millionaires. What would you do?

The paradox hinges on a conflict between two ways of reasoning. On the one hand, we still have the dominance argument:

	$1M	$0
Greedy	$1,001,000	$1,000
Modest	$1,000,000	$0

Rows correspond to your strategy, columns correspond to the state of the opaque box, and the entries denote your monetary payoff. Clearly, the first row dominates the second.

On the other hand, you observe a regularity that the greedy strategy leads to a payoff of \$1,000, whereas the modest, to \$1M. It is as if your choice changes the probabilities of the states of the world. How can that happen?

11.1.2   States as Functions from Acts to Outcomes

The answer is that this can happen if you misspecified the state space. The states in the table presuppose that you have no control over the content of the opaque box. But there is plenty of evidence that you actually do. That is, even though we started by telling the story as if the content of the box is independent of your choice, you never know. Maybe the guy who handles the box is a crook or a magician. Or maybe there are some amazing regularities that science has not yet deciphered. Whatever your favorite explanation is, you have to remain open to the possibility that there are some causal relationship that you have not yet fathomed. If you don't allow some states of the world to describe such relationships, how will you be able to recognize them once they are proved by scientific studies? Recall that if you are Bayesian, you can never add states to the model, nor update a zero probability to a positive one. Anything that might ever be a proven fact has to be a possibility, namely, has to have some states of the world consistent with it.

There is a simple and algorithmic way to avoid the pitfalls of prejudice and to allow for all possible causal relationships that might affect your life: to define states as functions from acts to outcomes.[1] That is, states should not be presumed given in the problem. Modeling a certain description of the world as a "state" is tantamount to assuming that your choice does not affect the probability of this state, and this can be a mistake. Rather, given the set of actions that are available to you, A, and the set of outcomes you can imagine (or describe in English), X, you should *define*

$$S = X^A;$$

that is, a state specifies what would be the outcome of each action. Since states are now functions of acts, they can be assumed independent of the acts: the dependence of the outcome on the act is reflected in the argument of the function, not in the function itself.

In Newcomb's example, there are four outcomes and two acts; hence, we should have 4^2 states. We can make a simplifying assumption, according to

---

[1] The exact origin of this idea is unclear. Savage's theory was attacked by Jeffrey (1965) for failing to take into account causal relationships. This definition of states was a reply that Savage gave. At the same time, as I emphasize next, this definition is a natural extension of the notion of a state as a truth function for propositions, which is an old idea. In the context of Newcomb's paradox, this resolution probably first appeared in Gibbard and Harper (1978).

which each act can result only in two possible outcomes, and reduce the number of states to 4: specifying whether $1M exist in the opaque box (i) if you decide to be greedy, and (ii) if you decide to be modest.

The states would therefore be

(1, 1) – the money is there anyway;
(1, 0) – $1M are found only by the greedy;
(0, 1) – $1M are given to the modest alone;
(0, 0) – the opaque box is empty.

Observe that only the states (1, 1) and (0, 0) were included in the previous analysis. Now we will have the matrix

	(1, 1)	(1, 0)	(0, 1)	(0, 0)
Greedy	$1,001,000	$1,001,000	$1,000	$1,000
Modest	$1,000,000	$0	$1,000,000	$0

Clearly, there is no dominance in this matrix. There exists a state, (0, 1), in which modesty pays off. After seeing about 1,000 observations that fit the state (0, 1) so perfectly, you would be wise to assign it a high probability. If you think that the state is selected once and for all, (0, 1) will be the only state consistent with observations. If you think that the state is drawn afresh for each player, but from a given distribution in an i.i.d. (independently and identically distributed) manner, you will find (0, 1) very likely due to its high likelihood value.

The main message is quite simple: defining states as functions from acts to outcomes allows all possible causal relationships to be reflected in the analysis. It is also consistent with the "canonical state-space" approach: defining states as truth functions whose domain is the set of propositions of interest. Since the propositions "If I am greedy, I will find $1M in the opaque box" and "If I am modest, I will find $1M in the opaque box" are among the propositions we should consider, a state should at least specify the truth values of these two.

11.1.3 A Problem

The preceding resolution is very compelling. However, you may feel uncomfortable with the number of states it generates. In our example, after making a simplifying assumption, we ended up with 4 states where we had only 2 acts. This doesn't seem to be enough to find a unique probability measure. Indeed, the preference between the two acts will give us one inequality that the probabilities have to satisfy. Since the dimensionality of the simplex of probabilities is 3, one inequality will not suffice.

Indeed, Savage's model requires that we have a complete preference on F. *All* the functions from states to outcomes should be considered, at least as "conceivable acts" if not actual ones. If we start with a set of actually available acts A and construct $S = X^A$, we now have to proceed to define

$$F = X^S = X^{(X^A)}$$

and assume that $\succsim$ is a complete order on F. In our example, with $|A| = 2$ and $|X| = 2$, we obtained $|S| = 4$ and will have $|F| = 16$. The relation $\succsim$ requires the comparison of $\binom{16}{2} = 120$ pairs of alternatives, out of which only one comparison is actually observable.

You might be tempted to expand the set of acts that the decision maker can choose from to include all of F. But this will result in a new state space, X^F, and a new set of conceivable acts, and so forth. This explosion in the cardinality of the set of acts will be even more dramatic when the sets involved are infinite.

When we have a given state space, it is natural to require that the model include all conceivable acts. But the problem we encounter here is that the choices between elements of F cannot be observable *in principle*. That is, if we wish to formulate Savage's model in such a way that it accommodates all possible causal relationships, we obtain a model that is inherently not related to observations. As a result, we will not be able to derive subjective probability from observed behavior.

11.2   HEMPEL'S PARADOX OF CONFIRMATION

11.2.1   Are All Ravens Black?

Hempel (1945, 1966) presented the following "paradox of confirmation." Suppose we wish to test the rule or hypothesis that all ravens are black. An acceptable procedure is to randomly select ravens and test each of them for blackness. One counterexample would suffice to refute the rule, though the rule will never be proved by examples. However, the more ravens we test, the stronger is our belief in the truthfulness of the general rule, should they all turn out to be black.

Notice that "all ravens are black" is logically equivalent to "all that is not black is not a raven." We may therefore test the second formulation of the rule rather than the original one. Applying the same scientific method, one may randomly select nonblack objects, test them for "ravenhood," and then either refute the rule or increase its plausibility.

From here to embarrassment the way is short. Pick a nonblack item in the classroom, or consider a red herring. As a nonblack object, it qualifies for the sample; as a nonraven, it should lend support to the rule tested. Yet it seems patently absurd to use such evidence to confirm the blackness of ravens.

It is often argued that the problem with testing nonblack objects is that there are so many of them. But if you get into such considerations, you have to take the cost of testing into account as well. After all, it is easier to find nonblack objects than it is to find ravens. Moreover, most of our statistical tests depend on the size of the sample but not on the size of the population from which it is drawn – this is typically assumed infinite. In any event, it seems that something else is at work here. Testing a red herring to find whether all ravens are black is not simply an inefficient sampling strategy. It is ridiculous. But why?

11.2.2   A State-Space Formulation

To see the problem, it is useful to resort to the state space within which the problem is couched. Using the state-space approach, as we will see, imposes certain restrictions on the type of resolutions we can consider. Yet, it will help us see where the problem is.

Let there be a set of objects, A, each of which can be a raven or not, black or not. For simplicity, assume that A is finite. The status of object $i \in A$ is an element of $\{0, 1\}^2$, where $(0, 0)$ is an object that is neither a raven nor black, $(1, 0)$ designates a raven that is not black, and so forth. The state space is given by

$$S = \{s : A \rightarrow \{0, 1\}^2\}.$$

The event "object i confirms the rule," equated with "object i is not a counterexample to the rule," is

$$C_i = \{s \in S \mid s(i) \neq (1, 0)\}$$

and the event "all ravens are black" is

$$C = \cap_{i \in A} C_i.$$

Observe that in this formulation the rule "all ravens are black" is completely equivalent to "all nonblack objects are nonravens." That is, the state-space formulation does not allow us to distinguish between the two rules.[2]

11.2.3   What Is a Confirmation?

It is not obvious what we mean when we argue that an observation confirms a rule. In fact, Hempel was attempting an axiomatic approach to this relation between observations and theories. Let us take a Bayesian point of view. For a Bayesian with subjective beliefs, confirmation would naturally be defined as an increase in the probability. That is, if the posterior probability of a theory, given the observation, is higher than the prior probability of that theory, we could argue that the observation confirmed the theory.

Is it the case that observations that are consistent with the theory always confirm it? Well, almost. Assume that we observe object i and find that it does not contradict the theory; that is, C_i is the case. Then

$$P(C|C_i) = \frac{P(C)}{P(C_i)} \geq P(C).$$

Hence, a weak inequality always holds. However, a strict one would hold only if $P(C_i) < 1$, that is, if there used to be an a priori positive probability that observation i would indeed refute the theory.

---

[2] Such distinctions have been suggested in the literature as a possible resolution of the paradox.

11.2.4   A Resolution

It is now obvious what the problem is with the red herring as a confirmation of the theory that all ravens are black: the red herring had been known not to be a raven, even before tested. If we know that i is not a raven, $s(i) \notin \{(1,1),(1,0)\}$ and, in particular, we know C_i. Since $P(C_i) = 1$, the preceding inequality holds as an equality. Observing that the herring is not a nonblack raven does not change our belief in the theory, because we already knew that it wouldn't be a refutation.

Testing a herring, which is known not to be a raven, and therefore also known not to be a counterexample, is similar to testing the same raven again and again. After the first observation, once it has been established that the particular raven is black, our probability already reflects this observation, namely, $P(C_i) = 1$. Observing C_i again will not change our beliefs.

By contrast, it is worth emphasizing that the problem does not lie in the contrapositive. It is indeed true that "all ravens are black" is logically equivalent to "all that is not black is not a raven." Further, we can imagine scenarios in which testing nonblack objects for ravenhood is the right way to go. Suppose that you send me on this sampling mission. The sad truth is that I can't tell ravens from nonravens. I can, however, tell black birds from other birds. I might sample many nonblack birds and bring them to an ornithologist. Suppose I ask her to have a look at my sample, and she tells me that none of them is a raven. I will be justified in increasing my belief that all ravens are black. The point is that when sampling a nonblack bird, I have to have some positive probability that it might be a counterexample (i.e., a raven) to learn something from it. If I already know it's not a counterexample, testing it becomes silly.

11.2.5   Good's Variation

Good (1967, 1968, 1986) has suggested a variation of Hempel's paradox. The following is a simplified version of Good's paradox that highlights the issues discussed previously.

Consider a population containing two objects. It is known that one of the two holds: either both objects are red herrings or both are ravens, in which case one is black and one is red. Let us suppose, for simplicity, that both possibilities are equally likely. Hence the prior probability of the rule "all ravens are black" is 50%, since it holds true in the herring population but does not hold in the raven population.[3]

We are now told that object 1 is a black raven. It follows that the population consists of ravens, in which case the posterior probability that "all ravens are black" has decreased to 0. How can this be reconciled with the preceding calculation?

---

[3] This example does not rely on the fact that the theory is vacuously true. In fact, Good's original example did not involve empty sets.

It may be helpful to spell out the states of the world in this example. Having two objects, we have 16 states of the world, each of which specifies, for each of the two objects, one of the four possibilities: the object is a black herring (BH), black raven (BR), red herring (RH), or red raven (RR). The prior probability we stipulated can be represented by the following table, in which rows designate the status of object 1, and columns, of object 2:

	BH	BR	RH	RR
BH				
BR				0.25
RH			0.50	
RR		0.25		

(Blank entries denote zero probability.) For the raven population, it is assumed here that objects 1 and 2 are equally likely to be the red (hence also the black) raven.

The event "all ravens are black" (denoted by C previously) consists of the 3×3 northwest matrix. Its prior probability is 50%. The event "object 1 does not contradict the rule" is represented by the top three rows. Indeed, given this event alone, the posterior probability of C is $2/3$, that is, larger than the prior. However, given that object 1 is also a raven, it becomes zero. In fact, this latter piece of information would have sufficed: the event "object 1 is a raven," which is represented by rows 2 and 4, leaves zero probability on the event C.

To conclude, what decreases the probability of the rule "all ravens are black" is *not* the positive example per se; it is additional information, which does not follow from the fact that the item sampled does not contradict the rule.

11.2.6 What Do We Learn from This?

Hempel's paradox is supposed to convince us that the state space is a powerful analytical tool. If you couple it with Bayesian reasoning, you are very well equipped to deal with puzzles and paradoxes. The Bayesian approach is a very effective tool to sort out our intuition. We will later criticize it and argue that in many situations, one cannot specify the prior probabilities needed to use the Bayesian machinery. But in order to follow qualitative reasoning, this is a remarkably coherent setup.

It is also worth recalling that modeling uncertainty by a state-space formulation does not necessitate a Bayesian approach. That is, one can use a state-space model, but not specify a prior over it or only partially specify it.

Two comments are in order regarding Hempel's paradox of confirmation. First, whereas the Bayesian approach helps us, in the preceding analysis, to resolve the paradox, it is not essential for the resolution. The crux of the matter is that when I sample a red herring, knowing it is not a raven, I learn nothing. This argument can be made independently of the state-space model. The point of the example is that the state-space model forces us to think about some issues that can otherwise be lost.

Second, as briefly mentioned earlier, Hempel's interest was in formulating general rules of confirmation. For instance, he suggested the rule, or axiom, that if evidence e confirms hypothesis h and h implies h', then e should also confirm h'. When I first read Hempel, it was after I had already been brought up as a Bayesian. Reading this axiom, I tested how intuitive it is by checking whether Bayesian update satisfies it. It is easy to see that it doesn't. That is, you may have events A, B, C such that $A \subset B$, $P(A|C) > P(A)$, but $P(B|C) < P(B)$. When you go through the analysis, you see the reason: C may make A more likely, but it may make $B \backslash A$ less likely, and overall there is no reason that it would make B more likely.

Of course, one may start with Hempel's conditions and dismiss the Bayesian approach because it fails to satisfy these conditions. However, Hempel's conditions where shown to lead to unreasonable conditions (see Goodman, 1954). I believe that there is a rather wide consensus today that there is little hope to obtain valid axioms of the type that Hempel sought.

11.3 MONTY HALL THREE-DOOR GAME

In the famous TV game "Let's make a deal," a contestant has to choose one of three doors, behind one of which a prize was hidden. Before opening any door, the moderator, Monty Hall (MH), opens a door and gives the contestant the chance to switch. For simplicity, let us assume that MH has to open a door and that he has to open one which is neither the one hiding the prize nor the one named by the contestant.[4] Should the contestant switch after such a door was opened?

It is easy to see that the answer is in the affirmative and that switching obtains the prize with probability of 2/3, as opposed to 1/3 probability of getting the prize if one's strategy is not to switch. One can also find various intuitive explanations for the advantage of switching. For example, it is worth pointing out that the strategy "switch" does not always mean the same door. It uses the information provided by MH, who helps the contestant by ruling out some of the bad choices that the latter could have made.

Another explanation that sometimes helps seeing the point involves more doors. Suppose, for example, that there are 100 doors, of which MH has to open 98, where he still cannot open the door that the contestant named or the one hiding the prize. Assume that you are the contestant and that you chose door 17. MH walks around, flinging open 98 doors, leaving shut only numbers 17 and 82. Now you ask yourself, which door is more likely to hide the prize – 17 or 82? We knew that door 17 would be left shut if only because you named it. No

---

[4] In reality, MH had more choices. He could decide not to open any door, offer financial incentives for switching, and so forth. It is an amusing exercise to analyze the situation as a two-person zero-sum game, where the only choice MH has is whether to open a door, possibly conditioning it on whether the contestant's initial guess was correct. While the game is a bit complicated, it's not hard to see that its value is 1/3 (for the contestant). Clearly, MH's objective function was not to keep the car with the highest probability, but to have a show with high ratings. In any event, for our purposes it is simpler to assume that he had to open a door.

additional assumptions are needed to explain why it is now shut. By contrast, it seems that door 82 has survived a tougher test in order to be among the last two doors left shut. More formally, you can apply a likelihood reasoning: the theory "the prize is behind door 82" has a likelihood value of 1; under this theory, we'd expect to see precisely doors 17 and 82 shut. The theory "the prize is behind door 17" has a lower likelihood value: under this theory, one needs to explain why door 82 was the one selected to be left shut. Assuming that MH makes a random choice when he indeed has a choice, the probability of this particular door to be left shut was only 1/99. Hence, the likelihood value of the former theory is 99 higher than that of the latter. With only three doors the explanation is similar, though less dramatic.

But the question we need to resolve is "what's wrong with the intuitive argument that switching doesn't improve our probabilities?" Assume that I named door A, and MH opens door B. If a priori I had the probabilities $P(A) = P(B) = P(C) = 1/3$, and state B was crossed out, don't I get $P(A|\{A, C\}) = P(C|\{A, C\}) = 1/2$?

The answer is that this is a perfectly correct calculation, applied to the wrong model. A model with three states, A, B, C, tells us where the prize is, but it is not rich enough to describe MH's strategy, namely, which door he would open given where the prize really is. Rather than a model with 3 states, we need a model with (at least) 9 states. Suppose that I named door A. Consider the 9 states defined by combinations of (i) where the prize is (A, B, C), and (ii) which door MH opens (OA, OB, OC):

	OA	OB	OC	
A	0	1/6	1/6	1/3
B	0	0	1/3	1/3
C	0	1/3	0	1/3
	0	1/2	1/2	1

where the rows denote where the prize really is, the columns denote which door MH opens, and the last row and last column are the marginal probabilities. The diagonal consists of 0s because MH is not allowed to reveal the prize. The first column consists of 0s because he is not allowed to open the door that I named (assumed to be A). Since each row adds up to 1/3, the only freedom in filling up the numbers is in the case that the prize is indeed behind A, and MH can open door B or C (where I chose to assume a random choice on his part).

Given this matrix, conditioning on "the prize is not behind B," namely, crossing out the middle row, we obtain $P(A|\{A, C\}) = P(C|\{A, C\}) = 1/2$ as earlier. However, conditioning on "MH opened door B," namely, focusing on the middle column, the conditional probabilities are

$$P(A|OB) = \frac{1/6}{1/2} = \frac{1}{3}$$

and

$$P(C|OB) = \frac{1/3}{1/2} = \frac{2}{3}.$$

This analysis would change if the probabilities of $A \cap OB$ and $A \cap OC$ were not symmetric, but the conclusion that one has a higher probability of winning by switching than by not switching will be valid. To see this more clearly, assume that, in case the prize is actually behind door A, MH opens door B with probability $\alpha \in [0, 1/3]$. We then have the matrix

	OA	OB	OC	
A	0	α	$1/3 - \alpha$	$1/3$
B	0	0	$1/3$	$1/3$
C	0	$1/3$	0	$1/3$
	0	$1/3 + \alpha$	$2/3 - \alpha$	1

In this case, if, once a door was opened, you ask yourself what is the conditional probability that switching will win the prize, it is not necessarily 2/3, and it will generally depend on which door was opened. If, for instance, $\alpha = 1/3$, there is no reason to switch in case MH opens door B, but in case he opens C, the contestant can switch, knowing that he is going to get the prize with conditional probability of 1. Clearly, it is still true that the a priori probability of winning the prize by the switching strategy is 2/3, and this a priori probability will equal the expected conditional probability (given OB and given OC):

$$\frac{2}{3} = \left(\frac{1}{3} + \alpha\right) \frac{1/3}{1/3 + \alpha} + \left(\frac{2}{3} - \alpha\right) \frac{1/3}{2/3 - \alpha}.$$

The point of this example is, again, that the states of the world should be informative enough. Whereas Newcomb's example reminded us that the states should describe potential causal relationships, MH's example shows that the way in which we obtain information may be informative in and of itself.[5] Hence the state should describe not only the information, but also the protocol by which it was revealed to us.

---

[5] This general message of the MH game was pointed out to me by Roger Myerson.

CHAPTER 12

A Critique of Savage

Savage's "technical" axioms, P6 and P7, have been discussed in Chapter 10. They are not presented as canons of rationality, rather as mathematical conditions needed for the proof. We therefore do not discuss them any further.

There is also little to add regarding axiom P5. It is worth emphasizing its role in the program of behavioral derivations of subjective probabilities, but it is hardly objectionable.

By contrast, P1–P4 have been, and still are, a subject of heated debates, based on their reasonability from a conceptual viewpoint. We start the discussion with P3 and P4. We will attempt to delineate their scope of applicability as clearly as we can, briefly discuss alternatives, and move on. Only then will we get to P1 and P2. The problems with these axioms will motivate the discussions that follow.

12.1 CRITICIZING CRITIQUES

It may be useful to agree what constitutes a violation of an axiom and when we would like to retain an axiom despite what appears to be a violation thereof. This will also serve as an example of an application of the discussion in Section 7.2.

12.1.1 An Example

Consider the IIA (independence of irrelevant alternatives) axiom in consumer theory. You probably know it from Mas-Colell *et al.* (1995) or from Kreps (1988). It is stated in the context of a choice function, mapping nonempty sets of alternatives, A, to nonempty subsets of themselves, $C(A) \subset A$. The axiom says that if $x, y \in A \cap B$, $y \in C(A)$, and $x \in C(B)$, then also $y \in C(B)$.

Next consider the following example: assume that the alternatives are clearly ranked by a linear order $\succ$, reflecting, for instance, which amount of money is larger, which seat is more comfortable, and so on. You would like to get an alternative that is as high as possible in this order, but you do not want to take the best one for various reasons. Say, you don't want to appear greedy to your friends, or you want to leave the best one for your child to pick, and so forth.

Then, if $a \succ b \succ c$, you will choose b out of $\{a, b, c\}$, but (only) c out of $\{b, c\}$, thus violating the IIA.

What do we make of it? Should we discard the IIA axiom, or at least restrict its applicability to situations in which no social or emotional payoffs are relevant? For some applications, we may have to do that. In particular, if we attempt to seriously predict choices, either by estimating utility functions or by other means, we will have no choice but to admit that, as far as we can observe, the IIA axiom is violated. Indeed, empirical economic research is generally very careful in asking what unobservable factors might be interfering with the observable choice data.

But suppose that we focus on theoretical applications, which tend to be more rhetorical in nature. To go back to our example, choice theory will be applied, at the end of a long road, to questions such as the welfare theorems and the organization of markets. Do we wish to dismiss the IIA axiom and the notion of utility maximization due to the preceding example?

I think not. It appears that the IIA axiom is basically a very reasonable axiom and that the application of the IIA axiom as earlier does not give the theory a fair chance, so to speak. In these examples there are two dimensions to the choice problem: what you get to consume, and another dimension such as what your friends think of you or what your child gets to consume. It is quite rational to take such considerations into account. Your social standing affects your well-being directly. It also gets to be reflected in material outcomes, say, whether you will be invited to parties. Similarly, caring about our children is, at least in the eyes of some, the epitome of rationality. If these choices are rational, they can probably be described by constrained optimization. Indeed, this can and has been done. Many authors in "behavioral economics" retained the rational choice paradigm but added more factors as determinants of utility. Using the basic paradigm of utility maximization, this approach surely retains the IIA axiom as well. Only it applies the IIA axiom to a richer set of alternatives.

12.1.2   The General Lesson

Amos Tversky used to say, "Give me an axiom and I will design an experiment that refutes it." He was not just bragging – the remarkable record of experiments that he and Daniel Kahneman developed more or less proves the point. In a sense, Tversky's challenge was in line with Popper's view that theories are always false.

One should not be overly depressed by this fact. Many of the experiments of Kahneman and Tversky came themselves under attack for being cast in artificial environments (see Gigerenzer and Hoffrage, 1995). Also, one should worry about the prevalence of deviations from a certain theory. The fact that for every theory there exists an experiment that violates it, chosen after the theory was stated, need not imply that the theory will be refuted in most or even in many of the possible applications we have in mind for it.

But despite these defenses, there is no denial that we do observe a large body of evidence that indicates failures of many of our theories and of specific assumptions. When confronted with such failures, it will be useful to develop the habit of stopping to ask whether the theory or assumption was meant to be used in the strict sense or as a conceptual framework. These interpretations are so different that they warrant two separate paragraphs.

Viewed as a specific theory, we are wedded to particular types of datasets that may be observed. We may, for instance, observe saving behavior, but not the way that children's utility enters that of their parents. If we believe, for instance, that bequest motives affect saving behavior, we will have to think how we account for the unobservable data in the analysis. We can use structural models or use proxy variables, or otherwise try to measure the unobservable data.

Viewed as a conceptual framework, we have already discussed (in Section 7.1) the role of theories as metaphors. When theories are used mostly as frameworks within which our intuition can be sharpened, or as rhetorical devices, we can and should let our imagination soar and consider factors that are measurable in principle even if not in practice.

When judging an axiom for the sake of theoretical or rhetorical applications, we should not be quick to dismiss it because of an observed violation. If one can plausibly redefine the mapping from theoretical concepts to real-life entities in such a way that the axiom regains its plausibility, it may still be a powerful tool for reasoning. We should worry more about the cases in which a certain axiom fundamentally misses the point, in a way that cannot be salvaged by an intuitive (even if not easily measurable) redefinition of terms.

12.2 CRITIQUE OF P3 AND P4

12.2.1 Example

The main difficulty with both P3 and P4 is that they assume a separation of tastes from beliefs. That is, they both rely on an implicit assumption that an outcome x is just as desirable, no matter at which state s it is experienced.

The best way to see this is, perhaps, by a counterexample. The classical one, mentioned earlier, is considering a swimsuit, x, versus an umbrella, y. You will probably prefer y to x in the event A, in which it rains, but x to y in the event B, in which it doesn't rain.[1]

This is a violation of P3. As explained earlier, P3 can be viewed as follows: For every nonnull event A, define $\succsim_A \subset X \times X$ by

$$x \succsim_A y \quad \text{iff} \quad f_A^x \succsim f_A^y$$

---

[1] For the sake of the argument, let us suppose that if it doesn't rain it is also warm enough to go to the beach. Of course, the same analysis also holds if A and B are not complements.

for some $f \in F$. P2 guarantees that the choice of f does not matter. This implies that $\succsim_A$ is transitive and, in fact, that $x \succ_A y$ iff there exists $f \in F$ with $f_A^x \succ f_A^y$. That is, the event A suggests a possible way to measure the relative desirability of the outcomes: it defines an order on X. P3 requires that this order be independent of the event A. The swimsuit example shows that it may not.

Similarly, the same example can be used to construct a violation of P4. Suppose that I am trying to find out which is more likely in your eyes, event A (that it rains) or event B (that it doesn't rain). For any pair of outcomes z, w such that $z \succ w$, define the relation $\succsim_{z,w} \subset 2^S \times 2^S$ by

$$A \succsim_{z,w} B \quad \text{iff} \quad w_A^z \succsim w_B^z.$$

P4 requires that $\succsim_{z,w}$ be independent of the choice of $z \succ w$. To see why it is violated in this example, consider, first, a neutral pair of outcomes, say, \$100, denoted by z, and \$0, denoted by w. You probably prefer z (for sure) to w (for sure). Suppose that you also exhibit the preference $w_B^z \succ w_A^z$, suggesting that you find rain less likely than no rain. Next, compare x (for sure) to y (for sure). Irrespective of your beliefs about the rain, I would be willing to bet that you would exhibit the preference $x_A^y \succ x_B^y$. Indeed, x_A^y is just what you want: to have a swimsuit if it doesn't rain, and an umbrella if it does, whereas x_B^y is the disastrous mismatch in which you get the umbrella on the beach and the swimsuit to run in the rain. That is, the preference $x_A^y \succ x_B^y$ follows from the matching between the outcomes and the states, and it reveals nothing about beliefs. It is therefore not surprising that we may get the contradiction $A \succ_{x,y} B$ and $B \succ_{z,w} A$.

12.2.2 Defense

Examples such as those given in the preceding paragraph have been discussed for a long time. In particular, they appeared in an exchange of letters between Aumann and Savage in 1970–1971.[2] The standard response, given by Savage, is that the definition of an "outcome" should be precise and elaborate enough so as to fully specify the decision maker's well-being. Thus, concrete goods such as a swimsuit and an umbrella may not qualify as outcomes, because the utility we derive from them is uncertain. An outcome could be, for instance, "lying on the beach in the sun," "walking in the rain dressed in a swimsuit," and the like.

With this understanding of outcomes, the assumption that all functions in $F = X^S$ are available to choose from involves hypothetical choices. For example, since we haven't changed the definition of the states, there is still an event A where it rains. One possible act f may attach to the event A the outcome "lying on the beach in the sun." How can we envisage a situation in which this outcome is experienced when it does, in fact, rain? This is as if

---

[2] These letters were published in Dreze (1987, appendix 2A).

someone promised you that should it rain where you are, you'd immediately be transported to a calm tropical beach. Indeed, this is a hypothetical choice, but it can be imagined with some effort. And if you do imagine it, you can try to elicit your subjective probability for the event of rain irrespective of how much you like rain and the outcomes associated with it.

Savage was well aware that the hypothetical choices involved may be a bit of a stretch. In what has become a very famous quote, Savage wrote to Aumann, "I don't mind being hanged as long as my reputation and good health are unharmed." Caricaturizing his own argument, Savage suggested that we imagine state–outcome combinations that may be hypothetical.

The image of Savage hanged and enjoying good health may never leave your mind. It is a good warning. Yet, let us also consider an example in which Savage's defense of P3–P4 is compelling. Imagine that you are getting stock options. The value of the options depends on the state of the world. One could argue that Savage's model is inappropriate to analyze options because P3 and P4 are violated when the value of the outcome changes with the state. Alternatively, one may say that the outcome is measured in money and that the option, despite being a concrete financial asset, is still an uncertain act. In this case the uncertainty will be described as usual in Savage's model, namely, by representing an option as a function from states to outcomes.

I believe that the option example does not make you question P3 or P4. It seems perfectly reasonable to define outcomes as monetary payoffs. Some degree of hypothetical reasoning may still be involved. For instance, I can ask you to imagine that your portfolio is very valuable in a state in which the market crashes and trade is suspended. But this degree of hypothetical reasoning may be a small price to pay for the simplicity of the model in which we can assume that tastes and beliefs are separable.

12.2.3   State-Dependent Utility

Still, the image of Savage at the gallows comes back to haunt us. There are situations in which the hypothetical reasoning we are required to engage in goes beyond the limits of good taste. What shall we do then?

Dreze (1961) was probably the first to suggest the model of expected utility maximization with a state-dependent utility. In such a model, the utility function is defined as $u : X \times S \to \mathbb{R}$ and the decision maker maximizes

$$U(f) = \int_S u\left(f(s), s\right) d\mu(s), \tag{12.1}$$

where μ, as in Savage's model, is the subjective probability over the state space S.

There is an obvious theoretical drawback to such a state-dependent model: the pair (u, μ) in (12.1) is not unique. To see this more clearly, assume that we have finitely many states, $S = \{1, \ldots, n\}$, and

$$U(f) = \sum_i u\,(f(i), i)\,\mu(i).$$

For every set of coefficients $\lambda_i > 0$, we can define

$$u'\,(f(i), i) = u\,(f(i), i)\,/\lambda_i$$

$$\mu'(i) = \frac{\lambda_i \mu(i)}{\sum_j \lambda_j \mu(j)}$$

and find that (u, μ) and (u', μ') represent the same preferences. This implies that μ is very far from being unique. In fact, the only agreement that is guaranteed to hold between μ and μ' will consist in the set of zero-probability events. We can still do economic theory with such models, but we do not have a definition of subjective probabilities based on observed choices.

Karni *et al.* (1983) and Karni (1985) axiomatize models of state-dependent utilities. In Karni and Schmeidler (1981) and Karni (1985, ch. 1), uniqueness of the probability measure can be reinstated if one allows more data to be considered observable. Typically, these involve some hypothetical choices.

12.2.4   The Definition of Subjective Probability

There is another example of state-dependent preferences that I find particularly illuminating. It is based on an example of Aumann, and it is discussed in Karni (1996) and Karni and Mongin (2000). In this example a decision maker satisfies all of Savage's axioms, and yet state independence appears inappropriate. It goes as follows:

Mr. and Mrs. Jones have been happily married for many years. Unfortunately, Mrs. Jones is seriously ill and she has to undergo a dangerous operation. The doctors tell Mr. Jones that, on the basis of reliable data, his wife will survive the operation with probability .5. Mr. Jones has no reason to doubt this assessment.

Now you are trying to find out Mr. Jones's subjective probability regarding the outcome of the operation. You may ask him a de Finetti–Savage question such as to rank the following two acts:

$$f = \begin{cases} \$0 & \text{wife survives} \\ \$3,000 & \text{wife dies} \end{cases} \qquad g = \$1,000.$$

Let us put aside the emotional stress that Mr. Jones in under, as well the ethical problems involved. Mr. Jones may find that he is indifferent between f and g. The reason is that, should his wife die, he is likely to be depressed. Nothing that he enjoys now will be as enjoyable in this case. He won't feel like going on trips on his own, he won't enjoy concerts, and so forth.

Suppose that Mr. Jones's utility, as long as his wife is alive, is the identity function, but should his wife die, the utility he will derive from any outcome x will be reduced by $1/2$. It is easy to see that if Mr. Jones computes his state-dependent expected utility relative to the prior 50%–50%, he will report indifference between f and g. An outside observer may conclude that he has a linear utility function, but that he's more optimistic than are the doctors, and attaches a subjective probability of only $1/3$ to his wife dying.

Thus, even if a decision maker satisfies all of Savage's axioms, and we elicit a unique probability measure that describes the decision maker's preferences through the simple formula of expected utility maximization with a state-independent utility function, we can still not be sure that what we measured is the decision maker's subjective probabilities. In the preceding example, when you ask Mr. Jones what are the chances that his wife would die, he will give the same answer as his doctors, 50%. If he has to provide advice to a third party, who is not directly affected by the outcome of the operation, he will base his answer on the 50% probability. For example, imagine that his wife's bridge partner is delicately trying to find out when Mrs. Jones will be playing again. Mr. Jones can sadly tell them that there is a 50% probability that she won't be coming back at all. That is, to find out what is Mr. Jones subjective probability we should simply ask him. A direct question will lead to a more accurate answer than the behavioral definition, relying on "willingness to bet."

It is important to recall that the uniqueness of the utility and probability in Savage's representation are *relative to that representation*. If you allow yourself a more general framework, such as (12.1), uniqueness is lost even if preferences do satisfy Savage's axioms.[3] Having said that, we should also note that the preceding example does not appear very robust. In particular, it relies on a limited set of outcomes. To see this, assume that we extend the set of outcomes to include pairs of outcomes that differ only in ways that do not affect Mr. Jones directly. For example, outcomes might specify (i) all that is relevant to Mr. Jones' personal well-being, as well as (ii) the number of casualties in an earthquake on the other side of the globe. We might assume (and hope) that for any fixed level of personal well-being, Mr. Jones would prefer there to be fewer casualties in the earthquake. This would mean that his preferences will not satisfy Savage's axioms after all, because for *some* pairs of outcomes the utility differences will be state independent, while for others they will be state dependent. In other words, when utility is indeed state dependent, we should expect to observe violations of P3 and P4 in a reasonably rich model. Taking the contrapositive of this claim, we can argue that, in a reasonably rich model, *should* a decision maker satisfy all of Savage's axioms, interpreting the resulting measure as her subjective probability does not seem unwarranted.

12.2.5   When Is State Dependence Necessary?

Given the considerable cost of giving up the uniqueness of the probability measure, one may wonder how far can Savage's defense go and when do we truly have to reject state dependence (and with it, P3 and P4)?

---

[3] Edi Karni argues that due to this reason, the choice of the subjective probability that corresponds to the state-independent utility is only a matter of convention.

Savage's caricature implicitly admits that when an event such as death is concerned, state-dependent utility might be a necessity. The same would apply to other catastrophic events, in which the decision maker may become paraplegic, insane, and so on. The example of Mr. Jones shows that uncertainty need not apply to one's person in order to change utility in a way that state-independent utility would be misleading or simply false. What distinguishes these examples, in which state-dependent utility is crucial, from simple misapplications of the model as in the options example?

A natural guideline emerges if we remind ourselves of the nature of the exercise we perform. Again, the name of the game, following the Ramsey–de Finetti–Savage line, is to elicit beliefs from preferences. That is, we observe the results of a decision process and try to reason back and ask what beliefs might have driven the choices we observed.

People make choices based on their beliefs, but also based on what they like and dislike. In other words, the decision maker's "hedonic engine," her ability to enjoy or suffer from experiences, is part of the measurement tool that Ramsey, de Finetti, and Savage designed to measure beliefs. If the measurement tool is itself subject to uncertainty, we should not be surprised to find problems. Our situation is analogous to an astronomer who observes the stars, but does not know how their motion affects the operation of his own telescope.

All the examples of state-dependent utility in which one cannot restate the model along the line of Savage's defense, I would argue, have one thing in common: they describe uncertainty that affects the decision maker's hedonic engine, that is, her ability to enjoy life. This is true of death, illness, death of a loved one, and so forth. Conversely, in examples that do not involve uncertainty about one's hedonic engine, it is quite possible that Savage's defense is convincing and one may redefine outcomes so as to obtain a state-independent utility.

Considering economic applications, we find that problems that have to do with physical and mental health, problems that involve life insurance, and so forth are likely to require state-dependent utility model. These would also be problems for which the Savage approach does not provide a satisfactory definition of subjective probabilities.

12.3   CRITIQUE OF P1 AND P2

12.3.1   The Basic Problem

The main difficulty with axioms P1 and P2, as well as with Savage's theorem and with the entire Bayesian approach is, in my mind, the following: for many problems of interest, there is no sufficient information based on which one can define probabilities.[4] Referring to probabilities as subjective rather than

---

[4] Much of the material in this section appeared in Gilboa *et al.* (2004, 2007). See also Shafer (1986).

objective is another symptom of the problem, not a solution thereof. It is a symptom, because, were one capable of reasoning one's way to probabilistic assessments, one could have also convinced others of that reasoning and result in a more objective notion of probability. Subjective probabilities are not a solution to the problem: subjectivity may save us needless arguments, but it does not give us a reason to choose one probability over another. Interpreting probabilities subjectively, each of us is entitled to his or her own opinion. But when left to our devices, it is only rational that we ask ourselves, why do other people have different beliefs? How can I be so sure that I'm right and they're wrong? Maybe I should give some credence to their beliefs as well?

This difficulty can manifest itself in violations of P1 and/or P2. If one takes a strict view of rationality and asks what preferences can be justified based on evidence and reasoning, one is likely to end up with incomplete preferences.[5] One may take a weaker view of rationality and explicitly model preferences that are not necessarily justified, but are also not contradicted by evidence and reasoning. This approach has the advantage of satisfying the completeness axiom, but it does so at a cost: many preference pairs will have to be determined quite arbitrarily. As a result, one may find that one violates other axioms. In particular, P2 is a likely victim, because it is the axiom that implies, among other things, that the decision maker should be indifferent between likelihood judgments that are well reasoned and those that are arbitrary.

We now turn to discuss these issues in more detail.

12.3.2   Reasoned Choice versus Raw Preferences

As mentioned in Section 6.1, in consumer theory the completeness axiom is typically considered to be rather weak. Descriptively, it says that something will have to be chosen. Normatively, it adds that it is better to explicitly model that something. The completeness axiom may help us elicit the utility function of the consumer by observing their choices and reasoning backward. This process may even be followed by the decision maker herself. For example, if I observe that there are two types of mustard in my refrigerator, one is consumed and the other isn't, I may infer from this that I like the first more than the second.

When my preferences are well defined and require no reasoning, a similar process may help me elicit my subjective probabilities. For example, if I notice that I do not buckle up for a short trip of half a mile, I can infer that I probably do not find it very likely that an accident would occur in such short a trip. I do not need to consciously think about the probability of an accident in order to define my preferences. My preferences are given and, on careful inspection, they can be viewed as reflecting subjective probabilities.

Next assume that I have to decide whether to invest in a certain firm in an emerging economy. Should I or should I not invest? I can try to inspect my

---

[5]   See the discussion in Chapter 13.

mind for preferences, but as opposed to the case of the mustard or the seat belt, there are no preferences in my head. I do not know what I prefer.

Trying to figure out my preferences, I may start thinking what would be the probability of this economy continuing to grow at the current pace, what is the probability of the particular firm succeeding, and so forth. In assessing these probabilities no gain would be obtained from asking myself what my preferences are. In fact, this would lead me back to the probability question.

We are therefore led to a distinction between types of choices. On one extreme there are choice situations in which preferences are well defined and require no inference.[6] Let us refer to these as "raw preferences." On the other extreme we find decision problems that require thinking and reasoning to construct our preferences. Call these "reasoned choices." The interpretation of a relation $\succsim$ is quite different in these situations.[7]

When $\succsim$ refers to raw preferences, as in simple consumer problems, completeness may be viewed as a very weak axiom, whereas the other axioms impose restrictions on preferences. When $\succsim$ models reasoned choice, by contrast, completeness is the challenge: one attempts to find out one's preferences. The other axioms, being restrictions on the preferences one may consider, can be viewed as aids to decision. By restricting the set of possible preference relations, axioms such as transitivity and P2–P4 provide the decision maker with hints, as it were, regarding her preferences. Relatedly, such axioms provide reasons for various preferences. The decision maker might think, "Since I prefer f to g and I know I also prefer g to h, I should prefer f to h." Or, "I notice that f is preferred to g given A and also given A^c. I conclude that I actually prefer f to g unconditionally as well."

For reasoned choice, the completeness axiom is the goal. This goal might be attained only after the reasoning process is complete and a probability measure has been assessed. At that point it will be too late to use the completeness axiom to derive a probability measure. We should find a probability measure based on other grounds if we wish to satisfy the completeness axiom.

12.3.3   Schmeidler's Critique and Ellsberg's Paradox

Cognitive Unease

Assume now that one has decided to bring forth all one's preferences. Choices will be made; let us make them explicit. But now we have choices that are justified by reasoning (and evidence) and choices that are not. One problem of the Bayesian approach is that it does not distinguish between these.

---

[6] The phrase "preference requires no inference" is borrowed from Zajonc (1980).

[7] This point was made in Gilboa *et al.* (2004). There are many situations that present us with intermediate cases, for instance, when one follows a reasoning process to conclude that a is preferred to b, while one's gut feeling still prefers b.

David Schmeidler was bothered by these issues in the early 1980s. He suggested the following mind experiment: you are asked to bet on a flip of a coin. You have a coin in your pocket, which you have tested often and found to have a relative frequency of head of about 50%. I also have a coin in my pocket, but you know nothing about my coin.

If you wish to be Bayesian, you have to assign probabilities to each of these coins coming up head. The coin for which relative frequencies are known should probably be assigned the probability .5. It has been flipped many times and it has honestly earned this probability. My coin is a wild card. You know nothing about it, but your ignorance is symmetric. You have no reason to prefer one side to the other. If you were not convinced by the principle of indifference, you may prefer not to assign any probability to my coin coming up head. Still, you have to. So you assign the probability of .5, based on symmetry considerations alone.

Now that probabilities were assigned, the two coins have the same probability. But Schmeidler's intuition was that they feel very different. There is some sense that .5 assigned based on empirical frequencies is not the same as .5 that was assigned based on default.

I emphasize the fact that Schmeidler's work started with this intuition. As we will see later, this intuition has a behavioral manifestation in Ellsberg's paradox. But Schmeidler did not start out by attempting to explain the experimental evidence. I think that this is partly the reason that Schmeidler's work had a very significant impact: sometimes we should trust our intuition more than experiments in finding when the theory doesn't make sense.[8]

Ellsberg's Two-Urn Paradox

Ellsberg (1961) suggested two experiments. His original paper does not report an experiment run in a laboratory, only replies obtained from economists. The two-urn experiment is very similar to the two-coin example:

There are two urns, each containing 100 balls. Urn I contains 50 red balls and 50 black balls. Urn II contains 100 balls, each of which is known to be either red or black, but you have no information about how many of the balls are red and how many are black. A *red bet* is a bet that the ball drawn at random is red and a *black bet* is the bet that it is black. In either case, winning the bet, namely, guessing the color of the ball correctly, yields $100. First, you are asked, for each of the urns, if you prefer a red bet or a black bet. For each urn separately, most people say that they are indifferent between the red and the black bet.

Then you are asked whether you prefer a red bet on urn I or a red bet on urn II. Many people say that they would strictly prefer to bet on urn I, the urn with

---

[8] Observe that in Section 6.4 we also concluded that our intuition (about decreasing marginal utility) should have been trusted more than it had been.

known composition. The same pattern of preferences is exhibited for black bets (as, indeed, would follow from transitivity of preferences given that one is indifferent between betting on the two colors in each urn). That is, people seem to prefer betting on an outcome with a known probability of 50% than on an outcome whose probability can be anywhere between 0 and 100%.

It is easy to see that the pattern of choices described previously cannot be explained by expected utility maximization for any specification of subjective probabilities. Such probabilities would have to reflect the belief that it is more likely that a red ball will be drawn from urn I than from urn II and that it is more likely that a black ball will be drawn from urn I than from urn II. This is impossible because in each urn the probabilities of the two colors have to add up to 1. Thus, Ellsberg's findings suggest that many people are not subjective expected utility maximizers. Moreover, the assumption that comes under attack is not the expected utility hypothesis per se: any rule that employs probabilities in a reasonable way would also be at odds with Ellsberg's results. The questionable assumption here is the basic tenet of Bayesianism, namely, that all uncertainty can be quantified in a probabilistic way. Exhibiting preferences for known versus unknown probabilities is incompatible with this tenet. It violates Machina and Schmeidler's probabilistic sophistication.

To see why P2 is violated in this example, we should embed it in a state space. In principle, we should define the states as functions from acts to outcomes. But we can save ourselves some writing if we agree that it is impossible that both a red bet and a black bet, on the same urn, would win $100. Thus, what a state should specify is only, for each urn, which color would be the ball drawn from that urn. Formally,

$$S = \{R, B\}^{\{I,II\}} = \{s : \{I, II\} \to \{R, B\}\}.$$

If we agree that the first coordinate denotes $s(I)$ and the second, $s(II)$, we can refer to the states as $\{RR, RB, BR, BB\}$.

Let there be four acts, denoted IR, IB, IIR, IIB, where IR means betting on a red ball out of urn I; IIR, on a red ball out of urn II; and so on. We now have the following decision matrix, where 1 denotes $100, and 0, $0:

	RR	RB	BR	BB
IR	1	1	0	0
IB	0	0	1	1
IIR	1	0	1	0
IIB	0	1	0	1

Considering $A = \{RR, BB\}$, we find that

$$IR(s) = IIB(s) \quad IB(s) = IIR(s) \quad \forall s \notin A$$

and

$$IR(s) = IIR(s) \quad IB(s) = IIB(s) \quad \forall s \in A.$$

In words, on A^c, the two acts IR and IIB are equal. This means that if we change them on A^c, but keep them equal to each other, preferences between them should not be reversed. But after we change IR and IIB on A^c to equal $IB = IIR$, IR becomes IIR and IIB becomes IB. P2 would therefore imply that

$$IR \succsim IIB \quad \Leftrightarrow \quad IIR \succsim IB$$

whereas modal preferences are

$$IR \sim IB \succ IIR \sim IIB.$$

Ellsberg's Single-Urn Paradox

The two-urn example has two main advantages. First, I find its intuition very clear. Second, you need to work a bit to define the states of the world for it, and this is a good exercise. By contrast, the single-urn example is more straightforward in terms of the analysis.

This time there are 90 balls in an urn. We know that 30 balls are red and that the other 60 balls are blue or yellow, but we do not have any additional information about their distribution. There is going to be one draw from the urn. Assume first that you have to guess what color the ball will be. Do you prefer to bet on the color being red (with a known probability of $1/3$) or being blue (with a probability that could be anything from 0 to $2/3$)? The modal response here is to prefer betting on red, namely, to prefer the known probability over the unknown one.

Next, with the same urn, assume that you have to bet on the ball *not being* red, that is, being blue or yellow, versus *not being* blue, which means red or yellow. This time your chances are better – you know that the probability of the ball not being red is $2/3$, and the probability of not being blue is anywhere from $1/3$ to 1. Here, for similar reasons, the modal response is to prefer not-red, again, where the probabilities are known. (Moreover, many participants simultaneously prefer red in the first choice situations and not-red in the second.)

Writing down the decision matrix, we obtain

	R	B	Y
red	1	0	0
blue	0	1	0
not-red	0	1	1
not-blue	1	0	1

It is readily seen that *red* and *blue* are equal on Y. If P2 holds, changing their value from 0 to 1 on Y should not change preferences between them. But when we make this change, *red* becomes *not-blue* and *blue* becomes *not-red*. That is, P2 implies

$$red \succsim blue \quad \Leftrightarrow \quad not\text{-}blue \succsim not\text{-}red,$$

which is violated by the observed preferences

$$red \succ blue \qquad not\text{-}red \succ not\text{-}blue.$$

Ellsberg as a Metaphor

Ellsberg's examples are very neat. They show an exact violation of P2, relying on a large degree of symmetry in the problems. But this degree of symmetry may also be misleading. In particular, people are often tempted to come up with the symmetric prior and, cognitive unease aside, decide to make decisions in accordance with this prior.

For example, in the two-urn experiment, it is tempting to assume that the probability of a black draw from the unknown urn is 50%. You can obtain this by applying the principle of indifference to the two sides of the coin. Alternatively, you may think about second-order probabilities, asking what the distribution of the urn is likely to be, and if you have a symmetric prior over the urn distribution, your overall probability for black (and for red) will be 50%. After such calculations, you can convince yourself that even if these were not your original preferences, then these should be your preferences. And the conclusion might be that since you were convinced by Savage that it makes sense to be Bayesian, decision makers who were tricked by Ellsberg, as it were, should repent and adopt the natural prior.

This conclusion would be misleading, because in most questions of interest there is no natural prior. David Schmeidler often says, "Real life is not about balls and urns." Indeed, important decisions involve war and peace, recessions and booms, diseases and cures. In these examples there are no symmetries and no natural priors, and the principle of indifference cannot lead us very far.

It is important to remember that while Ellsberg needed all these symmetries to generate counterexamples to P2, these counterexamples should only be taken as metaphors. The urn with the unknown composition may be thought of as the unknown probability of a stock market crash. And the question raised by Ellsberg's paradox is, is it realistic to suppose that in questions involving stock market crashes, wars, and the like, people will satisfy P2?

12.3.4 Observability of States

If you try to think about this last question seriously, you may find that the answer is that we don't know and that there is probably no way to tell. P2 has a clear meaning when we draw Savage acts on the blackboard, as well as when we draw balls from urns. But let us consider a real problem such as determining what should be the US foreign policy. It may be very difficult to come up with four acts that are actually available to the United States and that are constrained by P2.

One of the problems we will encounter in such a model is that the states of the world are not directly observable. We typically will not know what states of the world the decision maker has in mind. When we have participants in an experiment in which balls are drawn from urns, there is but one reasonable model to describe the uncertainty they face. But when we consider a real-life choice, different people may think of different eventualities, different possible outcomes, and plan for different time horizons. Actual choices may not satisfy P2 when embedded in a given model, and yet they may satisfy it when embedded in a larger model. It is thus not always easy to tell whether people satisfy Savage's axioms and, correspondingly, whether they have a subjective probability.[9]

12.3.5   Problems of Complexity

Finally, I should mention that the notion of a state space is likely to involve problems of daunting complexity. We have been freely defining state spaces as set of functions from here to there, but such definitions involve exponential growth in the number of states. If you consider a contract that refers to n possible binary conditions, writing down the state space that corresponds to the contract involved 2^n states. Similarly, there are 2^n different regression models that may be relevant for the explanation of one variable, if there are n candidates for the predictors.[10] It follows that for many problems that we can think of, actually writing down the state-space model is not a practical undertaking.

Complexity considerations are relevant for descriptive and normative purposes alike. In a descriptive interpretation of the theory, it is unreasonable to assume that people think of very many states, and it is therefore unclear whether they would miraculously exhibit behavior as if they did. In a normative interpretation, the recommendations we make should also be practicable.

---

[9] Dekel *et al.* (2001) derive a subjective state space from preferences over sets of lotteries. This derivation assumes a notion of probabilities used in the lotteries. For the decision problems in question, these probabilities would probably have to be interpreted as subjective. It is interesting that states can be derived from probabilities, as opposed to the Savage's derivation. Yet, this derivation presupposed that subjective probabilities are a meaningful concept.

[10] See Aragones *et al.* (2005).

CHAPTER 13

Objectivity and Rationality

There is no fundamental reason for this chapter to come at this point in the discussion. However, if we haven't discussed these issues yet, it might be a good idea to do it now, after Savage's theorem was discussed, and before we look for alternative approaches.

13.1 SUBJECTIVITY AND OBJECTIVITY

When subjective probability was introduced, and even when it was championed by de Finetti, people tended to believe that certain things have existence that is objective and unrelated to the observer, that is, to us. On this background, de Finetti said, "Probability does not exist," meaning that it is not an objective feature of the world around us, but only a concept that is in our minds, something that we impose on reality around us, trying to make sense of our observations.

Since then many things happened, and reality is not what it used to be. Many people think that objective reality does not exist, that the most we can refer to is intersubjectivity, and so forth.

Personally, because of my inability to understand ontology, I never quite understood what can be "objective" in the classical sense. I was therefore excited to read the definition of objective probabilities in Anscombe and Aumann (1963). They argue that all probabilities are subjective, but if subjective probabilities happen to coincide, we call them objective. That is, "objective" is simply a nickname for a subjective term that happens to be in agreement, not far from the meaning of "intersubjective."

After many years, David Schmeidler convinced me that this is hardly a satisfactory definition. His example was the following: suppose that the two of us are looking at a crater and wondering how deep it is. Each of us provides his subjective assessment, and let's suppose it turns out that both assessments are the same, 20 feet. Next assume that David also has a meter. He pulls it out of his pocket, rolls it down, and shows me that the depth is 20 feet. Again, we agree on the assessments, but this time it feels that there is something more "objective" about it.

The difference is that after having measured the depth I believe that the agreement between our assessments is not coincidental. I have a theory as to why we had to agree on the assessment. Similarly, if a third person would now join us and be asked to assess the depth of the crater, there will be a difference between the two scenarios. In the first case, I may well believe that the coincidental agreement with David will not be shared with the third person. In the second, I am rather confident that I will be able to convince the third person that our view is correct.

In Gilboa and Schmeidler (2001) we used this definition of objectivity, namely, one that is likely to be shared by others. Obviously, some theorizing about the world is needed to judge claims to objectivity. To find out that David and I have the same assessment we only need our assessments. To reason about what a third person would agree to, we need to make some speculation about the kind of person we might encounter, the fact that the measurement of the crater depth will be consistent, and so forth. Moreover, there may be disagreements about these theories. For instance, David may believe that any reasonable person would be convinced by his meter measurement, and I may think that reasonable people might disagree with him. In short, this definition is not making any reference to any reality that exists outside of our minds. But our minds are asked to imagine a few more scenarios involving convincing other people.

13.2 OBJECTIVE AND SUBJECTIVE RATIONALITY

I have warned you earlier that I use the term "rationality" differently than most economic theorists. The standard definitions are purely behavioral, and these equate rationality with a concept such as behaving in compliance with Savage's axioms or some other set of axioms.[1] I prefer a definition of rationality that has to do not only with behavior, but also with cognition, and, specifically, with reasoning about behavior.

Let us perhaps start with defining irrationality. My favorite definition is the following: a mode of behavior is *irrational* for a given decision maker, if, when the decision maker behaves in this mode and is then exposed to the analysis of her behavior, she feels embarrassed.[2] Clearly, this definition is subjective, quantitative, and not purely behavioral. According to this definition, the same mode of behavior can be irrational for one person and not for another. The measurement of irrationality depends on a rather nebulous concept such as embarrassment. Worse still, if we consider two decision makers who behave in the same way but differ in their intelligence, we may find that the less intelligent one is more rational, simply because she fails to see the logic of some axioms. That is, one may not be dubbed "irrational," thanks to failing to see what's

---

[1] See Arrow (1986), and Simon (1957, 1986).

[2] The term "embarrassed" in this context was suggested to me by Amos Tversky. A slightly less provocative version of this definition is used in Gilboa and Schmeidler (2001).

wrong with one's decisions. I tend to view all these features as advantages of the definition.

Why is it a good definition? Let me try to convince you that it is a useful concept for the type of discussions in which we are involved. We recognize that almost all the axioms of choice theory are under empirical and experimental attacks, and we admit that for practically every axiom there will be an experiment refuting it. What do we do then? If we are still interested in the social science enterprise, there are two main lines of progress: we can try to adapt our theories to reality, making them more accurate descriptive theories. Or we can try to preach our theories and teach decision makers to behave in accordance with our theories. That is, we can bring the theory closer to reality or try to bring reality closer to the theory. Which path should we take? I argue that the preceding definition of irrationality is precisely what should guide our choice.

Consider, for example, framing effects (Tversky and Kahneman, 1981). I have tried them in many classes, and I found that, if the students had not been exposed to them before, framing effects work: for many students, choices depend on the representation of the choice problem. In all of these classes I went on to explain the equivalence of two representations of the same problem, and I have yet to meet a student who insists that representation should, indeed, matter. People who make different choices are embarrassed to discover that.[3] By the same token, I argue that the same people are less likely to fall prey to similar framing effects the next time they are exposed to them. Indeed, it has happened to me that I tried to trick students only to discover that they had already heard about framing effects from another teacher. Moreover, it is possible that today many more people hear about framing effects in the popular or semipopular press than 20 years ago. It is not unthinkable that future generations will be much more sophisticated than ours in this respect. I do not wish to argue that framing effects will disappear. But the prevalence of the phenomenon is sensitive to our preaching.

This is not the case, for instance, with Ellsberg's paradox. Many people hold on to their choices even after P2 was explained to them. Indeed, we do not have simple algorithms to generate prior probabilities, and a decision maker who violates P2 need not feel embarrassed about it. Correspondingly, Ellsberg's phenomenon may be less responsive to the teachings of decision theory than are framing effects.[4]

---

[3] I refer here to framing effects that are simple to understand, as in the experiments of Tversky and Kahneman. When the equivalence of two representations requires a proof, such as Savage's theorem, for example, I would not expect anyone to be embarrassed for not having recognized the equivalence a priori.

[4] Observe that complexity considerations also play a role in this definition of irrationality. It is not irrational not to play chess optimally, because one cannot compute an optimal strategy in chess. Correspondingly, one need not be embarrassed if one fails to see a very sophisticated strategy in chess.

It follows that the question of irrationality may be related to the decision problem we are facing as theorists, namely, to preach our theories as normative or to improve their predictions as descriptive. If most people can be convinced by our theories, there is hope to change people's behavior. This may be relevant especially when the choices in question are important ones, when they are done by teams that engage in brainstorming, and so on.[5] If, however, people shrug their shoulders when we explain the logic of our axioms, or admit that these are nice axioms but argue that they are impractical, we should better refine the theories.[6]

What is a *rational* mode of behavior, then? One can simply argue that all that is not irrational is rational. Yet, the discussion of the completeness axiom, as given earlier, suggests that it may be useful to distinguish between the two. An arbitrary choice (of a prior, or of a decision) may not be irrational in the same sense that framing effects are. Yet, it is also not "rational" in the sense that it can be argued, justified, and found convincing by others. Thus, we will use *subjective rationality* to refer to any mode of behavior that is not irrational. The term *objective rationality* will be used for modes of behavior that can be explained to others so that these are convinced by them. A decision is objectively rational if the decision maker can convince others that she is right in making it. It is subjectively rational for her if others cannot convince her that she is wrong in making it.

In the usage suggested here, "irrationality" is not necessarily a disparaging term, and "rationality" need not be a compliment. According to this view, rationality is not a medal of honor bestowed on selected decision makers by the theorist. Rather, "irrational" means "is likely to change his mind" whereas "rational" means "is likely to insist on her behavior." The terms are used to facilitate discussion, while the decision maker remains the ultimate judge of the choices that are rational for her.

---

[5] For example, see Charness *et al.* (2008) on the example of the conjunction fallacy (the celebrated Linda).

[6] Naturally, many modes of behavior will be considered by some people as irrational and not by others. How irrational a mode of behavior is, is an empirical question that will depend on the education, intelligence, personal tastes, and cultural biases of the decision makers.

CHAPTER 14

Anscombe–Aumann's Theorem

The result by Anscombe and Aumann (1963) has already been mentioned twice in earlier chapters, and their setup is used twice next, so it seems like a perfect time to introduce their model and result. As in the case of von Neumann–Morgenstern (vNM), we use the simpler setup introduced by Fishburn (1970a).

The Anscombe–Aumann model has outcomes X and states S as does Savage's. However, acts do not map states directly into outcomes, but into the (mixture) space of vNM lotteries over outcomes. Formally, we remind ourselves that the vNM lotteries are

$$L = \left\{ P : X \to [0,1] \;\middle|\; \begin{array}{c} \#\{x \,|\, P(x) > 0\} < \infty, \\ \sum_{x \in X} P(x) = 1 \end{array} \right\}$$

and it is endowed with a mixing operation: for every $P, Q \in L$ and every $\alpha \in [0,1]$, $\alpha P + (1-\alpha)Q \in L$ is given by

$$(\alpha P + (1-\alpha)Q)(x) = \alpha P(x) + (1-\alpha)Q(x).$$

Now we wish to state that acts are functions from S to L. In general we would need to endow S with a σ-algebra and deal with measurable and bounded acts. Both of these terms have to be defined in terms of preferences, because we don't yet have a utility function. Instead, we will simplify our lives and assume that S is finite. (After all, this is one of the advantages of this model as compared to Savage's – in Savage's model this assumption isn't possible.) We will also retain this assumption in the two theorems that we present later in this setup. However, all three theorems hold for general measurable spaces.

After this apology, we can indeed define the set of acts to be $F = L^S$. We will endow F with a mixture operation as well, performed pointwise. That is, for every $f, g \in F$ and every $\alpha \in [0,1]$, $\alpha f + (1-\alpha)g \in F$ is given by

$$(\alpha f + (1-\alpha)g)(s) = \alpha f(s) + (1-\alpha)g(s) \qquad \forall s \in S.$$

We will denote the decision maker's preference order by $\succsim \subset F \times F$ and we will abuse this notation as usual. In particular, we can write, for $P, Q \in L$,

$P \succsim Q$, understood as $f_P \succsim f_Q$, where, for every $R \in L$, $f_R \in F$ is the constant act given by $f_R(s) = R$ for all $s \in S$.

To make sure that we understand the structure, observe that there are two sources of uncertainty: the choice of the state s, which is sometimes referred to as "subjective uncertainty," because no objective probabilities are given on it, and the choice of x, which is done with objective probabilities once you chose your act and Nature chose a state. Specifically, if you choose $f \in F$ and Nature chooses $s \in S$, a roulette wheel is spun, with distribution $f(s)$ over the outcomes X, so that your probability to get outcome x is $f(s)(x)$.

For a function $u : X \to \mathbb{R}$, we will use the notation

$$E_P u = \sum_{x \in X} P(x)u(x)$$

for $P \in L$.

Thus, if you choose $f \in F$ and Nature chooses $s \in S$, you will get a lottery $f(s)$, which has the expected u-value of

$$E_{f(s)}u = \sum_{x \in X} f(s)(x)u(x).$$

The Anscombe–Aumann axioms are the following. The first three are identical to the vNM axioms. Observe that they now apply to more complicated creatures: rather than to specific vNM lotteries, we now deal with functions whose values are such lotteries or, if you will, with vectors of vNM lotteries, indexed by the state space S. The next two axioms are almost identical to de Finetti's last two axioms, guaranteeing monotonicity and nontriviality:

AA1. **Weak order**: $\succsim$ is complete and transitive.
AA2. **Continuity**: For every $f, g, h \in F$, if $f \succ g \succ h$, there exist $\alpha, \beta \in (0, 1)$ such that

$$\alpha f + (1 - \alpha)h \succ g \succ \beta f + (1 - \beta)h.$$

AA3. **Independence**: For every $f, g, h \in F$, and every $\alpha \in (0, 1)$,

$$f \succsim g \quad \text{iff} \quad \alpha f + (1 - \alpha)h \succsim \alpha g + (1 - \alpha)h.$$

AA4. **Monotonicity**: For every $f, g \in F$, $f(s) \succsim g(s)$ for all $s \in S$ implies $f \succsim g$.
AA5. **Nontriviality**: There exist $f, g \in X$ such that $f \succ g$.

If you feel a little bit like putting together the vNM and de Finetti axioms, this is fine. This is in fact the point: justifying de Finetti's assumption of linearity by replacing payoffs by probabilities of payoffs.

In stating the Anscombe–Aumann theorem, we will still use the language of integration and measures, despite the fact that we assumed S to be finite. This will make the theorem look more impressive, and it will remind us that it also holds for more general spaces.

Theorem 14.1 *(Anscombe–Aumann)* $\succsim$ *satisfies AA1–AA5 if and only if there exist a probability measure μ on S and a nonconstant function $u : X \rightarrow \mathbb{R}$ such that, for every $f, g \in F$*

$$f \succsim g \quad \text{iff} \quad \int_S (E_{f(s)}u)d\mu(s) \geq \int_S (E_{g(s)}u)d\mu(s)$$

Furthermore, in this case, μ is unique and u is unique up to positive linear transformations.

The Anscombe–Aumann representation thus involves double integration: the outer one is over the state space, and relative to the subjective probability measure μ, and the inner one is the vNM expected utility calculation, where the objective probabilities are dictated by the act and the state.

As in Savage's model, the monotonicity axiom says a bit more than monotonicity: it actually implies separation of tastes from beliefs. In Savage's model the ordinal ranking of the outcomes was independent of the state to which they were associated. Here we get the same result, but this time the values of the functions, $f(s)$, are vNM lotteries. Since these lotteries are ranked the same at all states, we can attach to each state a vNM function, but these functions are positive linear transformations of each other. The multiplicative coefficients used to transform one function into another will turn out to be the ratios of the probabilities of the respective states.

The Anscombe–Aumann theorem is relatively easy to prove (see Fishburn, 1970a, pp. 176–178; Kreps, 1988, pp. 99–111), and it was not suggested as a major mathematical achievement. It was supposed to be a much simpler derivation of subjective probability than Savage's, one that can accommodate finite state spaces, and that made explicit the derivation of subjective probabilities from objective ones. As a (probably unintended) by-product, Anscombe and Aumann provided a very convenient setup in which alternative models of decision under uncertainty can be developed.

PART III

ALTERNATIVE BEHAVIORAL THEORIES

We ended the discussion of Savage's theorem by criticizing his axioms on descriptive and normative grounds alike. If the axioms do not always hold, and, furthermore, they might be dubious even as standards of rationality, we can proceed in two directions, which might be combined. One is to cling to the notion of probability, but to abandon the behavioral derivations of Ramsey–de Finetti–Savage and seek an alternative definition of probabilities. The other is to remain loyal to the behavioral approach and ask what alternative notions of belief can describe the way that people make decisions or the way that they can be convinced to make decisions when they attempt to be rational. And a combination of the two would allow for both different notions of beliefs (not only probabilities) and different types of definitions (not necessarily behavioral).

In the following chapters you will see all three. We begin by the second route, which adheres to the behavioral definition but allows different notions of beliefs, namely, nonadditive probabilities (including a digression to study prospect theory under risk) and multiple priors. We will then drop the behavioral approach and adopt a cognitive one. (This will mark the beginning of Part IV.) Within the cognitive direction we will consider models that use probabilities but also others that have less structured notions of beliefs.

CHAPTER 15

Choquet Expected Utility

15.1 SCHMEIDLER'S INTUITION

If you recall the discussion of Schmeidler's two-coin example and Ellsberg's paradox (Section 12.3.3), we find that P2 is too strong. What could be an alternative?

Schmeidler's starting point was that should probability reflect the decision maker's willingness to bet, this probability cannot be additive. To distinguish it from standard probabilities, let us denote the nonadditive one by v.[1] Then, for the unknown coin, we may find that

$$v(H) = v(T) = .4,$$

while

$$v(H \cup T) = 1.$$

That is, a nonadditive measure need not satisfy $v(A \cup B) = v(A) + v(B)$ whenever A and B are disjoint. So we are led to consider real-valued set functions, that is, functions from subsets[2] of S to the real line, or, to remind ourselves of probabilities, into $[0, 1]$.

It will still be natural to require the following properties:

    i. $v(\varnothing) = 0$;
    ii. $A \subset B$ implies $v(A) \leq v(B)$;
    iii. $v(S) = 1$.

A set function v that satisfies the preceding conditions will be called a *nonadditive probability* or a *capacity*.[3]

---

[1] A nonadditive set function is also what is known as a transferable utility game, where $v(A)$ is the value of a coalition A, or what the coalition can guarantee itself.

[2] If S is finite, we will consider all subsets. If it is infinite, one has to endow it with a σ-algebra of events.

[3] Choquet (1953–1954) defined the concept of a capacity, sometimes also called a *charge*, with applications to physics in mind. His definition involved additional continuity requirements, which are vacuously satisfied when S is finite.

Having the concept of a nonadditive probability, one can now explain such phenomena as the preference for betting on a coin with known probabilities or Ellsberg's experiments. In both of these there are but two possible outcomes. This means that the preference order is no more than a ranking of events, which may fail to satisfy de Finetti's cancellation axiom, but satisfies monotonicity. It should not be hard to represent such a preference relation by a real-valued function, and even a monotone one. Such a function will not be unique. In fact, it will only be ordinal. This may be a bit of a problem from a theoretical point of view, if we are after a definition of some notion of belief. Yet, a numerical representation of preferences will exist.

But what do we do with acts that have more than two possible outcomes? How do we represent preferences between them? We would like to have a notion of integration that works for nonadditive probabilities.

The natural way to define an integral is to follow Riemann's definition. Assume that f is a real-valued function, taking the value x_i on the event E_i, where $\{E_1, \ldots, E_m\}$ is a partition of S.[4] That is, $f = \sum_i x_i 1_{E_i}$, where 1_A is the indicator function of $A \subset S$. We will also write $f = (x_1, E_1; \ldots; x_m, E_m)$. Then, given a nonadditive measure v, it makes sense to define

$$R(f, v) = \sum_i x_i v(E_i),$$

that is, to sum the "areas" of the rectangles, each constructed on E_i with height x_i.

Such an intuitive definition turns out to suffer from three related difficulties:

1. **Ambiguity:** The integral will depend on the way we write the function f. Specifically, consider disjoint A and B and observe that

   $$(1, A; 1, B; 0, (A \cup B)^c) = (1, (A \cup B); 0, (A \cup B)^c),$$

   but in general it will not be the case that $v(A \cup B) = v(A) + v(B)$. This means that when we get a representation of a function $f = (x_1, E_1; \ldots; x_m, E_m)$, we have to ask ourselves whether some of the x_i's appear more than once and then decide how to treat them. The most reasonable definition is to take the maximal event over which f equals a certain x_i, and use these. (In a finite state space you can also think of the minimal events, but the maximal events idea makes just as much sense in general.)

2. **Discontinuity:** Consider now $f_\varepsilon = (1 + \varepsilon, A; 1, B; 0, (A \cup B)^c)$. As $\varepsilon \to 0$, f_ε converges (in any reasonable topology) to $f_0 = (1, (A \cup B); 0, (A \cup B)^c)$, but

   $$R(f_\varepsilon, v) = (1 + \varepsilon)v(A) + v(B) \to v(A) + v(B)$$

---

[4] Later on we will consider acts that do not assume real numbers as values. But we will have a utility function to do the translation for us. For the time being let's understand how we can integrate a real-valued function.

and, in general,

$$R(f_0, v) = v(A \cup B) \neq v(A) + v(B);$$

that is, the integral $R(f, v)$ is not continuous in the integrand.

3. **Violation of monotonicity:** With the preceding notation, assume that $v(A \cup B) > v(A) + v(B)$. Then, for a small enough ε, $R(f_\varepsilon, v) < R(f_0, v)$, even though f_ε dominates f_0 pointwise. Similarly, if $v(A \cup B) < v(A) + v(B)$, a violation of monotonicity will result when we consider $\varepsilon < 0$.

These are too many flaws. Something else needs to be found.

15.2   CHOQUET INTEGRAL

The idea of Choquet integration is to look at the rectangles sideways.[5] Suppose that we have a function $f \geq 0$. Say, $f_\varepsilon = (1 + \varepsilon, A; 1, B; 0, (A \cup B)^c)$ with $\varepsilon > 0$. Imagine that you are pouring water, trying to fill the area under the curve of f. You start out, and until the water gets to height 1, you have to cover all of $A \cup B$. Let us stop when you got to this height. So far you filled a rectangle whose height is 1 and whose basis is the event $A \cup B$. This will take you

$$1 \cdot v(A \cup B)$$

gallons of water. At this point the water reaches the graph of f_ε over the event B, but not over A. Continue to pour to reach the graph of f_ε also under A. You will need to cover another rectangle whose height is ε and whose basis is the event A. This will require additional

$$\varepsilon \cdot v(A)$$

gallons. Altogether, the integral of f_ε according to v will be

$$1 \cdot v(A \cup B) + \varepsilon \cdot v(A).$$

This water-pouring story will also be the general definition. Before we define it formally, observe that this definition (at least in this simple case) solves all the problems of the Riemann-style definition. First, there is no problem of ambiguity: as you pour water in, you don't really care how f is represented algebraically; only the graph of f matters. Second, if ε is very small, positive or negative, the amount of water that you pour under the graph of f_ε converges to that you pour under the graph of f_0. Finally, as long as v is monotone with respect to set inclusion (as we required), you will find that the integral is monotone with respect to pointwise domination.

For the general definition, let us start with a nonnegative f. Since S is finite, we know that f takes finitely many values. Let us order them from the largest to the smallest: that is, $f = (x_1, E_1; \ldots; x_m, E_m)$ with $x_1 \geq x_2 \geq \cdots \geq x_m \geq 0$.

---

[5] The original definition is in Choquet (1953–1954).

If you follow the water-pouring procedure, you will first get to cover $\cup_{i=1}^{m} E_i$ up to height x_m. Then E_m will drop out and you will have to cover only $\cup_{i=1}^{m-1} E_i$ to an additional height of $(x_{m-1} - x_m)$, and so on. We will therefore define the *Choquet integral* of f according to v to be

$$\int_S f \, dv = \sum_{j=1}^{m} (x_j - x_{j+1}) v \left(\cup_{i=1}^{j} E_i \right) \tag{15.1}$$

with the convention $x_{m+1} = 0$. If v is additive, this integral is equivalent to the Riemann integral (and to $\sum_{j=1}^{m} x_j v(E_j)$). You can also verify that (15.1) is equivalent to the following definition, which applies to any bounded nonnegative f (even if S were infinite, as long as f were measurable with respect to the algebra on which v is defined):

$$\int_S f \, dv = \int_0^\infty v(f \geq t) dt,$$

where the integral on the right is a standard Riemann integral. (Observe that it is well defined, because $v(f \geq t)$ is a nonincreasing function of t.)

And if you wonder how the integral is defined for functions that may be negative, the answer is simple: we want it to have the nice property that for every function f and constant c,

$$\int_S (f + c) dv = \int_S f \, dv + c,$$

a property that holds for nonnegative f and c. So we make sure the property holds: given a bounded f, take a $c > 0$ such that $g = f + c \geq 0$, and define $\int_S f \, dv = \int_S g \, dv - c$.

15.3 COMONOTONICITY

The Choquet integral has many nice properties – it respects "shifts," namely, the addition of a constant, as well as multiplication by a positive constant. It is also continuous and monotone in the integrand. But it is not additive in general. Indeed, if we had

$$\int_S (f + g) dv = \int_S f \, dv + \int_S g \, dv$$

for every f and g, we could take $f = 1_A$ and $g = 1_B$ for disjoint A and B, and show that $v(A \cup B) = v(A) + v(B)$.

However, there are going to be pairs of functions f and g for which the Choquet integral is additive. To see this, observe that (15.1) can also be rewritten as

$$\int_S f \, dv = \sum_{j=1}^{m} x_j \left[v \left(\cup_{i=1}^{j} E_i \right) - v \left(\cup_{i=1}^{j-1} E_i \right) \right].$$

Assume, without loss of generality, that E_i is a singleton. (This is possible because we required only a weak inequality $x_j \geq x_{j+1}$.) That is, there is some permutation of the states, $\pi : S \to S$, defined by the order of the x_i's, such that $\cup_{i=1}^{j} E_i$ consists of the first j states in this permutation. Given this π, define a probability vector p_π on S by $p_\pi(\cup_{i=1}^{j} E_i) = v(\cup_{i=1}^{j} E_i)$. It is therefore true that

$$\int_S f \, dv = \int_S f \, dp_\pi;$$

that is, the Choquet integral of f equals the integral of f relative to some additive probability p_π. Note, however, that p_π depends on f. Since different f's have, in general, different permutations π that rank the states from high f values to low f values, the Choquet integral is not additive in general.

Assume now that the two functions, f and g, happen to have the same permutation π. They will have the same p_π and then

$$\int_S f \, dv = \int_S f \, dp_\pi \quad \text{and} \quad \int_S g \, dv = \int_S g \, dp_\pi.$$

Moreover, in this case, $f + g$ will also be decreasing relative to the permutation π, and

$$\int_S (f+g) dv = \int_S (f+g) dp_\pi,$$

and it follows that $\int_S (f+g) dv = \int_S f \, dv + \int_S g \, dv$.

In other words, if f and g are two functions such that there exists a permutation of the states π, according to which both f and g are nonincreasing, we will have additivity of the integral for f and g. When will f and g have such a permutation? It is not hard to see that a necessary and sufficient condition is the following:

f and g are *comonotonic* if there are no $s, t \in S$ such that $f(s) > f(t)$ and $g(s) < g(t)$.

15.4 AXIOMS AND RESULT

Schmeidler (1989) uses the Anscombe–Aumann setup. This requires a new definition of comonotonicity, because now the acts assume values in L, rather than in $\mathbb{R}$. For two acts $f, g \in F$, we say that f and g are *comonotonic* if there are no $s, t \in S$ such that $f(s) \succ f(t)$ and $g(s) \prec g(t)$.

To understand the notion of comonotonicity between acts and its role in the presence of uncertainty, one may go back to Ellsberg's examples. Why do decision makers violate P2 in these examples? One explanation is that the changes in the values of the functions, over the event A^c, where the two functions are equal, affect their degree of uncertainty in an asymmetric way. In the single-urn example, for instance, *red*, which has a known probability, becomes *not-blue*, with an unknown probability, and vice versa for *blue*.

This type of asymmetric effect on uncertainty can also occur when you mix acts that are not comonotonic. Consider a simple case, with $S = \{s, t\}$, and denote functions simply by vectors with two components. Assume also that we have already translated von-Neumann–Morgenstern (vNM) lotteries to real numbers. Suppose that f is $(0,100)$ and g is $(100,0)$. Further, assume complete symmetry between the states, so that $f \sim g$. Now consider mixing both f and g with $h = g$. Mixing g with h will leave us with g, of course. But g can offer some hedging against f. If you consider $(1/2)f + (1/2)g$, you will get an act whose expected value is $(50, 50)$. That is, when you mix two acts that are not comonotonic, you can have hedging effects. If h hedges better against f than it does against g, you can find that the independence axiom fails.

It follows that it would make sense to weaken the independence axiom and require that it hold only in those cases where no hedging is possible. Indeed, Schmeidler defined

Comonotonic independence: For every pairwise comonotonic $f, g, h \in F$, and every $\alpha \in (0, 1)$,

$$f \succsim g \quad \text{iff} \quad \alpha f + (1 - \alpha)h \succsim \alpha g + (1 - \alpha)h.$$

That is, the sole modification needed in the Anscombe–Aumann model is that now independence is required to hold only when the acts involved are comonotonic. And the only modification in the theorem is that the probability may be nonadditive.

Theorem 15.1 *(Schmeidler)* $\succsim$ *satisfies AA1, AA2, comonotonic independence, AA4, and AA5 if and only if there exist a nonadditive probability measure v on S and a nonconstant function $u : X \to \mathbb{R}$ such that, for every $f, g \in F$,*

$$f \succsim g \quad \text{iff} \quad \int_S (E_{f(s)}u)dv \geq \int_S (E_{g(s)}u)dv$$

(where the integrals are in the sense of Choquet). Furthermore, in this case, v is unique and u is unique up to positive linear transformations.

The proof is given in Schmeidler (1989, pp. 579–581, relying on Schmeidler, 1986). To understand how it works, observe that restricting attention to acts that are constant over S, we basically have vNM lotteries, and they satisfy the vNM axioms. (Importantly, a constant act is comonotonic with any other act, and in particular, all constant acts are pairwise comonotonic.) Thus we can find a utility function that represents preferences over lotteries, and we can plug it in. This simplifies the problem to one dealing with real-valued functions. Furthermore, if S is indeed finite, we have real-valued vectors.

Now consider all vectors that are nondecreasing relative to a given permutation of the states, π. They generate a convex cone, and they are all pairwise comonotonic, so that the independence axiom holds for any three of them. Moreover, these vectors generate a mixture space – when we mix two of them, we are still inside the set. Applying a generalization of the vNM theorem such as Herstein and Milnor (1953), one gets an equivalent of the Anscombe–Aumann representation, restricted to the cone of π-non-decreasing vectors. For this cone, we therefore obtain a representation by a probability vector p_π. One then proceeds to show that all these probability vectors can be described by a single nonadditive measure v.

CHAPTER 16

Prospect Theory

16.1 BACKGROUND

When I was teaching this course 20 years ago and, in fact, even 10 years ago, I could find many students in class who had never heard of Kahneman and Tversky. I would then spend some time on their various findings and on prospect theory (PT). These dark ages are over. Today everyone knows about their project and about behavioral economics, and there is no need to argue with the extreme assumptions of rationality that were religiously held by economists throughout most of the 1970s and the 1980s. In fact, I sometimes marvel at how fast the pendulum swings. While behavioral economics often comes under attack, it is nowadays considered acceptable to introduce highly irrational modes of behavior into economic models. From assuming that economic agents are just as rational as the modeler, know all mathematical theorems, and know even unknowable things such as a prior probability over an overarching state space, the field suddenly started accepting agents who are systematically overoptimistic, ignore information at will, and violate dynamic consistency on a daily basis.

Behavioral economics is beyond the scope of this course, which focuses on the definition of probability from a rational point of view. Most of Kahneman and Tversky's contributions are too far in the realm of biases and mistakes as to be considered rational or normative. Moreover, from the remarkable body of work that they did, relatively little is devoted to the very definition of probability. Because of that, and due to the popularity of their work, I could imagine skipping it here. However, there is a striking similarity between the evolution of prospect theory into cumulative prospect theory (Tversky and Kahneman, 1992; Wakker, 2008) on the one hand and Choquet integration on the other, and this calls for a short discussion, if only for the historical anecdote.

16.2 GAIN–LOSS ASYMMETRY

The most important idea in PT is, I believe, the notion of gain–loss asymmetry.[1] The idea that people react to changes and not to absolute levels is intuitive,

---

[1] Daniel Kahneman expressed the same opinion in a personal conversation. The idea also appeared in Markowitz (1952), and is in line with adaptation level theory of Helson (1964).

powerful, and empirically convincing. Incidentally, it does not involve too much irrationality. People can be embarrassed in some examples of the phenomena, but not in all.

Consider the following example. There are two choice situations:

Problem 1:
You are given $1,000 for sure. Which of the following two options would you prefer?

(a) To get additional $500 for sure
(b) To get another $1,000 with probability 50%, and otherwise nothing more (and be left with the first $1,000)

Problem 2:
You are given $2,000 for sure. Which of the following two options would you prefer?

(a) To lose $500 for sure
(b) To lose $1,000 with probability 50%, and otherwise to lose nothing

Many people choose (a) in Problem 1 and (b) in Problem 2. This can be an example of the gain–loss asymmetry: when people are faced with the prospect of gaining something they do not have, they make decisions in a certain way, often in accordance with the assumption of risk aversion. But when people are faced with the prospect of losing something that they already have, they behave quite differently. Kahneman and Tversky argued that loss aversion, namely, our extreme dislike of losing what we have, can make us behave in a risk-loving way in the domain of losses.

This example is striking because it can also be thought of as a framing effect. After all, you are asked to make the choice a priori, before you received $1,000 or $2,000. Writing down options (a) and (b) before the game begins shows that these are the same options in Problem 1 and Problem 2; they are only represented differently, as gains relative to $1,000 or as losses relative to $2,000.

Indeed, people are embarrassed to find that they make different choices in these two problems. But this is embarrassing mostly because the game has not yet been played, no money has been given, and there is no real reason to think of the two options in Problem 2 as losses. By contrast, when real-life choices are concerned, and we have enough time to allow people to adapt to, say, a certain income level, gain–loss asymmetry cannot be described as a mere framing effect. And it is not necessarily irrational to exhibit such behavior.

Similarly, the endowment effect, namely, the tendency to value a good more because it is ours (Kahneman *et al.*, 1991), is not necessarily irrational. When applied to financial assets, most people would be embarrassed to find that they find it hard to part from an asset just because they have it (the "disposition effect," see Odean, 1998; Shefrin and Statman, 1985). But, when applied to other goods, ranging from family heirloom to one's house, the endowment effect appears very reasonable.

I therefore believe that gain–loss asymmetry is not only a powerful phenomenon, but also one that will probably be quite stubborn and hard to uproot. Even if decision theory gets into high school curricula and we are allowed to preach our theories to the minds of the young, I doubt that this phenomenon will disappear.

16.3 DISTORTION OF PROBABILITIES

The other important idea in PT was the notion that probabilities are "distorted" in the decision-making process, that is, that people react to a probability p as if it actually were $f(p)$ for some function $f : [0, 1] \to [0, 1]$. This idea dates back to Preston and Baratta (1948) and Mosteller and Nogee (1951). Applying this idea to the evaluation of a lottery $(x_1, p_1; \ldots; x_n, p_n)$, we are led to replace the expected utility formula

$$\sum_i p_i u(x_i)$$

by a "probability transformation" model

$$\sum_i f(p_i)u(x_i), \tag{16.1}$$

where $f : [0, 1] \to [0, 1]$ is nondecreasing with $f(0) = 0$ and $f(1) = 1$ (see also Edwards, 1954).

Kahneman and Tversky (1979) dealt with "prospects," which are the same mathematical entities as are "lotteries," only interpreted differently: a monetary outcome x_i in a prospect is considered to be the *change* from current wealth level, rather than overall (or net) wealth. PT dealt with prospects with only two nonzero outcomes. Because the generalization to many outcomes has not been spelled out in the original paper, many took PT to mean formula (16.1) applied to positive x_i's and to negative x_i's separately.[2] This interpretation is actually incorrect, as was pointed out by Peter Wakker: PT for the case of two positive or two negative outcomes was actually following the rank-dependent formula, which we discuss in the next section. Thus, formula (16.1) can be thought of as a "separate-outcome probability transformation model" or a variant of PT.[3]

The typical finding, when assuming this model and fitting data, is that f is above the 45° line for small values of p and below it for values of p closer to 1. That is, small probabilities tend to be overestimated, while large ones,

---

[2] With a "value" function v replacing the utility function u.
[3] I wish to thank Peter Wakker for pointing out this to me.

underestimated. This can explain various phenomena such as Allais's paradox (Allais, 1953) or the certainty effect (Kahneman and Tversky, 1979).[4]

However, formula (16.1) raises several difficulties. We have to assume that f is not additive. (Function f is additive if it satisfies

$$f(p + q) = f(p) + f(q)$$

whenever $p + q \leq 1$.) For if it were, you could first prove that $f(1/n) = 1/n$ for every $n \geq 1$ and then that $f(k/n) = k/n$ for every $n \geq k \geq 1$, and finally, by monotonicity, that is, $f(p) = p$ for all $p \in [0, 1]$, in which case (16.1) would boil down to von-Neumann–Morgenstern (vNM) expected utility (as long as gains are considered).

Consider, then, two probabilities p, q such that $f(p + q) \neq f(p) + f(q)$, say,

$$f(p + q) > f(p) + f(q).$$

Imagine that the decision maker is offered two equivalent representations of the same prospect:

$$(\$10, p; \$10, q; \$0, (1 - p - q))$$

and

$$(\$10, p + q; \$0, (1 - p - q)).$$

Assuming $u(\$0) = 0$, the first will be evaluated by $[f(p) + f(q)]u(\$10)$, while the second, by $f(p + q)u(\$10)$. These are not equal. Hence, we have to decide which representation of the prospect applies. It makes sense to take the latter representation, uniquely defined by using the minimal number of components (x_i, p_i) in the representation of the prospect. Kahneman and Tversky assumed, indeed, that an editing phase precedes the choice (as are some other phases, including cancellation of identical components).

Next assume that we compare this prospect with

$$(\$10 + \varepsilon, p; \$10, q; \$0, (1 - p - q)).$$

This one is a distinct prospect, and editing would not make it identical to the previous one. Thus, we have to evaluate it by

$$f(p)u(\$10 + \varepsilon) + f(q)u(\$10).$$

As $\varepsilon \to 0$, we would expect $u(\$10 + \varepsilon) \to u(\$10)$. In fact, since u is assumed to be nondecreasing, it can only have countably many points of discontinuity. If $\$10$ happens to be one of them, we can take another monetary outcome that

---

[4] A famous example of the certainty effect is the following: people often prefer \$3,000 with certainty to \$4,000 with probability .8, but they prefer \$4,000 with probability .2 to \$3,000 with probability .25, in violation of the vNM independence axiom. See Rubinstein (1988) for an alternative explanation of the certainty effect.

isn't. Let's therefore, assume, with no loss of generality, that u is continuous at \$10. As $\varepsilon \to 0$, we get

$$f(p)u(\$10 + \varepsilon) + f(q)u(\$10) \to [f(p) + f(q)]u(\$10)$$
$$< f(p+q)u(\$10),$$

which is a violation of both continuity and monotonicity. And if we have $f(p+q) < f(p) + f(q)$, the same would hold for $\varepsilon < 0$.

No, you didn't flip back a few pages without noticing, and this is not a déjà vu. Well, literally it is: you have seen precisely these arguments when we explained why one cannot use the standard Riemann definition of an integral with nonadditive probabilities.[5]

16.4   RANK-DEPENDENT PROBABILITIES AND CHOQUET INTEGRATION

The solution to the difficulties of PT in aggregating distorted probabilities was suggested by several authors, including Quiggin (1982) and Yaari (1987).[6] The basic idea was that rather than distorting the probability of a particular outcome, that is, of the event $X = a$, one should apply the function f to decumulative events, that is, events of the form $X \geq a$.

To be more precise, assume that we are given a lottery $(x_1, p_1; \ldots; x_n, p_n)$ with $x_1 \geq \cdots \geq x_n \geq 0$.[7] Let us start with standard expected utility, which can be written as

$$U((x_1, p_1; \ldots; x_n, p_n)) = \sum_{i=1}^{n} p_i u(x_i)$$

$$= \sum_{i=1}^{n} \left(\sum_{j=1}^{i} p_j \right) [u(x_i) - u(x_{i+1})]$$

with the convention $x_{n+1} = 0$.

Let $f : [0, 1] \to [0, 1]$ be non-decreasing with $f(0) = 0$ and $f(1) = 1$, and consider

$$V((x_1, p_1; \ldots; x_n, p_n)) = \sum_{i=1}^{n} f\left(\sum_{j=1}^{i} p_j \right) [u(x_i) - u(x_{i+1})]$$

---

[5] Kahneman and Tversky were aware of most of these difficulties, and some of them were dealt with by the assumptions about the preprocessing that people perform on prospects. Fishburn (1982) noted that PT does not respect first-order stochastic dominance, namely, the monotonicity referred to earlier.

[6] The same mathematical structure was axiomatized also in Weymark (1981) in the context of social choice theory.

[7] Quiggin and Yaari did not emphasize gain–loss asymmetry. It is therefore more natural to think of the objects of choice in their models as lotteries (over final wealth) rather as prospects (of gains or losses).

and observe that V can also be written as

$$V((x_1, p_1; \ldots; x_n, p_n)) = \sum_{t=1}^{n} \left[f\left(\sum_{j=1}^{i} p_j\right) - f\left(\sum_{j=1}^{i-1} p_j\right) \right] u(x_i).$$

Defining a probability vector by

$$q_i = f\left(\sum_{j=1}^{i} p_j\right) - f\left(\sum_{j=1}^{i-1} p_j\right)$$

we observe that V looks like expected utility formula for a certain probability vector that is derived from p and f. However, it also depends on the x-values, because different lotteries would give rise to a different ordering of the p_i's. In other words, q depends on x only via the ranking of the x_i's. This is why these models are called *rank-dependent expected utility*, or *rank-dependent utility* for short.

Clearly, the rank-dependent models are very similar to Choquet integration. To be precise, if you let μ denote the underlying measure, relative to which the objective probabilities p_i are given, and if you then define $v = f(\mu)$, the Choquet expected utility relative to v coincides with the rank-dependent model defined by f.[8]

However, it is important to note that rank-dependent models are, in a sense, a very special case of Choquet expected utility: a case in which there is an underlying probability measure that contains sufficient information to define v. This is not the case in Ellsberg's examples, for instance. In these examples there is no underlying measure that can summarize all we need to know about events. More generally, Choquet expected utility allows us to say something about situations in which we do not have enough information to define probability, whereas the rank-dependent models do not.

---

[8] The rank-dependent models in the context of risk were developed independently of Schmeidler's Choquet expected utility. In 1984 I was present at a seminar in which Yaari pointed out the relationship. I believe he was the first to note this fact.

CHAPTER 17

Maxmin Expected Utility

17.1 CONVEX GAMES

Schmeidler (1986, 1989) defined a notion of uncertainty aversion, given a nonadditive probability v, by[1]

$$v(A) + v(B) \leq v(A \cup B) + v(A \cap B).$$

This condition is known in transferable utility (TU) cooperative game theory as "convexity" of v. A TU game may be identified with a nonadditive probability as defined earlier, where $v(A)$ is interpreted as the "value" of a coalition A, namely, the payoff that A can guarantee itself without the cooperation of the other players.

The notion of convexity has an interpretation of increasing marginal contribution. You can verify that convexity of v is equivalent to the following condition: for every three coalitions W, R, T with $R \subset T$ and $W \cap T = \varnothing$,

$$v(T \cup W) - v(T) \geq v(R \cup W) - v(R),$$

namely, the marginal contribution of the coalition W can increase only if W joins a larger coalition (in the sense of set inclusion). Convexity of v is also known as 2-monotonicity, supermodularity, and complementarity.

Convexity of TU games was defined by Shapley (1965), who showed that they have a nonempty core. The *core* of game v is defined as all the ways that total value (normalized to $v(S) = 1$) can be split among the players, so that no subcoalition has an incentive to deviate. Formally,

$$Core(v) = \left\{ p \left| \begin{array}{c} p \text{ is a probability measure} \\ p(A) \geq v(A) \qquad \forall A \subset S \\ p(S) = v(S) \end{array} \right. \right\}.$$

[1] There has since been many contributions to the study of uncertainty aversion, and this definition is not considered satisfactory by most authors.

Schmeidler (1986) has shown that the following is true: a game v is convex if and only if

(i) $Core(v) \neq \varnothing$, and
(ii) for every $\varphi : S \to \mathbb{R}$,

$$\int_S \varphi \, dv = \min_{p \in Core(v)} \int_S \varphi \, dp.$$

Similar results appear in Rosenmueller (1971, 1972).

17.2   A COGNITIVE INTERPRETATION OF CEU

The preceding result suggests the following cognitive interpretation of Choquet integration with respect to a convex v: Consider $Core(v)$, which is a set of probability measures. Assume that the decision maker does not know what the probability measure that actually governs the process she observes is, but she believes it is one of the probabilities in the set $Core(v)$. She has to evaluate an act f. If she wants to be cautious, she may compute the expected utility (EU) of f with respect to each possible measure $p \in Core(v)$ and take the minimal one. This level of EU is what the act f guarantees her. If she now wishes to maximize this minimal level, she might as well maximize the Choquet expected utility (CEU) of f relative to the nonadditive measure v.

This interpretation has the advantage that we can imagine the reasoning process involved in the decision. Choquet integration is not a very familiar concept, and it doesn't remind us of any process that we can recognize by introspection. By contrast, thinking of a set of measures and looking at the worst case is something that we can think of as a model of human reasoning, albeit a highly idealized one. Moreover, a nonadditive probability is a notion with which most people are not familiar. Typically, the information that the decision maker has will not be presented in the form of a nonadditive probability. By contrast, a set of probabilities is a much more natural way to describe the partial information we may have about a problem. In fact, this is the standard way to describe information in classical statistics: by a set of distributions.

If we continue this line of reasoning, we are led to ask, is the set of probabilities that we consider as possible necessarily the core of a game? What happens if my information says that the true probability is in some closed subset C, and I still want to use the maxmin approach?[2,3]

---

[2] C is assumed closed to make the minimum well defined. Alternatively, you can think of infimum EU. However, it is hard to think of realistic examples in which a set of measures is considered possible, but an accumulation point thereof isn't.

[3] The maxmin expected utility approach was also suggested by Levi (1980).

It is easy to see that if I intend to find an f with the maximal value of

$$J(f) = J_{u,C}(f) = \min_{p \in C} \int_S u(f) dp \tag{17.1}$$

I might as well assume that C is convex. That is, considering any set C and its convex hull $conv(C)$ would yield the same J value for every f. Still, not every closed and convex set of probabilities is a core of a game. Consider, for instance, $S = \{1, 2, 3\}$, so that probability measures are points in the two-dimensional simplex. A game is characterized by six numbers (since there are $2^3 = 8$ subsets of S, and two values are fixed: $v(\varnothing) = 0$ and $v(S) = 1$). By contrast, if you are allowed to choose any closed and convex subset of probabilities, you have infinitely many degrees of freedom.

To see some examples of sets of probabilities that are not cores of games, consider, for instance,

$$C_1 = \{p = (p_1, p_2, p_3) \in \Delta^2 \,|\, 2p_1 \geq p_2\}.$$

C_1 is defined by a simple linear inequality, but this inequality compares the probabilities of two events, and it cannot be written by constraints of the form $p(A) \geq \alpha$. Such inequalities may arise if we do not know probabilities of events, but we know conditional probabilities. For example, if we know that $p(\{1\}|\{1, 2\}) \geq 1/3$, we would get $2p_1 \geq p_2$.

Alternatively, we might have a guess that the true probability is, say, $(.5, .5, 0)$, but feel that we should have a "confidence set" around it, for instance,

$$C_2 = \{p = (p_1, p_2, p_3) \in \Delta^2 \,|\, \|p - (.5, .5, 0)\| < .2\}$$

or we may feel that the probability cannot be too far from two possible guesses:

$$C_3 = \left\{ p = (p_1, p_2, p_3) \in \Delta^2 \,\middle|\, \begin{array}{l} \|p - (.5, .5, 0)\|^2 + \\ \|p - (0, .5, .5)\|^2 < .1 \end{array} \right\}.$$

Clearly, neither C_2 nor C_3 can be described by finitely many inequalities, and, in particular, they are not the cores of convex games.

There is therefore an interest in a model of maxmin expected utility (MMEU), that is, maximization of $J(f)$ as in (17.1). However, before we axiomatize such a model, let us stress that it does not generalize the CEU model. If you consider the latter model with a nonadditive measure v that is not convex, the Choquet integral does not equal $J(f)$ for any subset of measures C. It may also be the case that v has an empty core, in which case we don't have any candidates to be in the set C. Conceptually, CEU does not presuppose any notion of uncertainty aversion. We considered convex v's, but we can similarly define concave ones (with the reverse inequality) and reflect uncertainty liking just as much as we do uncertainty aversion. This is not the case in the MMEU model, where uncertainty aversion (understood as focusing on the minimal EU value) is built into the decision rule.

17.3 AXIOMS AND RESULT

Anscombe–Aumann's (AA) independence condition can be further weakened as follows:

C-independence: For every $f, g \in F$, every constant $h \in F$, and every $\alpha \in (0, 1)$,

$$f \succsim g \quad \text{iff} \quad \alpha f + (1 - \alpha)h \succsim \alpha g + (1 - \alpha)h.$$

On the other hand, an additional condition is needed:

Uncertainty aversion: For every $f, g \in F$, if $f \sim g$, then for every $\alpha \in (0, 1)$,[4]

$$\alpha f + (1 - \alpha)g \succsim f.$$

Thus, uncertainty aversion requires that the decision maker have a preference for mixing. Two equivalent acts can improve simply by mixing or "hedging" between them. Observe that uncertainty aversion is also a weakened version of the AA independence axiom (which would have required $\alpha f + (1 - \alpha)g \sim f$ whenever $f \sim g$).

Theorem 17.1 *(Gilboa and Schmeidler, 1989)* $\succsim$ *satisfies AA1, AA2, C-independence, AA4, AA5, and uncertainty aversion if and only if there exist a closed and convex set of probabilities on S, $C \subset \Delta(S)$, and a nonconstant function $u : X \to \mathbb{R}$ such that for every $f, g \in F$,*

$$f \succsim g \quad \text{iff} \quad \min_{p \in C} \int_S (E_{f(s)}u)dp \geq \min_{p \in C} \int_S (E_{g(s)}u)dp.$$

Furthermore, in this case, C is unique and u is unique up to positive linear transformations.

The uniqueness of C is relative to the conditions stated. Explicitly, if there is another set C' and a utility function u' that satisfy the preceding representation, $C' = C$ and u' is a positive linear transformation of u.

The proof is to be found in Gilboa and Schmeidler (1989, pp. 145–149).

17.4 INTERPRETATION OF MMEU

In the informal description building up to the theorem, I emphasized the intuitive idea that the set C captures our information and that the functional J reflects uncertainty aversion. But this is not the only interpretation possible. Indeed, Theorem 17.1 is in the behavioral tradition of Savage and Anscombe–Aumann. It can be interpreted as a mathematical account that is completely divorced from, or at least silent on, the mental processes in which the decision maker engages. We can interpret the theorem as a story about a black box, getting pairs of acts as

---

[4] It suffices to require this condition for $\alpha = 1/2$.

inputs and providing choices as outputs, where the mathematical representation is simply an analytical tool describing the black box.

Such an interpretation is particularly tempting when people wonder why is uncertainty aversion so extreme in the MMEU model. When asked, "But why are your decision makers choosing the minimal EU of all those possible? Why are they so pessimistic?" it is tempting to reply, "I never said that the set C is what they really know. It is what comes out of the axioms. If you accept the axioms, you agree that people behave *as if* they had such a set C etc."[5]

While this is true, I try not to resort to this answer, because MMEU enjoys the appeal of the simplicity of the formula and the cognitive account one can provide thereof. It follows that other approaches are welcome (see later).

At the same time, we need not assume that the set C is always identical to the set of probabilities that cannot be ruled out based on hard evidence. For example, in Ellsberg's two-urn experiment, we know nothing about the composition of urn II. This means that the set of measures we cannot rule out is

$$C_1 = \{(p, 1 - p)|0 \leq p \leq 1\}.$$

Yet, maximizing the minimal EU with respect to C_1 is quite extreme indeed. In particular, it means that getting \$100 on red and nothing on black will be equivalent to getting nothing for sure. It is possible that in this situation a decision maker will satisfy the preceding axioms, and when we elicit her set of measures, we find, for example,

$$C_2 = \{(p, 1 - p)|.4 \leq p \leq .6\}.$$

When compared to CEU, the MMEU model has two main advantages. First, it appears more intuitive. Second, it has many more degrees of freedom. To use CEU one needs to specify the state space and define a nonadditive measure on it, v. To use the MMEU model, one may take any standard model (with a unique probability) and relax any assumption, such that allowing a certain parameter to vary in a certain range. Even if the model is very complex, we know that, by definition, we get a set of measures C. The set may not be convex (and it may be hard to tell whether it is), but we also know that every set C is observationally equivalent (under the MMEU model) to its convex hull, and we can therefore compute the minimal EU of every act for the agent under consideration.[6]

---

[5] The same type of question is not raised in the context of CEU, even when v is convex. The reason is probably that people barely understand what Choquet integration is, and they do not find that their intuition guides them about its reasonableness.

[6] However, Peter Wakker argues that when it comes to actual applications, involving real decision makers whose beliefs are to be assessed, the parsimony of the CEU model makes it much easier to use than the MMEU model.

17.5   GENERALIZATIONS AND VARIATIONS

The interpretational difficulties discussed previously prompted research in several directions. One approach was suggested by Gajdos *et al.* (2007). They explicitly model a set of objectively given probabilities, that is, the decision maker's information or state of knowledge. Preferences are defined over acts in the context of such sets of known probabilities. They then derive an MMEU model for each given set and discuss the relationship between the set that represents information, namely, the "cognitive" one, and the set that governs behavior, that is, the "behavioral" one.

Klibanoff *et al.* (2005) and Seo (2007) suggest to replace the minimum EU by some aggregation of all possible expected utilities. To this end, they need some second-order probability, namely, a probability over the probabilities in $\Delta(S)$. Furthermore, they need to introduce some nonlinearity in order to capture a nonneutral attitude to ambiguity. (Otherwise, a prior over all priors would boil down to a Bayesian model again.) Their approaches to the problem are axiomatic.

The MMEU model was extended to a dynamic setup by Epstein and Schneider (2003). The maxmin model, as well as CEU, were greatly generalized by Ghirardato and Marinacci's (2001) "biseparable" preferences (see also Ghirardato *et al.*, 2005).

Another variation was introduced by Maccheroni *et al.* (2006*a*), who introduce a concave cost function for every probability $p \in \Delta(S)$, with the maxmin model being the special case for which the cost function takes only the values $\{0, \infty\}$. Maccheroni *et al.* (2006*b*) provides the dynamic version of this model.

17.6   BEWLEY'S ALTERNATIVE APPROACH

Another approach to decision under uncertainty is due to Bewley (2002). His model also suggests that there is a set of priors, C, but the decision rule is different: act f is preferred to act g if and only if, according to each prior $p \in C$, the EU of f is higher than that of g. Clearly, if C is not a singleton, this defines a partial order. Indeed, Bewley starts out by weakening the completeness axiom.[7] In Bewley's theory, when there was no preference between f and g, choice was determined by a status quo.[8]

---

[7] Bewley wrote his first working paper in 1986. It was independently developed of the maxmin model, which also appeared as working paper in 1986. My MA thesis, in 1984, contained a chapter that axiomatized the same decision rule as Bewley's. It was not a very elegant axiomatization and I never translated it into English. Needless to say, Bewley's work was independent of it. Both results relied on Aumann (1962), who provided a representation theorem for partial orders in a von Neumann–Morgenstern (vNM) model. Aumann (1962) dealt with incompleteness of preferences in general, and was not concerned with uncertainty. Kannai (1963) generalized Aumann's theorem to infinitely many dimensions.

[8] Bewley did not have a theory of the emergence of the status quo, and this was one of the reasons that he dropped the theory. By 1989 he had about five very exciting papers on the topic, none of which had been published. I asked him about their publication and he said that he might publish

17.7 COMBINING OBJECTIVE AND SUBJECTIVE RATIONALITY

Following the discussion of objective and subjective rationality given previously, one may represent a decision maker by two binary relations, $\succsim^*$ and $\succsim^0$.[9] The first denotes choice that is rational in the objective sense, and it is potentially incomplete: when a preference $f \succsim^* g$ can be justified, we express it. Otherwise, we remain silent. That which cannot be justified does not exist. You can think of $f \succsim^* g$ as "Based on evidence, logic, and perhaps some sound decision theoretic reasoning, one can prove that g is better than f." Any reasonable person, who honestly adopts the utility function of our decision maker, would agree that f is at least as good as g.

This approach is appealing, especially when the right to remain silent is given. Indeed, classical statistics, which attempts to draw objective conclusions from evidence, can neither prove nor refute many claims, and science remains silent on a variety of issues. But whereas objective rationality suffices for science, it doesn't for decision making, because the need to act is unavoidable. Eventually, something will be chosen even if neither $f \succsim^* g$ nor $g \succsim^* f$ holds. Leaving this choice unmodeled may be dangerous. If we insist on stating only the preferences that are rational in the objective sense, we may find ourselves making choices that are not even rational in the subjective sense. You can think of $\succsim^*$ as the advice given by an expert to a decision maker. If this relation leaves many pairs of acts unranked, the expert can then discover that the decision maker did not even satisfy transitivity and kept cycling among acts that were unranked by $\succsim^*$.

It therefore seems more reasonable to bring forth the choices made and to try to guarantee that they are at least not irrational. Let $\succsim^0$ denote these choices. It will be a complete relation, because we do not wish to leave anything unmodeled. But, apart from completeness, it may satisfy only weaker axioms than does $\succsim^*$. For example, consider the AA independence axiom. We can expect $\succsim^*$ to satisfy it in its original form. Indeed, assume that $f \succsim^* g$. That is, on the basis of evidence, scientific studies, statistics, and logic, you manage to convince people that f is at least as desirable as g. This now gives you a way to convince your audience that $\alpha f + (1-\alpha)h$ is at least as desirable as $\alpha g + (1-\alpha)h$, for any h. In fact, the (vNM)–AA axiom *is* the reasoning: it provides the link between the preference $f \succsim^* g$ and the preference $\alpha f + (1-\alpha)h \succsim^* \alpha g + (1-\alpha)h$. In other words, if asked what are the pairs of comparisons that can be justified, this set should be closed under transitivity, under AA independence, under monotonicity, and so on. As argued earlier, for

---

them together as a book. Two years later he decided that economic theory (at large) was not the answer to the problem that bothered him, which had originally been wage rigidity. He dropped this remarkable project without publishing most of it. He later agreed to publish the papers only if they required minimal or no revisions, and this is why his 1986 paper was published only in 2002.

[9] This section is a sketchy description of Gilboa *et al.* (2008).

reasoned choice, the completeness axiom is the challenge, and all the other axioms can be viewed as modes of reasoning that may help us cope with this challenge. In an attempt to "prove" that f is preferred to g, such axioms can be the inference rules.

By contrast, $\succsim^0$ need not satisfy the AA independence axiom in all its strength. It is possible that, out of ignorance, I will behave according to $f \sim^0 g$, say, be indifferent between betting on red or on black in Ellsberg's unknown urn. This does not mean that I truly believe that f is as good as g, and I do not purport to be able to convince others that f and g should really be equivalent. Someone else might come along, and with the same utility function and the same information that I have, they might conclude that they strictly prefer f to g. I cannot say that they would be irrational in doing so. Nor would they be able to say that I am irrational in expressing indifference between f and g. When we now consider $\alpha f + (1 - \alpha)h$ and $\alpha g + (1 - \alpha)h$, preferences might change. It is possible, for instance, that $\alpha f + (1 - \alpha)h$ is risky, while $\alpha g + (1 - \alpha)h$ is uncertain. Because of the problem of uncertainty, I do not necessarily subscribe to AA's independence. I will not be embarrassed to violate it in some cases. In short, subjective rationality will satisfy certain axioms of AA, such as transitivity, but it need not satisfy all of them. Importantly, not all the axioms that can be used as reasoning templates, or inference rules, with $\succsim^*$ can also be similarly applicable to $\succsim^0$. Because $\succsim^*$ deals only with objectively rational preferences, it serves as a sounder basis for construction of new preferences than does $\succsim^0$. The latter, including certain arbitrary choices, can be used for construction of new preferences only when we feel that the axiom (the inference rule) is a very compelling one, such as transitivity.

Clearly, which axioms are reasonable ones for either of the two relations, $\succsim^*$ and $\succsim^0$, is a matter of subjective judgment. As an example, assume that we agree that objective rationality, $\succsim^*$, should satisfy certain axioms that guarantee a Bewley-type representation and that subjective rationality, $\succsim^0$, should satisfy the MMEU axioms. Then there exists a set of probabilities C_{obj} such that[10]

$$f \succsim^* g \quad \text{iff} \quad \int_S (E_{f(s)}u)dp \geq \int_S (E_{g(s)}u)dp \quad \forall p \in C_{obj}. \quad (17.2)$$

and another set of probabilities C_{sub} such that

$$f \succsim^0 g \quad \text{iff} \quad \min_{p \in C_{sub}} \int_S (E_{f(s)}u)dp \geq \min_{p \in C_{sub}} \int_S (E_{g(s)}u)dp.$$

We can now state axioms that explicitly relate the two relations and, equivalently, the two sets of probabilities. For instance, a basic consistency axiom would state

$$f \succsim^* g \quad \text{implies} \quad f \succsim^0 g;$$

---

[10] Gilboa *et al.* (2008) offer such a characterization result. It differs from Bewley's (2002) in several ways. In particular, it represents weak preference by a collection of weak inequalities, whereas Bewley represents strict preference by a collection of strict inequalities.

that is, a preference that is objectively rational should also be subjectively rational; what we are convinced of we should actually do. This can be shown to be equivalent to $C_{sub} \subset C_{obj}$.[11] One can also impose another axiom, reflecting extreme caution, which says that when comparing an uncertain act f to a constant one c, unless there is a good reason to prefer the uncertain one, that is, if $f \succsim^* c$ doesn't hold, we should go for the certain one, that is, $c \succsim^0 f$. This axiom is equivalent to $C_{obj} \subset C_{sub}$. Together, the two axioms imply that the decision maker has a single set of probabilities, which is used to describe objective rationality by the anonymous rule (17.2) and subjective rationality by the maxmin rule. However, one may consider other alternatives, in particular, models in which C_{sub} is a proper subset of C_{obj}.

17.8 APPLICATIONS

There are several applications of CEU and of MMEU. The majority of the applications of CEU involve a convex nonadditive measure, so they can be considered applications of MMEU as well. The following is a very sketchy description of some applications.

Dow and Werlang (1992) showed that in the CEU/MMEU model, a person may have a range of prices at which she wishes neither to buy nor to sell a financial asset. To see the basic logic, consider an unknown probability on two states, say, $p \in [0.4, 0.6]$, and a financial asset X that yields 1 in the first state and -1 in the second. The MMEU model would value both X and $-X$ at -0.2. Thus, it is no longer the case that an agent would switch, at a certain price p, from demanding X to offering it. This may explain why people refrain from trading in certain markets. It can also explain why at times of greater volatility one may find lower volumes of trade: with a larger set of probabilities that are considered possible, there will be more decision makers who prefer neither to buy nor to sell.[12]

Epstein and Miao (2003) use uncertainty aversion to explain the "home bias" phenomenon in international finance, namely, the observation that people prefer to trade in their own country's stock market, even though foreign ones are also available. The intuition is very similar to Ellsberg's two-urn experiment: the home country is analogous to the known urn, where probabilities can presumably be assessed. The foreign country is similar to the unknown urn. A trader can decide whether to buy or to sell a stock in the foreign market, just as she can decide to choose a red or a black bet on the unknown urn. Still, people may prefer neither.

The multiple prior model has also been employed in a job search model by Nishimura and Ozaki (2004). They ask how an unemployed agent will react

---

[11] See also Nehring (2002, 2008) for similar reasoning.

[12] This argument assumes that the decision maker starts with a risk-free portfolio. A trader who already holds an uncertain position may be satisfied with it with a small set of probabilities, but wish to trade in order to reduce uncertainty if the set of probabilities is larger.

to increasing uncertainty in the labor market. In a Bayesian model, greater uncertainty might be captured by higher variance of the job offers the agent receives. Other things being equal, an increase in variance should make the agent less willing to accept a given offer, knowing that he has a chance to get better ones later on. This conclusion is a result of the assumption that all uncertainty is quantifiable by a probability measure. Nishimura and Ozaki (2004) show that in a multiple prior model (assuming, again, an "uncertainty averse" agent, say, one who uses the maxmin rule) the conclusion might be reversed: in the presence of greater uncertainty, modeled as a larger set of possible priors, agents will be more willing to take an existing job offer rather than bet on waiting for better ones in the future.

Hansen and Sargent (2001, 2003, 2008) apply a multiple prior model to macroeconomic questions starting from the viewpoint that whatever is the probability model a policy maker might have, it cannot be known with certainty. Considering a set of priors around a given model and asking how robust economic policy would be to variations in the underlying probability, they revisit and question classical results. Hansen *et al.* (1999) compare savings behavior under EU maximization with savings behavior of a "robust decision maker" who behaves in accordance with the multiple prior model. They show that the behavior of a robust decision maker puts the market price of risk much closer to empirical estimates than does the behavior of the classical EU maximizer.

Other applications to finance include Epstein and Wang (1994, 1995), where the authors explain financial crashes and booms using the MMEU model. Mukerji (1998) used CEU with a convex nonadditive measure to explain incompleteness of contracts.

This list is not exhaustive. The main point is that the multiple prior model can yield qualitatively different and sometimes more plausible results than a Bayesian model. Of course, there are also many models in which multiple priors beliefs would not change anything of importance. For example, I do not see an urging need to change Akerlof's lemon model to allow for multiple priors (Akerlof, 1970). The basic result of Akerlof seems robust to the details of the modeling of uncertainty. By contrast, the no-trade theorem of Milgrom and Stokey (1982) does hinge on additive beliefs. As a very general guideline, I would suggest considering the MMEU model when a Bayesian result seems to crucially depend on the existence of a unique, additive prior, which is common to all agents. When you see that, in the course of some proof, things cancel out too neatly, this is the time to wonder whether introducing a little bit of uncertainty may provide more realistic results.

PART IV

COGNITIVE ORIGINS

We made a rather long detour into theories of decision under uncertainty seeking a way to define subjective probabilities based on observed behavior. The idea was one of "reverse engineering": observing behavior and inferring what beliefs might have induced it. Sadly, I have to admit that I do not view the project as a great success. This is not because the theories of decision under uncertainty that we have reviewed are flawed. In fact, I think that they are rather good theories. Expected utility maximization in general, and with subjective probabilities in particular, is not a bad approximation of actual behavior in many problems. Moreover, this theory provides compelling recommendations in an even wider array of problems. It may convince us that with the appropriate choice of the utility function, we need not take higher moments into account, nor consider other choice criteria. As long as we know what probabilities are, I believe that the theory is quite impressive.

However, when we do not know what the probabilities should be, I do not see that we have made much progress. In problems such as (3) and (4) in Chapter 1, we may find that our preferences are too ill defined, too incomplete, and too likely to violate other Savage's axioms in order to serve as a basis for the definition of probabilities. Savage's axioms can help us elicit our subjective probability measure if we have well-defined preferences that satisfy the axioms. The axiomatization might even convince us that we would like to have a subjective probability. But it does not help us determine which subjective probability we should adopt if we don't already have one.

The approach followed in Part III was to consider other decision theories, to be used when probabilities cannot be defined. Here we take a different path. We drop the behavioral approach and try to ask how probabilities should be constructed. In some cases, this approach might help us define probabilities when these are not reflected in our preferences. In others, we may find that the current approach does not lead us far enough to generate probabilities.

As hinted in Section 4.3, when there are many observations that can be assumed to be causally independent, as in the medical example (3) (Chapter 1), there are plausible definitions of beliefs and probabilities. One approach to these definitions, roughly corresponding to kernel methods in statistics, is axiomatically developed in the following two chapters. But when the observations, or "cases," are interwoven by causal relationships, the methods discussed here may be too naive to provide a definition of probability. This is also true of other definitions of "probability," which may be more or less intuitive, axiomatically justified or not. In fact, I remain skeptical about the possibility of defining probability in a meaningful way in such applications.

The analysis in this part is also axiomatic, but the axioms herein refer to cognitive judgments rather than to behavior. And, importantly, we explicitly refer to observations (or "cases") and try to model the mapping from databases of observations to beliefs. Because in this part you will not see decisions explicitly, but you will see observations as part of the model, you may feel that this is closer to statistics than to decision theory. Indeed, the following two chapters may be viewed as preliminary steps toward an axiomatic approach to statistical inference.

CHAPTER 18

Case-Based Qualitative Beliefs

In this chapter we deal with beliefs that may not be quantified by probabilities. Rather, we think in terms of binary relations interpreted as "at least as likely as" akin to de Finetti's qualitative probabilities. I first introduce a representation theorem and then show that the representation obtained generalizes several known statistical techniques. I then discuss the extent to which the theorem can apply to problems of inductive inference that are less structured than these well-established statistical techniques.

18.1 AXIOMS AND RESULT

We assume two primitives: *alternatives* to be ranked, A, and *observations* based on which ranking will take place, X. The alternatives can be possible predictions for a particular decision problem at hand, alternative theories, and so forth. Neither A nor X is endowed with any structure. Moreover, there is no a priori relationship between them. The ranking of alternatives in A based on observations from X will give rise to such relationships.

The set of databases is defined as

$$\mathbb{D} \equiv \{I \mid I : X \to \mathbb{Z}_+, \quad \sum_{x \in X} I(x) < \infty\},$$

where $\mathbb{Z}_+$ stands for the nonnegative integers. $I \in \mathbb{D}$ is interpreted as a counter vector, where $I(x)$ counts how many observations of type x appear in the database represented by I.

Algebraic operations on $\mathbb{D}$ are performed pointwise. Thus, for $I, J \in \mathbb{D}$ and $k \geq 0$, $I + J \in \mathbb{D}$, and $kI \in \mathbb{D}$ are well defined.

For $I \in \mathbb{D}$, we assume as given (and observable) a relation $\succsim_I \subset A \times A$, where $a \succsim_I b$ is interpreted as "given the database I, alternative a is at least as likely as alternative b." Thus, we assume that qualitative beliefs constitute legitimate data. These beliefs are similar to de Finetti's qualitative probabilities with two distinctions: (i) our relation is defined only on alternatives, and not on subsets thereof;[1] (ii) we deal with a collection of relations, defined on the set of alternatives and parameterized by the possible databases of observations.

The asymmetric and symmetric parts of $\succsim_I$, $\succ_I$ and $\sim_I$, respectively, are defined as usual.

The following result appears in Gilboa and Schmeidler (2001, 2003). To state it, we first define a matrix $v : A \times X \to \mathbb{R}$ to be *diversified* if no row in v is dominated by an affine combination of three (or fewer) other rows in it. That is, if there are no elements $a, b, c, d \in A$ with $b, c, d \neq a$ and $\lambda, \mu, \theta \in \mathbb{R}$ with $\lambda + \mu + \theta = 1$ such that

$$v(a, \cdot) \leq \lambda v(b, \cdot) + \mu v(c, \cdot) + \theta v(d, \cdot).$$

(Recall that an affine combination is similar to a convex combination, but the coefficients used in it may be negative.)

The first axiom is standard, and only requires that $\{\succsim_I\}_I$ be weak orders.

A1 order: For every $I \in \mathbb{D}$, $\succsim_I$ is complete and transitive on A.

The next two axioms are new: they do not restrict a given $\succsim_I$, but rather the relation among several such relations (for different Is).

A2 combination: For every $I, J \in \mathbb{D}$ and every $a, b \in A$, if $a \succsim_I b$ ($a \succ_I b$) and $a \succsim_J b$, then $a \succsim_{I+J} b$ ($a \succ_{I+J} b$).

The basic idea of the combination axiom is quite obvious: if the same conclusion, namely, that a is at least as likely as b, is reached given two distinct databases, it should also be reached given their union. Observe that a "union" of disjoint databases, represented by counter vectors I and J, is represented by the sum, $I + J$. We will discuss the limitations of the axiom later on.

A3 Archimedean axiom: For every $I, J \in \mathbb{D}$ and every $a, b \in A$, if $a \succ_I b$, then there exists $l \in \mathbb{N}$ such that $a \succ_{lI+J} b$.

The Archimedean axiom states that if database I gives you a reason to believe that a is (strictly) more likely than b, then sufficiently many replications of database I will eventually overwhelm the evidence provided by any other database, J. This axiom may not be very reasonable if a single observation can prove that an alternative is certain, or impossible. But if we are in a statistical frame of mind, in which noise variables make nothing impossible, it seems reasonable.

Finally, we need a richness condition. It is justified by mathematical necessity. Hopefully, you won't find it too objectionable.

A4 diversity: For every list (a, b, c, d) of distinct elements of A, there exists $I \in \mathbb{D}$ such that $a \succ_I b \succ_I c \succ_I d$. If $|A| < 4$, then for any strict ordering of the elements of A there exists $I \in \mathbb{D}$ such that $\succ_I$ is that ordering.

---

[1] One can extend this approach to rankings over sets of alternatives and impose de Finetti's cancellation axiom on the likelihood relations. See Gilboa and Schmeidler (2002).

Theorem 18.1 *(Gilboa and Schmeidler, 2001)* $\{\succsim_I\}_{I \in \mathbb{D}}$ *satisfy A1–A4 if and only if there is a diversified matrix* $v : A \times X \to \mathbb{R}$ *such that for every* $I \in \mathbb{D}$ *and every* $a, b \in A$,

$$a \succsim_I b \quad \textit{iff} \quad \sum_{x \in X} I(x)v(a, x) \geq \sum_{x \in X} I(x)v(b, x). \tag{18.1}$$

Furthermore, *in this case, the matrix* v *is unique in the following sense:* v *and* u *both represent* $\{\succsim_I\}_{I \in \mathbb{D}}$ *as in (18.1) iff there are a scalar* $\lambda > 0$ *and a matrix* $\beta : A \times X \to \mathbb{R}$ *with identical rows (i.e., with constant columns) such that* $u = \lambda v + \beta$.

The proof can be found in Gilboa and Schmeidler (2001, pp. 77–90). The theorem is stated and proved for a different setup, in which observations are modeled by sets rather than by counter vectors in Gilboa and Schmeidler (2003). (See pp. 5–8 for the statement of the theorem.) The proof uses Theorem 18.1. It is stated and proved in the appendix (Theorem 2, pp. 16–23). Some mathematical ideas go back to Gilboa and Schmeidler (1997).

18.2 FOUR KNOWN TECHNIQUES

There are several special cases of (18.1) that are well known in statistics and in machine learning.

Example A: A statistician is interested in estimating a discrete distribution. She observes the realizations of several i.i.d. (independently and identically distributed) random variables taken from this unknown distribution. She then takes the empirical distribution, namely, the relative frequencies of the various outcomes, as an estimate of the unknown distribution.

Given a discrete random variable taking values in some set N, let $A = X = N$. This is a special but interesting situation, in which past observations and future occurrences are precisely the same type of objects: the next random variable may assume one of the values in N (hence $A = N$), and past cases are values of similar random variables taking values in N (hence $X = N$).

Ranking alternatives in A by their empirical frequency can be modeled by

$$a \succsim_I b \quad \textit{iff} \quad \sum_{x \in X} I(x)1_{\{x=a\}} \geq \sum_{x \in X} I(x)1_{\{x=b\}},$$

namely, by setting

$$v(a, x) = 1_{\{a=x\}}.$$

Example B: As in example A, a statistician is estimating an unknown distribution. This time she believes that the random variable is real valued and has a continuous distribution.[2] In this case, the empirical distribution observed will

---

[2] This methods extends in a straightforward manner to random variables that assume values in Euclidean spaces of higher dimensions.

never be a good enough approximation of the "true" distribution, as the former is discrete and the latter is continuous. One approach to this problem is known as "kernel estimation" (see Akaike, 1954; Parzen, 1962; Rosenblatt, 1956; and for recent texts, Scott, 1992; Silverman, 1986): the statistician chooses a so-called kernel function $k : \mathbb{R} \times \mathbb{R} \to \mathbb{R}_+$ with $\int k(z, x)dx = 1$ and, given a sample $\{z_i\}_{i=1}^n$, generates the density

$$f(x) = \frac{1}{n} \sum_{i=1}^{n} k(z_i, x).$$

This is a straightforward extension of estimation by empirical frequencies, where each observation is "smoothed" and represented by a density around the actually observed value.

Here again the set of cases and the set of eventualities coincide: $A = X = \mathbb{R}$. The original problem involves the estimation of a density function. In our prediction problem, we ask the predictor to rank alternatives only by their plausibility. However, you can use the estimated density $f(x)$ to rank x values, so that a value with a higher density will be considered "more likely." Formally, define

$$x \succsim_{\{z_i\}_{i=1}^n} y \quad \text{iff} \quad f(x) \geq f(y).$$

You can then verify that the relations $(\succsim_{\{z_i\}_{i=1}^n})$ (when you range over all databases $\{z_i\}_{i=1}^n$) satisfy our axioms. In fact, they are represented by

$$v(a, x) = k(x, a).$$

Example C: An engineer has to program a machine whose task is to identify handwriting. The machine will learn by asking the user to provide several examples of each letter in the alphabet, and it will store these examples. When a new data point will be presented, the machine will compare it to the examples obtained in the learning phase and classify the new point accordingly. Assume that each data point is represented by a real-valued vector $z \in \mathbb{R}^k$. One possible classification method, based on the kernel methods discussed previously, is the following: equip the machine with a similarity function $s : \mathbb{R}^k \times \mathbb{R}^k \to \mathbb{R}_+$. Let there be given a new data point $w \in \mathbb{R}^k$. For each possible class x (the letters of the alphabet), let $\{z_j^x\}_{j=1}^{n_x}$ be the examples in the database that are known to belong to class x. Then, attach to each class x the index

$$S(w, x) = \sum_{j=1}^{n_x} s(w, z_j).$$

Finally, classify the input w as belonging to class x for an x in the argmax of $S(w, \cdot)$.

This technique, referred to as *kernel classification*, involves more structure than the previous ones. To see that it is also a special case of the preceding representation, let the set of possible classes be A and the set of observations be

$X = \mathbb{R}^k \times A$. An observation $x = (z, a)$ is interpreted as an example, in which the data point z was found to belong to class a. Defining

$$v(a, (z, c)) = s(z)1_{\{c=a\}},$$

(18.1) boils down to kernel classification.[3]

Example D: A statistician is interested in estimating a parameter of a distribution with a given functional form. He takes a sample of i.i.d. variables with this distribution and computes a maximum likelihood estimator of the parameter.

In this example, X is the set of values that the observed random variables might assume. A is the set of values of the unknown parameter. Observe that these sets are typically different. They are related by the statistical model, namely, a family of distributions over X, parameterized by A. The statistical model is given by $\{f(x|a)\}_{a \in A}$, where for each $a \in A$, $f(\cdot|a)$ is a distribution or a density function over X. Maximum likelihood estimation selects, for a sample $\{x_i\}_{i=1}^n$, the maximizers of $\prod_i f(x_i|\cdot)$ over A. It is natural to extend maximum likelihood to a ranking of any two values of the unknown parameter as follows:

$$a \succsim_I b \quad \text{iff} \quad \prod_i f(x_i|a) \geq \prod_i f(x_i|b).$$

Clearly, we obtain (18.1) by setting

$$v(a, x) = \log(f(x|a)).$$

18.3   THE COMBINATION AXIOM IN GENERAL ANALOGICAL REASONING

We saw that four known statistical techniques satisfy the axioms and are special cases of (18.1). This gives room for hope that this representation of likelihood rankings will be a reasonable way to represent beliefs also in less structured environments.

Consider Example (3) from Chapter 1 again. In this example, I ask my physician about the probabilities of possible outcomes of my surgery. This problem will be discussed in the next chapter. At this point, let us start with a simpler task, of qualitative ranking of possible eventualities. That is, assume that I will be content to have a statement such as "you are more likely to survive the surgery than not."

The physician is facing a classification problem, as the handwriting identification problem in Example C. Classification problems range from pattern and speech recognition to computer-aided diagnosis and weather forecasting.

---

[3] Kernel classification is akin to k-nearest neighbor approaches (see Cover and Hart, 1967; Fix and Hodges, 1951, 1952). These approaches, however, do not satisfy the Archimedean axiom (for any k) and they also violate the combination axiom if $k > 1$.

In fact, classification problems may be viewed as rather general decision problems, with the important caveat that the decision being made does not affect the
process predicted. For example, the weather forecaster may be right or wrong in
her prediction, thus affecting her own payoff, but we assume that her prediction
does not affect the weather. This renders classification problems conceptually
simpler than are general decision problems. In particular, the predictor can
look back at history and figure out what would have been the result of each
prediction she could have made. By contrast, the same type of learning in a
general decision problem leads to counterfactual reasoning. For example, we
do not know how history would have evolved had Hitler crossed the channel,
but we do know whether the weather forecaster would have been right had she
forecast rain yesterday.

   Since both the handwriting identification problem (Example C) and the
medical forecast problem (Example (3)) are classification problems, we may
wonder whether (18.1) might not apply to the latter just as it does to the former.
Specifically, we should ask ourselves whether the combination axiom is a
reasonable assumption in this context. This axiom requires that if we reach a
certain conclusion based on each of two databases separately, we should reach
the same conclusion based on their union. For concreteness, suppose that my
physician, on the basis of her database, tells me that I'm more likely to survive
the operation than not. I then seek a second opinion and consult with another
physician, who has been working in a different hospital, thus having access to a
different database (where the two databases may be assumed disjoint). Suppose
that he too thinks that I'm going to make it. Do I want them to share their data?
If not, that is, if I am happy to get the converging expert opinion, I implicitly
exhibit faith in the combination axiom: I probably find it hard to believe that,
should they share their data, their joint prediction would be changed. This
example suggests that the combination axiom may be a reasonable assumption
in this context, at least as a first approximation.[4]

   If we are willing to accept the other axioms as well, the theorem suggests
that there should be a function – denoted $s(w, z)$ previously – dictating my
physician's answer: she should simply check whether the sum of s values over
the patients that she has seen surviving is larger than the same sum for the
patients she has seen dying. She should predict that I am more likely to survive
than not if and only if the former is higher than the latter.

   We may think of the function s as the similarity that the physician finds
between the patients in her database and the patient for whom she is asked
to predict the outcome. This is in line with Hume (1748), who wrote, "From
causes which appear *similar* we expect similar effects. This is the sum of all our
experimental conclusions." The theory presented earlier can be thought of as a
model of the analogical reasoning that Hume viewed as the basis for prediction.
However, as we turn to discuss the weaknesses of this axiom, it is important to

---

[4] However, see the qualifications in the next section.

recall that (despite Hume's casual use of the word "sum") analogical reasoning need not be restricted to the combination axiom.

18.4 VIOLATIONS OF THE COMBINATION AXIOM

The combination axiom is extensively discussed in Gilboa and Schmeidler (2003, pp. 11–14). I will mention here only two major classes of problems in which it is likely to be violated.[5] The first involves problems in which the reasoner learns how to reason. To be more concrete, assume that the reasoner uses a similarity function to learn from the past regarding the future, but also learns the similarity function itself from observations. This process is referred to as "second-order induction" in Gilboa and Schmeidler (2001). It is clearly part of the way children learn. Also, the end result of this process, namely, the appropriate similarity function, is part of the definition of expertise. Experts are supposed to know many facts, but also be able to draw the "right" analogies between different cases. However, when the similarity function is learned from the data, the combination axiom is unlikely to hold.

The second class of problems involves reasoning that is not merely from past to future cases, but that engages in theorizing as well, that is, when we consider not only case-to-case induction but also case-to-rule induction. In the latter, the reasoner tries to learn general theories from her observations and then use these theories in a deductive way to generate predictions. When such a process takes place, the effect of cases on the eventual prediction need not be additive. For example, a reasoner who seeks trends in the data will not find any regularity in each single observation, but may observe a trend when the observations are considered together. It is easy to generate examples violating the combination axiom based on such intuition.

When cases are causally related to each other, case-to-case induction will not suffice. Causal relationships can be thought of as theories that relate cases to each other. For example, if we believe that one traumatic war is going to render another war less likely, this causal relationship can be captured by a rule, suggesting negative correlation between wars in consecutive periods. It will certainly not be captured by an additive formula such as (18.1).

The way we reason about wars or stock market crashes may still be based on past cases. Such reasoning involves case-to-case analogies, as well as case-to-rule theorizing. Finding a formal theory that unifies these types of reasoning in an elegant and insightful way is a challenge for future research.

---

[5] There are many other problems, such as Simpson's paradox (Simpson, 1951), which are resolved by a natural redefinition of "cases" or "alternatives."

CHAPTER 19

Frequentism Revisited

19.1 SIMILARITY-WEIGHTED EMPIRICAL FREQUENCIES

Consider the physician problem (Example (3) in Chapter 1) again, and (as opposed to the previous chapter), insist that the physician provide probabilistic predictions. As mentioned earlier, it is an example where many causally independent observations exist. They were not obtained under "identical" conditions, and so a frequentist definition of probability would not be a viable alternative in this case. The physician has already told me that if I insist on measuring everything, I will find that I am a unique case in human history and that no data were yet collected about me. Yet, there are past cases that are more and less similar to mine. A rather natural idea is to suggest that the notion of empirical frequencies be used, but with weights, such that a more similar case will have a higher weight in the calculation of the relative frequency than a less similar case.

To be more concrete, let the variable of interest be $y \in \{0, 1\}$, indicating success of a medical procedure. The characteristics of patients are $x = (x^1, \ldots, x^m)$. These variables are real valued, but some (or all) of them may be discrete. We are given a database consisting of past observations of the variables $(x, y) = (x^1, \ldots, x^m, y)$, denoted $(x_i, y_i)_{i \leq n}$. A new case is introduced, with characteristics $x_{n+1} = (x^1_{n+1}, \ldots, x^m_{n+1})$, and we are asked to assess the probability that $y_{n+1} = 1$.

This is the setup of logistic regression, which is the most common way of defining probabilities in such problems. You may think of logistic regression as a rule-based approach, resulting from case-to-rule induction. The approach presented here is case-based, following case-to-case induction.

Assume that we are also equipped with a similarity function s, such that for two vectors of characteristics, $x_i = (x^1_i, \ldots, x^m_i)$ and $x_j = (x^1_j, \ldots, x^m_j)$, $s(x_i, x_j) > 0$ measures the similarity between a patient with characteristics x_i and another patient with characteristics x_j. The similarity function s will later be estimated from the data. We propose to define the probability that $y_{n+1} = 1$, given the function s, by[1]

$$\hat{y}^s_{n+1} = \frac{\sum_{i \leq n} s(x_i, x_{n+1}) y_i}{\sum_{i \leq n} s(x_i, x_{n+1})}. \tag{19.1}$$

According to this formula, the probability that y_{n+1} will be 1, namely, that the procedure will succeed in the case of patient x_{n+1}, is taken to be the s-weight of all past successes, divided by the total s-weight of all past cases, successes and failures alike.

This formula is known to statisticians as "kernel estimation" of probability. It is known to psychologists as "exemplar learning." Apparently, it is another example in which descriptive models of the human mind came up with techniques that were independently developed in statistics. Such coincidences should make us feel good about ourselves: apparently, evolution has equipped us with rather powerful reasoning techniques.

19.2 INTUITION

Formula (19.1) is obviously a generalization of the notion of empirical frequencies. Indeed, should the function s be constant, so that all observations are deemed equally relevant, (19.1) boils down to the relative frequency of $y_i = 1$ in the database. If, however, one defines $s(x_i, x_j)$ to be the indicator function of $x_i = x_j$ (setting the similarity to 0 in case the vectors differ from each other and to 1 in case they are equal), then formula (19.1) becomes the conditional relative frequency of $y_i = 1$, that is, its relative frequency in the subdatabase defined by x_{n+1}. It follows that (19.1) suggests a continuous spectrum between the two extremes: as opposed to conditional relative frequencies, it allows us to use the entire database. This is particularly useful in the medical example, where the database defined by $x_i = x_{n+1}$ may be very small or even empty. At the same time, it does not ignore the variables x, as does simple relative frequency over the entire database. Formula (19.1) uses the entire database, but it still allows a differentiation among the cases depending on their relevance.

Observe that one may argue that the standard use of empirical frequencies is a special case of the formula not only from a mathematical but also from a conceptual viewpoint: no two cases in history are ever identical. When we collect data and assume that an experiment was conducted "under the same conditions," we are actually employing a similarity judgment and determining that observations in the sample are similar enough to each other to be considered identical.

---

[1] For simplicity, we assume that s is strictly positive, so that the denominator of (19.1) never vanishes. Leshno (2007) extends the axiomatization to this case and allows a sequence of similarity functions that are used lexicographically as in (19.1).

19.3 AXIOMATIZATION

The axiomatization of formula (19.1), with only two outcomes, can be found
in Gilboa *et al.* (2006). The case of $n \geq 3$ outcomes, which is more elegant, is
given in Billot *et al.* (2005). I follow this paper here.

Let $\Omega = \{1, \ldots, n\}$ be a set of *states of nature*, $n \geq 3$. Let C be a nonempty
set of *cases*.[2] C may be an abstract set of arbitrary cardinality. A *database*
is a sequence of cases, $D \in C^r$ for $r \geq 1$. The set of all databases is denoted
$C^* = \cup_{r \geq 1} C^r$. The concatenation of two databases, $D = (c_1, \ldots, c_r) \in C^r$ and
$E = (c'_1, \ldots, c'_t) \in C^t$, is denoted by $D \circ E$ and it is defined by $D \circ E =$
$(c_1, \ldots, c_r, c'_1, \ldots, c'_t) \in C^{r+t}$.

Observe that the same element of C may appear more than once in a given
database. As earlier, we are in a statistical mind-set and consider repetitions of
observations to constitute additional evidence.

As in the case of qualitative probabilities, the sets C and Ω have no particular
structure and are also unrelated a priori. Yet, the main application we have in
mind is comparable to a classification problem, with the important difference
that this time the prediction is probabilistic rather than deterministic. As in
a classification problem, it will be natural to assume that past cases include
observations of certain variables, say $x \in \mathbb{R}^k$, and a realization of one of the
states of nature. That is, it will be useful to bear in mind a concrete structure
$C \subset \mathbb{R}^k \times \Omega$.

The prediction problem at hand, namely, the patient who asks the physician
to provide prognosis, is fixed throughout this discussion. We therefore suppress
it from the notation.

For each $D \in C^*$, the reasoner has a probabilistic belief $p(D) \in \Delta(\Omega)$ about
the realization of $\omega \in \Omega$ in the problem under discussion.

For $r \geq 1$, let Π_r be the set of all permutations on $\{1, \ldots, r\}$, that is, all
bijections $\pi : \{1, \ldots, r\} \to \{1, \ldots, r\}$. For $D \in C^r$ and a permutation $\pi \in \Pi_r$,
let πD be the permuted database; that is, $\pi D \in C^r$ is defined by $(\pi D)_i = D_{\pi(i)}$
for $i \leq r$.

We formulate the following axioms:

Invariance: For every $r \geq 1$, every $D \in C^r$, and every permutation $\pi \in \Pi_r$,
$p(D) = p(\pi D)$.

Concatenation: For every $D, E \in C^*$, $p(D \circ E) = \lambda p(D) + (1 - \lambda)p(E)$ for
some $\lambda \in (0, 1)$.

The invariance axiom might appear rather restrictive, as it does not allow
cases that appear later in D to have a greater impact on probability assessments
than do cases that appear earlier. But this does not mean that cases that are
chronologically more recent cannot have a greater weight than less recent
ones. All we need to do in order to let recent cases matter more is to include

---

[2] The set of cases C plays the role of observations, X, given previously.

time as one of the variables defining a problem. If we use such a description, all permutations of a sequence of cases would contain the same information. More generally, if you don't like the invariance axiom because there is some information about the cases that is implicit in their order, you can make this information explicit by introducing another variable into the description of cases.

The concatenation axiom is a reincarnation of the combination axiom from the previous chapter, applied to probability vectors rather than to binary relations. The axiom states that the beliefs induced by the concatenation of two databases cannot lie outside the interval connecting the beliefs induced by each database separately. To understand its logic, it may be best to imagine its behavioral implications should the probabilities we generate be used for expected payoff maximization in a decision problem with states of nature Ω. The concatenation axiom could then be restated as follows: for every two acts a and b, if a is (weakly) preferred to b given database D as well as given database E, then a is (weakly) preferred to b given the database $D \circ E$, and a strict preference given one of $\{D, E\}$ suffices for a strict preference given $D \circ E$. By a standard separation argument, this condition holds for every possible payoff matrix if and only if the concatenation axiom is satisfied.

Theorem 19.1 *(BGSS, 2005) p satisfies the invariance axiom, the combination axiom, and not all $\{p(D)\}_{D \in C^*}$ are collinear if and only if there exists a function $\hat{p} : C \to \Delta(\Omega)$, where not all $\{\hat{p}(c)\}_{c \in C}$ are collinear, and a function $s : C \to \mathbb{R}_{++}$ such that for every $r \geq 1$ and every $D = (c_1, \ldots, c_r) \in C^r$,*

$$p(D) = \frac{\sum_{j \leq r} s(c_j) \hat{p}(c_j)}{\sum_{j \leq r} s(c_j)}. \qquad (*)$$

Moreover, in this case, the function $\hat{p}$ is unique and the function s is unique up to multiplication by a positive number.

This theorem may be extended to a general measurable state space Ω with no additional complications, because for every D, only a finite number of measures are involved in the formula for $p(D)$. The proof can be found in BGSS (2005, pp. 1130–1136).

The theorem provides a representation of $p(D)$ as a weighted average of the probability vectors $\hat{p}(c_j)$ for all cases c_j in D. If cases are, indeed, elements of $\mathbb{R}^k \times \Omega$, then a case $c_j = (x_j, \omega_j)$ tells a story of a problem with characteristics x_j that resulted in outcome ω_j. It is then natural to add an axiom that implies that $\hat{p}((x_j, \omega_j))$ assigns probability 1 to ω_j. This may sound a bit extreme if you really observed only one case. However, by this formula, $\hat{p}((x_j, \omega_j))$ is also the probability you will assign to states in Ω if you have a databases consisting of 1,000,000 replications of (x_j, ω_j) (and nothing else). In fact, one can restrict the function p to databases with many cases and then this assumption might seem less objectionable.

If indeed, $C \subset \mathbb{R}^k \times \Omega$, the similarity weight $s(c_j)$ might also depend on the outcome ω_j. This calls for another assumption, which would rule that out and guarantee that $s(c_j) = s((x_j, \omega_j))$ depends on x_j alone. With these two additional assumptions, the formula $(*)$ boils down to the similarity-weighted frequencies defined in (19.1).

This theorem is a version of a fundamental theorem in projective geometry, which has been known for about 400 years. The basic idea is that the concatenation axiom implies that intervals in the space of databases are mapped onto intervals in the simplex of probabilities. Functions that map intervals (and points) onto intervals (and points) are called projective functions, and they have been studied already in the 1400s, because such functions are at the basis of perspective drawing. Perspective was discovered in Florence at the very beginning of the fifteenth century, ushering the Renaissance. As befits Renaissance people, some artists could both draw and do the mathematics of their art. Piero della Francesca was perhaps the most prominent of them, and he wrote a book explaining drawing by the rules of perspective.[3]

To see the analogy between formula (19.1) and perspective drawing, consider a given database D. For each $c_j \in D$, draw $\hat{p}(c_j)$ on the simplex and extend it by s_j. Then, take the simple arithmetic average of all resulting vectors $s_j \hat{p}(c_j)$ and project it again onto the simplex to get $p(D)$. Assume now that you are a painter, put your eye at the origin, and let the simplex $\Delta(\Omega)$ be your canvas. Imagine that you are drawing the points $s_j \hat{p}(c_j)$ and their (regular, arithmetic) average. Each point $s_j \hat{p}(c_j)$ will map to $\hat{p}(c_j)$ on your canvas, but their average, to the similarity-weighted average, $p(D)$. In other words, cases c_j that are considered to be more similar to the case at hand (which is suppressed throughout this discussion) will have larger vectors $s_j \hat{p}(c_j)$ and will skew the average in their direction. This is equivalent to drawing a three-dimensional object on a two-dimensional canvas: the simple average (in $\mathbb{R}^3$) maps to a weighted average (in $\mathbb{R}^2$), where more remote points get a higher weight. In this sense, I like to argue that (19.1) defines probabilities as frequencies viewed in perspective.[4]

19.4 EMPIRICAL SIMILARITY AND OBJECTIVE PROBABILITIES

The generalization of empirical frequencies to similarity-weighted empirical frequencies is an appealing idea. It seems to deal with situations in which there are many observations that can be assumed causally independent, though not identical. However, it seems to veer away from the objectivity that relative frequencies used to have. Instead of asking people for their subjective probabilities directly, we have relegated the subjective problem to the choice of the similarity function.

---

[3] This was about 150 years before projective geometry was developed by Desargues.

[4] Some of my coauthors think that I get carried away here. Unfortunately, the referees thought so, too, and we could not include the perspective analogy in the published version of the paper.

The axiomatizations of the similarity-weighted formula (one of which we have just seen) can convince you that you might want to have a similarity function, but they do not tell you where you should get a similarity function from if you don't have one already. It appears that the same critique we raised in the context of Savage's theorem can be raised here.

But there is one difference: the similarity function can be computed from the data. That is, considering a database, and the similarity-weighted formula, one can ask, which similarity function would have best fit the data a priori? The similarity that does that is referred to as the "empirical similarity."

To understand this definition, assume that a database $((x_i, y_i))_{i \leq n}$ is given. Assume a certain parameterized family of similarity functions, such as[5]

$$s_w = e^{-d_w}$$

with

$$d_w(x, x') = \sqrt{\sum_{j \leq m} w_j (x^j - x'^j)^2}.$$

For each i, define

$$\hat{y}_i^s = \frac{\sum_{j \neq i} s(x_j, x_i) y_j}{\sum_{j \neq i} s(x_j, x_i)}$$

and

$$SSE(w) = \sum_{i=1}^{n} (y_i - \hat{y}_i^s)^2.$$

It is now a well-defined question, which vector $w \in \mathbb{R}_+^m$ minimizes $SSE(w)$ for the given database. This vector $\hat{w}$ will be used to define the empirical similarity, $s_{\hat{w}}$.

Gilboa *et al.* (2006) develop this idea and the statistical method for similarity estimation. Gilboa *et al.* (2007) further argue that when we use the empirical similarity to weigh relative frequencies, the resulting probabilities can be viewed as "objective." Objectivity should be taken here with a grain of salt: one may choose different functional forms of s, different metrics d, and various goodness-of-fit criteria. Still, the probabilities we obtain, say, in the medical example, can be computed by a statistician without any input from a physician. That is, the various choices we make in order to obtain these probabilities are of the type of choices that statisticians typically make when estimating models. There is no subjective, domain-specific intuition that is needed for the computation of these probabilities.

---

[5] The negative exponent of a norm is justified in Billot *et al.* (2008). The particular choice of the weighted Euclidean norm is but an example.

You may recall that the concatenation and combination axioms were not suggested as universal principles and that we identified some classes of counterexamples to them. One of these included situations in which the similarity function itself is learnt from the data. Unfortunately, this is precisely what we propose to do here: the "empirical similarity" is the similarity function that resulted from such learning. How can we still use the similarity-weighted formula, which was justified only when such learning does not take place?

One possible way out is to assume that learning of the similarity function takes place only in certain periods, between which there are long sequences of no-learning periods. This assumption seems psychologically realistic: people evidently learn from their experience what features of the similarity function are more important, but they do not appear to perform this type of learning with each and every new piece of evidence. One reason could be that this assumption also makes sense from a computational viewpoint: the computation of the similarity function is not a trivial task, and it does not seem efficient to recalculate it every period. Assume now that we are facing a long sequence of no-learning periods. Over this sequence, the concatenation axiom makes sense. Let us conjecture that Theorem 19.1 can be extended to the case in which all databases are bounded in their length, providing an approximation of formula (19.1). If this is true, one can try to learn the similarity function to be used in this approximated formula over the (long but finite) sequence of periods of no-learning that one is facing.

Another approach would be to relax the assumption that there is a unique similarity function and, correspondingly, a unique probability, and to allow a set of similarity functions, resulting in a set of probabilities.[6] This would seem a more consistent approach in the sense that, aware of the fact that the similarity function has still to be learned, the reasoner considers a set of similarity functions and does not commit to a single one too soon.

Be that as it may, the process by which observations are used for the generation of probabilistic beliefs clearly calls for further research.

Beyond these interpretational issues, you may not be excited about this definition of "objective" probabilities by similarity-weighted frequencies coupled with the empirical similarity function. One reason is that this definition captures only case-to-case induction. Indeed, we have mentioned that the combination and concatenation axioms do not appear reasonable when the reasoner engages in case-to-rule induction followed by deduction (from rules to specific cases in the future). As mentioned earlier, this type of rule-based learning in the context of probabilities is exemplified by logistic regression. Whereas formula (19.1) ignores trends and focuses on similarity, logistic regression does the opposite: it attempts to find (linear) rules and ignores similarity to particular cases. Human reasoning involves both analogies and generalizations, both cases and rules. A priori, none of them seems to have a stronger claim to "objectivity" than the other.

---

[6] Eichberger and Guerdjikova (2007) also extend Theorem 19.1 to a set of probabilities (or a "multiple prior") setup. They use a single similarity function.

Better definitions of objective probabilities would be obtained if we could (i) have reasonable criteria for the choice between rule-based and case-based probabilities, and (ii) have models that combine the two. Both of these are important challenges for future research.

In any event, it seems that neither similarity-weighted frequencies nor logistic regression would offer serious contenders for the title of "objective probabilities" in Example (4) (Chapter 1). In this example (involving war in the Middle East), observations are very different from each other, and they are also intricately causally related. We can try to identify patterns of causal relationships and redefine "observations" accordingly. But we will then find that our database involves very little observations, which are not very similar to the case at hand. It is not clear that one can indeed define objective probabilities in such examples. Recalling that this type of problem was also a major challenge for the behavioral definitions of subjective probabilities, I am left suspicious when I hear "probability" used in such contexts.

CHAPTER 20

Future Research

The discussion in the previous chapters offers several challenges to current research. The first is to develop better models of probabilities, in particular, of objective probabilities. It would be desirable to have probabilities that use analogies to cases, but that also employ general rules and theories. Beyond combination of case-based and rule-based reasoning, we may wish to model explicit causal theories, as is done by Bayesian networks (Pearl, 1986). These may be combined with similarity-weighted frequencies to generate better probabilistic assessments. In such a model, the Bayesian network reflects the presumed causal relationships, and the conditional probabilities attached to edges in the network can be derived from similarity-weighted frequencies employing an empirical similarity function.

Relaxing the requirement of probabilistic representation of beliefs, one can go back to models involving sets of probabilities, or nonadditive measures, and ask where do these emerge from, trying to model the cognitive processes that generate them. And if one continues to be more modest in one's demands, one may ask whether models of qualitative likelihood relations can be upgraded to include not only analogies and case-based reasoning, but also models, theories, and rules.

Going further down the line, we can also decide to forget about beliefs altogether. It is possible that there is no rational way to generate beliefs in some of the complicated examples we were discussing, and we may have to learn to live with this fact. This would probably mean that we will need models of decision making under uncertainty that do not make explicit references to beliefs. Such models will probably have a much more descriptive flavor, and their claim to rationality will be qualified. In Gilboa and Schmeidler (2001) we developed a theory of case-based decisions, which is of this type. The theory assumes that people choose acts that did well in similar past cases, but it makes no reference to beliefs, probabilistic or otherwise. However, the formal models in Gilboa and Schmeidler (2001) still relied on the combination axiom. Models that would involve more sophisticated reasoning would need to generalize the theory by relaxing this axiom.

One can also imagine a theory of rule-based decisions. Rules can be used (as hinted earlier) to generate predictions and define beliefs, where these are used for decision making. But we can also think of behavioral rules that directly specify which act to take. Mirroring the use of the combination axiom (and additive models) in case-based beliefs and case-based decisions, it is possible that there will be some similarity between models of rules as guides to the generation of beliefs and rules as guides to choices. In both applications, rules will have to be evaluated based on their past performance – be it success in predicting the future or success in obtaining desirable outcomes. In both applications one may also have a priori biases for or against certain rules, based on their simplicity, prior reasonability, and so forth. Moreover, it is possible that the combination axiom, which was found rather restrictive when applied to the learning from past to future cases, may be more reasonable when applied to learning from cases to rules, as exemplified by the likelihood maximization example (Example D in Section 17.2).[1]

There are many directions in which decision theory can be improved upon. We can certainly deepen our understanding of the meaning of probability, as of utility, and we also need to better understand when such concepts are useful and when other concepts are more appropriate. As in the example of case-based and rule-based reasoning, we probably need a variety of theories, elegant unifications thereof, as well as meta-theories that tell us when we should use each theory. While a unified, clean theory may not be around the corner, we definitely seem to be living in interesting times.

---

[1] This axiomatic derivation of the maximum likelihood principle was extended to an additive trade-off between the log-likelihood function and an a priori bias in Gilboa and Schmeidler (2007).

References

Aho, A. V., J. E. Hopcroft, and J. D. Ullman (1974), *The Design and Analysis of Computer Algorithms*, Addison-Wesley Series in Computer Science and Information Processing. Reading, MA: Addison-Wesley.

Akaike, H. (1954), "An Approximation to the Density Function," *Annals of the Institute of Statistical Mathematics*, **6**: 127–132.

———— (1974), "A New Look at the Statistical Model Identification," *IEEE Transactions on Automatic Control*, **19** (6): 716–723.

Akerlof, G. A. (1970), "The Market for 'Lemons': Quality Uncertainty and the Market Mechanism," *The Quarterly Journal of Economics*, **84**: 488–500.

Allais, M. (1953), "Le Comportement de L'Homme Rationnel devant le Risque: Critique des Postulats et Axiomes de l'Ecole Américaine," *Econometrica*, **21**: 503–546.

Alt, F. (1936), "On the Measurability of Utility," in J. S. Chipman, L. Hurwicz, M. K. Richter, and H. F. Sonnenschein (eds.), *Preferences, Utility, and Demand, A. Minnesota Symposium*. New York: Harcourt Brace Jovanovich, Inc., pp. 424–431, ch. 20. [Translation of "Uber die Messbarheit des Nutzens," *Zeitschrift fuer Nationaloekonomie*, **7**: 161–169.]

Anscombe, F. J., and R. J. Aumann (1963), "A Definition of Subjective Probability," *The Annals of Mathematics and Statistics*, **34**: 199–205.

Aragones, E., I. Gilboa, A. W. Postlewaite, and D. Schmeidler (2005), "Fact-Free Learning," *American Economic Review*, **95**: 1355–1368.

Arrow, K. J. (1951), "Alternative Approaches to the Theory of Choice in Risk-Taking Situations," *Econometrica*, **19**: 404–437.

———— (1986), "Rationality of Self and Others in an Economic System," *Journal of Business*, **59**: S385–S399.

Aumann, R. J. (1962), "Utility Theory without the Completeness Axiom," *Econometrica*, **30**: 445–462.

Bayes, T. (1763), "An Essay towards Solving a Problem in the Doctrine of Chances," Communicated by Mr. Price, *Philosophical Transactions of the Royal Society of London*, **53**: 370–418.

Beja, A., and I. Gilboa (1992), "Numerical Representations of Imperfectly Ordered Preferences (A Unified Geometric Exposition)," *Journal of Mathematical Psychology*, **36**: 426–449.

Bernoulli, D. (1738/1954), "Exposition of a New Theory on the Measurement of Risk," *Econometrica*, **22**: 23–36.

Bernoulli, J. (1713), *Ars Conjectandi*. Translated into German by R. Haussner (1899) as "Wahrscheinlichkeitsrechnung," in *Ostwald's Klassiker der Exakten Wissenschaften*, 107, 108. Leipzig: W. Englemann.

Bertrand J. (1907), *Calcul de Probabilité*, 2nd edition. Paris: Gauthiers Villars.

Bewley, T. (2002), "Knightian Decision Theory: Part I," *Decisions in Economics and Finance*, **25**: 79–110. Working Paper, 1986.

Billot, A., I. Gilboa, D. Samet, and D. Schmeidler (2005), "Probabilities as Similarity-Weighted Frequencies," *Econometrica*, **73**: 1125–1136.

Billot, A., I. Gilboa, and D. Schmeidler (2008), "Axiomatization of an Exponential Similarity Function," *Mathematical Social Sciences*, **55**: 107–115.

Blume, L., A. Brandenburger, and E. Dekel (1991), "Lexicographic Probabilities and Choice under Uncertainty," *Econometrica*, **59**: 61–79.

Cantor, G. (1915), *Contributions to the Founding of the Theory of Tranfinite Numbers*. Translated and provided with an introduction and notes by Ph. E. B. Jourdain. Chicago/London: The Open Court Publishing Company.

Carnap, R. (1923), "Uber die Aufgabe der Physik und die Andwednung des Grundsatze der Einfachstheit," *Kant-Studien*, **28**: 90–107.

Chaitin, G. J. (1966), "On the Length of Programs for Computing Binary Sequences," *Journal of the Association of Computing Machines*, **13**: 547–569.

Charness, G., E. Karni, and D. Levin (2008), "On the Conjunction Fallacy in Probability Judgment: New Experimental Evidence," mimeo.

Chernoff, H., and H. Teicher (1958), "A Central Limit Theorem for Sums of Interchangeable Random Variables," *Annals of Mathematical Statistics*, **29**: 118–130.

Chew, S. H. (1983), "A Generalization of the Quasilinear Mean with Applications to the Measurement of Income Inequality and Decision Theory Resolving the Allais Paradox," *Econometrica*, **51**: 1065–1092.

Choquet, G. (1953–1954), "Theory of Capacities," *Annales de l'Institut Fourier*, **5** (Grenoble): 131–295.

Connor, J. A. (2006), *Pascal's Wager*. New York: HarperCollins.

Cover, T., and P. Hart (1967), "Nearest Neighbor Pattern Classification," *IEEE Transactions on Information Theory*, **13**: 21–27.

de Finetti, B. (1930), "Funzione caratteristica di un fenomeno aleatorio," *Atti della Academia Nazionale dei Lincei Rendiconti, Class di Scienze Fisiche, Matematiche e Naturali*, **4**: 86–133.

——— (1937), "La Prévision: Ses Lois Logiques, Ses Sources Subjectives," *Annales de l'Institut Henri Poincaré*, **7**: 1–68.

Debreu, G. (1959), *The Theory of Value: An Axiomatic Analysis of Economic Equilibrium*. New Haven, CT: Yale University Press.

DeGroot, M. H. (1975), *Probability and Statistics*. Reading, MA: Addison-Wesley.

Dekel, E. (1986), "An Axiomatic Characterization of Preferences under Uncertainty: Weakening the Independence Axiom," *Journal of Economic Theory*, **40**: 304–318.

Dekel, E., B. L. Lipman, and A. Rustichini (2001), "Representing Preferences with a Unique Subjective State Space," *Econometrica*, **69**: 891–934.

Dow, J., and S. R. C. Werlang (1992), "Uncertainty Aversion, Risk Aversion, and the Optimal Choice of Portfolio," *Econometrica*, **60**: 197–204.

Dreze, J. H. (1961), "Les Fondements Logiques de l'Utilite Cardinale et de la Probabilité Subjective," *La Décision*. Paris: Colloques Internationaux du CNRS.

—— (1987), *Essays on Economic Decision under Uncertainty*. Cambridge, UK: Cambridge University Press.

Edwards, W. (1954), "The Theory of Decision Making," *Psycological Bulletin*, **51**: 380–417.

Eichberger, J., and A. Guerdjikova (2007), "Multiple Priors as Similarity-Weighted Frequencies," mimeo.

Ellsberg, D. (1961), "Risk, Ambiguity and the Savage Axioms," *Quarterly Journal of Economics*, **75**: 643–669.

Epstein, L. G., and J. Miao (2003), "A Two-Person Dynamic Equilibrium under Ambiguity," *Journal of Economic Dynamics and Control*, **27**: 1253–1288.

Epstein, L. G., and M. Schneider (2003), "Recursive Multiple Priors," *Journal of Economic Theory*, **113**: 32–50.

Epstein, L. G., and T. Wang (1994), "Intertemporal Asset Pricing under Knightian Uncertainty," *Econometrica*, **62**: 283–322.

—— (1995), "Uncertainty, Risk-Neutral Measures and Security Price Booms and Crashes," *Journal of Economic Theory*, **67**: 40–82.

Fechner, G. T. (1860), *Elemente der Psychophysik*, 2 vols. [Elements of Psychophysics]. English translation: *Elements of Psychophysics* (1966). New York: Holt, Reinhart and Winston.

Feller, W. (2005), *An Introduction to Probability Theory and Its Applications*, 2nd edition. New York: John Wiley and Sons.

Fishburn, P. C. (1970a), *Utility Theory for Decision Making*. New York: John Wiley and Sons.

—— (1970b), "Intransitive Indifference in Preference Theory: A Survey," *Operations Research*, **18**: 207–228.

—— (1982), "Foundations of Risk Measurement. II: Effects of Gains on Risk," *Journal of Mathematical Psychology*, **22**: 226–242.

—— (1985), *Interval Orders and Interval Graphs*. New York: John Wiley and Sons.

Fix, E., and J. Hodges (1951), "Discriminatory Analysis. Nonparametric Discrimination: Consistency Properties," Technical Report 4, Project Number 21-49-004. Randolph Field, TX: USAF School of Aviation Medicine.

—— (1952), "Discriminatory Analysis: Small Sample Performance," Technical Report 21-49-004. Randolph Field, TX: USAF School of Aviation Medicine.

Gajdos, T., T. Hayashi, J.-M. Tallon, and J.-C. Vergnaud (2007), "Attitude toward Imprecise Information," mimeo.

Ghirardato, P. (2002), "Revisiting Savage in a Conditional World," *Economic Theory*, **20**: 83–92.

Ghirardato, P., F. Maccheroni, and M. Marinacci (2005), "Certainty Independence and the Separation of Utility and Beliefs," *Journal of Economic Theory*, **120**: 129–136.

Ghirardato, P., and M. Marinacci (2001), "Risk, Ambiguity, and the Separation of Utility and Beliefs," *Mathematics of Operations Research*, **26**: 864–890.

Gibbard, A., and W. L. Harper (1978), "Counterfactuals and Two Kinds of Expected Utility," *Foundations and Applications of Decision Theory*, **1**: 125–162.

Gibbard, A., and H. Varian (1978), "Economic Models," *Journal of Philosophy*, **75**: 664–677.

Gigerenzer, G., and U. Hoffrage (1995), "How to Improve Bayesian Reasoning without Instructions: Frequency Formats," *Psychological Review*, **102**: 684–704.

Gilboa, I., and R. Lapson (1995), "Aggregation of Semi-Orders: Intransitive Indifference Makes a Difference," *Economic Theory*, **5**: 109–126.

Gilboa, I., O. Lieberman, and D. Schmeidler (2006), "Empirical Similarity," *Review of Economics and Statistics*, **88**: 433–444.

—— (2007), "On the Definition of Objective Probabilities by Empirical Similarity," mimeo.

Gilboa, I., F. Maccheroni, M. Marinacci, and D. Schmeidler (2008), "Objective and Subjective Rationality in a Multiple Prior Model," mimeo.

Gilboa, I., A. Postlewaite, and D. Schmeidler (2004), "Rationality of Belief," mimeo. Revised, 2007.

—— (2007), "Probabilities in Economic Modeling," mimeo.

Gilboa, I., and D. Schmeidler (1989), "Maxmin Expected Utility with a Non-Unique Prior," *Journal of Mathematical Economics*, **18**: 141–153.

—— (1995), "Case-Based Decision Theory," *The Quarterly Journal of Economics*, **110**: 605–639.

—— (1997), "Act Similarity in Case-Based Decision Theory," *Economic Theory*, **9**: 47–61.

—— (2001), *A Theory of Case-Based Decisions*. Cambridge: Cambridge University Press.

—— (2002), "A Cognitive Foundation of Probability," *Mathematics of Operations Research*, **27**: 68–81.

—— (2003), "Inductive Inference: An Axiomatic Approach," *Econometrica*, **71**: 1–26.

—— (2007), "Likelihood and Simplicity: An Axiomatic Approach," mimeo.

Good, I. J. (1967), "The White Shoe Is a Red Herring," *British Journal for the Philosophy of Science*, **17**: 322.

—— (1968), "The White Shoe qua Herring Is Pink," *British Journal for the Philosophy of Science*, **19**: 156–157.

—— (1986), "A Minor Comment Concerning Hempel's Paradox of Confirmation," *Journal of Statistics, Computation and Simulation*, **24**: 320–321.

Goodman, N. (1954), *Fact, Fiction, and Forecast*. Cambridge, MA: Harvard University Press.

Hacking, I. (1975), *The Emergence of Probability*. Cambridge: Cambridge University Press.

Halmos, P. R. (1950), *Measure Theory*. Princeton, NJ: Van Nostrand.

Handa, J. (1977), "Risk, Probabilities and a New Theory of Cardinal Utility," *Journal of Political Economics*, **85**: 97–122.

Hansen, L. P., and T. J. Sargent (2001), "Acknowledging Misspecification in Macroeconomic Theory," *Review of Economic Dynamics*, **4**: 519–535.

—— (2003), "Robust Control of Forward-Looking Models," *Journal of Monetary Economics*, **50**: 581–604.

—— (2008), *Robustness*. Princeton, NJ: Princeton University Press.

Hansen, L. P., T. J. Sargent, and T. D. Tallarini (1999), "Robust Permanent Income and Pricing," *Review of Economic Studies*, **66**: 873–907.

Hanson, N. R. (1958), *Patterns of Discovery*. Cambridge, England: Cambridge University Press.

Helson, H. (1964), *Adaptation Level Theory: An Experimental and Systematic Approach to Behavior*. New York: Harper and Row.

Hempel, C. G. (1945), "Studies in the Logic of Confirmation I," *Mind*, **54**: 1–26.

—— (1966), "Studies in the Logic of Confirmation," in *Probability, Confirmation and Simplicity*. New York: Odyssey Press, pp. 145–183.

Herstein, I. N., and J. Milnor (1953), "An Axiomatic Approach to Measurable Utility," *Econometrica*, **21**: 291–297.

Hume, D. (1748), *An Enquiry Concerning Human Understanding*. Oxford: Clarendon Press.

Jamison, D. T., and L. J. Lau (1977), "The Nature of Equilibrium with Semiordered Preferences," *Econometrica*, **45**: 1595–1605.

Jeffrey, R. C. (1965). *The Logic of Decision*. New York: McGraw-Hill.

Jensen, N.-E. (1967), "An Introduction to Bernoullian Utility Theory, I, II," *Swedish Journal of Economics*, **69**: 163–183, 229–247.

Kahneman, D., J. L. Knetsch, and R. H. Thaler (1991), "The Endowment Effect, Loss Aversion, and Status Quo Bias: Anomalies," *Journal of Economic Perspectives*, **5**: 193–206.

Kahneman, D., and A. Tversky (1979), "Prospect Theory: An Analysis of Decision under Risk," *Econometrica*, **47**: 263–291.

Kane, R. (2005), *A Contemporary Introduction to Free Will*. New York/Oxford: Oxford University Press.

Kannai, Y. (1963), "Existence of a Utility in Infinite Dimensional Partially Ordered Spaces," *Israel Journal of Mathematics*, **1**: 229–234.

Karni, E. (1985), *Decision Making under Uncertainty: The Case of State-Dependent Preferences*. Cambridge: Harvard University Press.

_____ (1996), "Probabilities and Beliefs," *Journal of Risk and Uncertainty*, **13**: 249–262.

Karni, E., and P. Mongin (2000), "On the Determination of Subjective Probability by Choices," *Management Science*, **46**: 233–248.

Karni, E., and D. Schmeidler (1981), "An Expected Utility Theory for State-Dependent Preferences," Working Paper 48-80. The Foerder Institute of Economic Research, Tel-Aviv University.

_____ (1991a), "Atemporal Dynamic Consistency and Expected Utility Theory," *Journal of Economic Theory*, **54**: 401–408.

_____ (1991b), "Utility Theory with uncertainty," in W. Hildenbrand and H. Sonnenschein (eds.), *Handbook of Mathematical Economics 4*. Amsterdam: North Holland, pp. 1763–1831.

Karni, E., D. Schmeidler, and K. Vind (1983), "On State Dependent Preferences and Subjective Probabilities," *Econometrica*, **51**: 1021–1031.

Keynes, J. M. (1921), *A Treatise on Probability*. London: MacMillan and Co.

Klibanoff, P., M. Marinacci, and S. Mukerji (2005), "A Smooth Model of Decision Making under Ambiguity," *Econometrica*, **73**: 1849–1892.

Knight, F. H. (1921), *Risk, Uncertainty, and Profit*. Boston/New York: Houghton Mifflin.

Kolmogorov, A. N. (1963), "On Tables of Random Numbers," *Sankhya Series A*, **25**: 369–376.

_____ (1965), "Three Approaches to the Quantitative Definition of Information," *Probability and Information Transmission*, **1**: 4–7.

Kopylov, I. (2007), "Subjective Probabilities on 'Small' Domains," *Journal of Economic Theory*, **133**: 236–265.

Kraft, C. H., J. W. Pratt, and T. Seidenberg (1959), "Intuitive Probability on Finite Sets," *Annals of Mathematical Statistics*, **30**: 408–419.

Kreps, D. (1988), *Notes on the Theory of Choice. Underground Classics in Economics*. Boulder, CO: Westview Press.

Kuhn, T. S. (1962), *The Structure of Scientific Revolutions*. Chicago, IL: University of Chicago Press.

Kyburg, H. E., and H. E. Smokler (1964), *Studies in Subjective Probability*. New York: John Wiley and Sons.

Leshno, J. (2007), "Similarity-Weighted Frequencies with Zero Values," mimeo.

Levi, I. (1980), *The Enterprise of Knowledge*. Cambridge, MA: MIT Press.

Luce, R. D. (1956), "Semiorders and a Theory of Utility Discrimination," *Econometrica*, **24**: 178–191.

Luce, R. D., and D. H. Krantz (1971), "Conditional Expected Utility," *Econometrica*, **39**, 253–271.

Maccheroni, F., M. Marinacci, and A. Rustichini (2006a), "Ambiguity Aversion, Robustness, and the Variational Representation of Preferences," *Econometrica*, **74**: 1447–1498.

——— (2006b), "Dynamic Variational Preference," *Journal of Economic Theory*, **128**: 4–44.

——— (2004), "Almost-Objective uncertainty," *Economic Theory*, **24**: 1–54.

Machina, M. J., and D. Schmeidler (1992), "A More Robust Definition of Subjective Probability," *Econometrica*, **60**: 745–780.

Markowitz, H. M. (1952), "The Utility of Wealth," *Journal of Political Economy*, **60**: 151–158.

Marks, L. E., and D. Algom (1998), "Psychophysical Scaling," in M. H. Birnbaum (ed.), *Measurement, Judgment, and Decision Making*. New York: Academic Press, pp. 81–136.

Mas-Colell, A., M. Whinston, and J. Green (1995), *Microeconomic Theory*. New York: Oxford Press.

Milgrom, P., and N. Stokey (1982), "Information, Trade, and Common Knowledge," *Journal of Economic Theory*, **26**: 17–27.

Mosteller, F., and P. Nogee (1951), "An Experimental Measurement of Utility," *Journal of Political Economy*, **59**: 371–404.

Mukerji, S. (1998), "Ambiguity Aversion and the Incompleteness of Contractual Form," *American Economic Review*, **88**: 1207–1232.

Nash, J. F. (1951), "Non-Cooperative Games," *Annals of Mathematics*, **54**: 286–295.

Nehring, K. (2002, 2008), "Imprecise Probabilistic Beliefs as a Context for Decision Making under Ambiguity," forthcoming.

Niebuhr, R. (1976), *Justice and Mercy*. New York: Harper and Row.

Nishimura, K., and H. Ozaki (2004), "Search and Knightian Uncertainty," *Journal of Economic Theory*, **119**: 299–333.

Nozick, R. (1969), "Newcomb's Problem and Two Principles of Choice," in *Essays in Honor of Carl G. Hempel*. Dordrecht Holland: Reidel, pp. 107–133.

Odean, T. (1998), "Are Investors Reluctant to Realize Their Losses?," *Journal of Finance*, **53**: 1775–1798.

Parzen, E. (1962), "On the Estimation of a Probability Density Function and the Mode," *Annal of Mathematical Statistics*, **33**: 1065–1076.

Pearl, J. (1986), "Fusion, Propagation, and Structuring in Belief Networks," *Artificial Intelligence*, **29**: 241–288.

Penrose, R. (1997), *The Large, the Small, and the Human Mind*. Cambridge: Cambridge University Press.

Popper, K. R. (1934), *Logik der Forschung*, English edition (1958), *The Logic of Scientific Discovery*. London: Hutchinson and Co. Reprinted (1961), New York: Science Editions.

Preston, M. G., and P. Baratta (1948), "An Experimental Study of the Auction Value of an Uncertain Outcome," *American Journal of Psychology*, **61**: 183–193.

Quiggin, J. (1982), "A Theory of Anticipated Utility," *Journal of Economic Behaviorand Organization*, **3**: 225–243.

Quine, W. V. (1953), "Two Dogmas of Empiricism," in *From a Logical Point of View*. Cambridge, MA: Harvard University Press.

——— (1969a), "Epistemology Naturalized," in *Ontological Relativity and Other Essays*. New York: Columbia University Press.

Ramsey, F. P. (1931), "Truth and Probability," in *The Foundation of Mathematics and Other Logical Essays*. London: Routledge and Kegan Paul, pp. 156–198.

Reiter, R. (1980), "A Logic for Default Reasoning," *Artificial Intelligence*, **13**: 81–132.

Rosenblatt, M. (1956), "Remarks on Some Nonparametric Estimates of a Density Function," *Annal of Mathematical Statistics*, **27**: 832–837.

Rosenmueller, J. (1971), "On Core and Value," *Methods of Operations Research*, **9**: 84–104.

——— (1972), "Some Properties of Convex Set Functions, Part II," *Methods of Operations Research*, **17**: 287–307.

Rostek, M. (2006), "Quantile Maximization in Decision Theory," forthcoming in the *Review of Economic Studies*.

Rubinstein, A. (1988), "Similarity and Decision-Making under Risk," *Journal of Economic Theory*, **46**: 145–153.

Russell, B. (1946). *A History of Western Philosophy*. Great Britain: Allen & Unwin.

Savage, L. J. (1954), *The Foundations of Statistics*. New York: John Wiley and Sons. Second edition in 1972, Dover.

Schmeidler, D. (1986), "Integral Representation without Additivity," *Proceedings of the American Mathematical Society*, **97**: 255–261.

——— (1989), "Subjective Probability and Expected Utility without Additivity," *Econometrica*, **57**: 571–587.

Scott, D. W. (1992), *Multivariate Density Estimation: Theory, Practice, and Visualization*. New York: John Wiley and Sons.

Searle, J. R. (2004), *Freedom and Neurobiology: Reflections on Free Will, Language, and Political Power*. New York: Cambridge University Press.

Seo, K. (2007), "Ambiguity and Second-Order Belief," mimeo.

Shafer, G. (1986), "Savage Revisited," *Statistical Science*, **1**: 463–486.

Shapley, L. S. (1965), "Notes on *n*-Person Games VII: Cores of Convex Games," The RAND Corporation R. M. Reprinted as Shapley, L. S. (1972), "Cores of Convex Games," *International Journal of Game Theory*, **1**: 11–26.

Shefrin, H., and M. Statman (1985), "The Disposition to Sell Winners Too Early and Ride Losers Too Long: Theory and Evidence," *Journal of Finance*, **40**: 777–790.

Silverman, B. W. (1986), *Density Estimation for Statistics and Data Analysis*. London/ New York: Chapman and Hall.

Simon, H. A. (1957), *Models of Man*. New York: John Wiley and Sons.

——— (1986), "Rationality in Psychology and Economics," *Journal of Business*, **59**: S209–S224.

Simpson, E. H. (1951), "The Interpretation of Interaction in Contingency Tables," *Journal of the Royal Statistical Society, Series B*, **13**: 238–241.

Sober, E. (1975), *Simplicity*. Oxford: Clarendon Press.

Solomonoff, R. (1964), "A Formal Theory of Inductive Inference I, II," *Information Control*, **7**: 1–22, 224–254.

Stevens, S. S. (1957), "On the Psychophysical Law," *Psychological Review*, **64**: 153–181.

Tversky, A., and D. Kahneman (1974), "Judgment under Uncertainty: Heuristics and Biases," *Science*, **185**: 1124–1131.

―――― (1981), "The Framing of Decisions and the Psychology of Choice," *Science*, **211**: 453–458.

―――― (1992), "Advances in Prospect Theory: Cumulative Representation of Uncertainty," *Journal of Risk and Uncertainty*, **5**: 297–323.

Villegas, C. (1964), "On Quantitative Probability σ-Algebras," *Annals of Mathematical Statistics*, **35**: 1787–1796.

von Neumann, J., and O. Morgenstern (1944), *Theory of Games and Economic Behavior*. Princeton, NJ: Princeton University Press.

Wakker, P. P. (1993a), "Unbounded Utility for Savage's 'Foundations of Statistics,' and other Models," *Mathematics of Operations Research*, **18**: 446–485.

―――― (1993b), "Clarification of Some Mathematical Misunderstandings about Savage's Foundations of Statistics, 1954," *Mathematical Social Sciences*, **25**: 199–202.

―――― (2008), *Prospect Theory*. Cambridge: Cambridge University Press, forthcoming.

Weber, E. H. (1978), *The Sense of Touch* (De Tactu – Der Tastsinn), 1st edition. Translated by H. E. Ross, and D. J. Murray. Preface by J. D. Mollon. London: Academic Press.

Weymark, J. A. (1981), "Generalized Gini Inequality Indices," *Mathematical Social Sciences*, **1**: 409–430.

Wittgenstein, L. (1922), *Tractatus Logico Philosophicus*. London: Routledge/Kegan Paul.

Yaari, M. E. (1987), "The Dual Theory of Choice under Risk," *Econometrica*, **55**: 95–115.

Zajonc, R. B. (1980), "Feeling and Thinking: Preferences Need No Inferences," *American Psychologist*, **35**: 151–175.

Index

accuracy, 113
  Cantor's theorem and, 56, 63–66
  determinism and, 5–6
  frequency approach and, 33–34
  measurement and, 6n2
  principle of indifference and, 19
  role of theories and, 73–74
  smooth beliefs and, 18–19
acts
  causality and, 114–15 (*see also* causality)
  definition of states and, 114–15
  Savage's theorem and, 96–97
additivity, 90–91, 94, 105–7
Aho, A. V., 24n7
Akaike, H., 176
Akerlof, G. A., 169
algebraic approach, 83–84, 142, 147n2, 173
Algom, Daniel, 65n14
algorithms
  Cantor's theorem and, 57, 62
  objectivity and, 140
  states definition and, 114
  Turing machines and, 24–25, 31
Allais's paradox, 157
Alt, F., 70n19
ambiguity axiom, 148–49, 165
Anscombe, F. J., 95, 138
Anscombe-Aumann theorem, 151
  axiomatic approach and, 142–44
  De Finetti's theorem and, 93n3
  model of maxmin expected utility (MMEU) and, 163
  Savage's theorem and, 142–44

Aragones, E., 137n10
Archimedeanity
  Cantor's theorem and, 61
  qualitative beliefs and, 174, 177n3
  Savage's theorem and, 103–4, 111–12
Arrow, Kenneth, 14n2, 22n5, 139n1
Arrow securities, 75
asymmetry, 154–56, 158n7
Aumann, R. J., 95, 126–27, 138, 165n7
aversion, 160–64, 168
axiomatic approach, 188–89
  Anscombe-Aumann theorem and, 142–44
  Cantor's theorem and, 51–55, 59–66
  Choquet expected utility and, 148–53
  de Finetti's theorem and, 90–93
  descriptive interpretation and, 63–64
  empirical similarity and, 185
  existential qualifiers and, 81n6
  frequentist approach and, 185–86
  Luce's theorem and, 66–69
  maxmin expected utility and, 163, 166–67
  meta-scientific interpretation and, 59–62, 64
  normative interpretation and, 52, 56–58, 62–63
  objectivity and, 140
  observable tests and, 81n5
  qualitative beliefs and, 173–75, 177–79
  role of theories and, 72
  Savage's theorem and, 97–107, 111–12, 123–32, 136–37
  splicing functions and, 99
  sufficiency and, 91–92

axiomatic approach (*cont.*)
  Tversky on, 124
  utility and, 51–55
  von Neumann-Morgenstern theorem
    and, 83–88
  See also specific axiom

Baratta, P., 156
Bayes, T., 79, 109
Bayesian statistics
  basic definitions and, 40–41
  vs. classical statistics, 40–48
  confidence and, 44–46
  court decisions and, 46–47
  definition of states and, 114
  exchangeability and, 42–44
  gambler fallacy and, 41–42
  goals of, 46–48
  God and, 41
  Hempel's paradox of confirmation and,
    117–20
  ideological position of, 40
  law of large numbers and, 41–44
  maxmin expected utility and, 169
  networks and, 188
  Savage's theorem and, 130–33
  state space and, 40–41
  updating and, 47
behavior
  Anscombe-Aumann model and, 95,
    142–44
  Cantor's theorem and, 51–66
  Choquet expected utility and, 147–53
  cognitive approach and, 161–62,
    171–87
  definitions of state, 113–22
  exemplar learning and, 181
  maximization of utility and, 51–71,
    160–69
  normative interpretation and, 52,
    56–58, 62–63
  objectivity and, 138–41
  prospect theory and, 154–59
  rationality and, 138–41 (*see also*
    rationality)
  role of theories and, 72–77
  Savage's theorem and, 94–112, 123–37
  von Neumann-Morgenstern theorem
    and, 79–88

Beja, A., 68n18, 69
beliefs, 8n4
  case-based qualitative, 173–79
  cognitive approach and, 171–89
  concatenation and, 182–83
  confidence and, 5, 21, 34, 40, 44–46,
    162
  evolutionary psychology and, 31–34
  faith and, 39–40
  free will and, 5–7
  frequentist approach and, 180–89
  future research for, 188–89
  God's existence and, 39–40
  intentional concepts and, 101
  intuition and, 185 (*see also* intuition)
  language dependence and, 23–26,
    31–34
  law of large numbers and, 20–21, 36,
    41–44
  Pascal's wager and, 38–40
  principle of indifference and, 18–19
  qualitative probabilities and, 173–74
  Savage's theorem and, 130 (*see also*
    Savage's theorem)
  simplicity and, 23–30, 33–34
  subjective approach and, 37–48
  Tversky-Kahneman experiment and,
    37–38
  utility and, 51–71
Bernoulli, Daniel, 70, 78–79
Bernoulli, Jacob, 14, 20–21
Bernoulli random variables, 40
Bertrand's paradox, 15n3
bets
  de Finetti's theorem and, 90
  gambler fallacy and, 41–42
  Savage's theorem and, 133–36
Bewley, T., 40, 165, 167
Billot, A., 182, 185n5
Billot-Gilboa-Samet-Schmeidler
    theorem, 182–84, 186
binary distribution
  canonical state space and, 14–17
  Cantor's theorem and, 51–55, 59–67
  de Finetti's theorem and, 90, 97
  frequentist approach and, 24–26, 183
  maxmin expected utility and, 166
  qualitative beliefs and, 173
  Savage's theorem and, 97, 110, 137

von-Neumann-Morgenstern theorem
 and, 80
biseperable preferences, 165
Blume, L. A., 100

cancellation, 87, 110, 148, 157, 174n1
canonical state space
 coin tossing and, 16
 principle of indifference and, 14–17
 sequences and, 14–17
 uniform distribution and, 15–16
Cantelli, 106n10
Cantor, G., 51
Cantor's theorem, 86, 87n10
 axiomatic approach and, 51–55,
   59–66
 as characterization of preference
   relation, 51–53
 choice theory and, 57, 71
 completeness and, 51–52
 consumer theory and, 51–52
 continuity and, 53
 convergent series and, 54
 descriptive interpretation, 63–64
 infinity and, 54
 intransitive indifference and, 65–66
 limitations and, 64–66
 meta-scientific interpretation and,
   59–62, 64
 normative interpretation, 52, 62–63
 proof and, 53–55
 semiorders and, 65–66
 separability and, 51–54
 transitivity and, 51–52, 60–61
 utility and, 53–55, 59–67
 Weber's law and, 65–66
capacity, 147–49
cards, 14, 18–19, 73
Carnap, R., 60
case-based qualitative beliefs
 axiomatic approach and, 173–75,
   177–79
 decisions problem and, 173, 178
 four techniques for, 175–77
 prediction problem and, 173, 176–79
causality
 acts and, 114–15
 cognitive approach and, 171–72
 Newcomb's paradox and, 113–15

 outcomes and, 114–15
 qualitative beliefs and, 179
 Savage's theorem and, 114n1, 115–16
 states and, 113–16
central limit theorem, 21, 44n9
Chaos theory, 6
Charness, G., 141n5
Chernoff, H., 44n9
Chew, S. H., 85n8
choice theory
 Cantor's theorem and, 57, 71
 objectivity and, 138–41
 prospect theory and, 158n6
 Savage's theorem and, 124
Choquet, G., 147n3, 149n5
Choquet expected utility
 ambiguity and, 148
 axiomatic approach and, 148–53
 cognitive interpretation of, 161–62
 discontinuity and, 148–49
 Ellsberg's paradox and, 147, 151
 formal statement of, 152
 independence and, 152
 intuition and, 147–49
 maxmin expected utility and, 161–62,
   164
 monotonicity and, 149–52
 nonadditive probability and, 147–49
 probability vectors and, 152–53
 prospect theory and, 154, 158–59
 Riemann integral and, 148, 150
 Schmeidler and, 147–49, 151–52,
   159n8
 von Neumann-Morgenstern lotteries
   and, 152–53
Choquet integral, 149–51, 158–59
Christians, 40
Church's thesis, 25n9
classical statistics, 3
 Bayesian statistics and, 40–48
 confidence and, 44–45
 court decisions and, 46–47
 description of, 40–41
 exchangeability and, 42–44
 gambler fallacy and, 41–42
 goals of, 46–48
 principle of indifference and, 14
 ridiculous outcomes from, 45–46
 state space and, 40–41

classification problem, 57–58, 176–78, 182
coalition, 147n1, 160–61
cognitive approach
  causality and, 171–72
  Choquet expected utility and, 161–62
  frequentist approach and, 180–89
  qualitative beliefs and, 173–79
coin tossing, 3, 49
  canonical state space and, 16
  frequentist approach and, 34
  Hume's critique and, 21–22
  knowledge level and, 6
  principle of indifference and, 14, 16–17
  randomness and, 6
  Savage's theorem and, 104n7
  smooth beliefs and, 18–19
combination axiom
  frequentist approach and, 176, 183, 188–89
  qualitative beliefs and, 174, 177–79
  violations of, 179
comonotonicity, 150–52
completeness axiom, 51–52, 132
complexity
  evolutionary psychology and, 33–34
  Goodman's grue-bleen paradox and, 29
  Kolmogorov's, 23–26, 28n12
  Savage's theorem and, 137, 140n3
computers
  PASCAL programs and, 25, 28
  Turing machines and, 24–25, 31
concatenation axiom, 182–83, 186
conceptual frameworks, 74–76, 125
confidence
  free will and, 5
  frequentist approach and, 21, 34
  maxmim expected utility and, 162
  subjective probabilities and, 40, 44–46
confirmation
  concept of, 117
  Good's variation and, 118–19
  Hempel's paradox and, 116–20
  null set and, 118n3
  state-space formulation and, 117
Connor, J. A., 39n3
consistency axiom, 167–68
consumer theory
  decision theory and, 51–52, 80, 96
  de Finetti's theorem and, 90

Savage's theorem and, 96
  utility maximization and, 51–52
  von Neumann-Morgenstern theorem and, 80
consumption bundles, 75
continuity axiom
  Anscombe-Aumann theorem and, 143
  de Finetti's theorem and, 90
  Savage's theorem and, 106, 111–12
  von Neumann-Morgenstern theorem and, 80–81
  utility maximization and, 61
convergent series, 54
convex games, 160–62, 164
Cover, T., 177n3

Debreu, G., 52, 53, 90n1
decision matrices, 7, 183
  definition of states and, 115, 119, 121–22
  free will and, 12–13
  God's existence and, 39
  Monty-Hall three-door game and, 120–22
  Pascal and, 39
  qualitative beliefs and, 174–75
  Savage's theorem and, 134–35
  subjective probabilities and, 39, 43
decision theory, 1
  cognitive approach and, 171–87
  consumer theory and, 51–52, 80, 96
  definition of states and, 113–20
  dominance argument and, 67, 87, 113–15, 158n5
  embarrassment and, 139–40
  free will and, 5–13
  future research and, 188–89
  gambler fallacy and, 41–42
  game theory and, 78–79
  intransitive indifference and, 66
  knowledge and, 6–12
  Monty Hall three-door game and, 120–22
  multiple priors and, 40
  normative interpretation and, 52, 62–63
  objectivity and, 138–41
  Pascal's wager and, 38–40
  preference theory and, 67–69, 73, 97–103

prospect theory and, 154–59
rationality and, 10–12, 139–41 (*see also* rationality)
role of theories and, 72–77
rule-based theory and, 189
St. Petersburg paradox and, 70, 78–79
Savage's theorem and, 94–112, 123–37
subjective approach and, 37–48
utility and, 39–40, 49, 51–71, 109–10 (*see also* utility)
weakly dominant strategy and, 39
deduction, 22n4, 186
de Finetti, B., 90, 145
  Anscombe-Aumann theorem and, 143
  cancellation and, 148, 174n1
  exchangeability and, 42–44
  Choquet expected utility and, 148
  qualitative probabilities and, 110–11, 173–74
  Savage's theorem and, 103, 106, 110–11
  subjective approach and, 128, 130
de Finetti's theorem, 95, 100
  axiomatic approach and, 90–93
  bet function and, 90
  consumer theory and, 90
  formal statement of, 91
  meta-scientific interpretation and, 92
  normative interpretation and, 93
  proof, 91–92
  subjective approach and, 89–94
DeGroot, M. H., 15n3, 45n10
Dekel, E., 85n8, 137n9
Desargues, 184n3
descriptive interpretation, 63–64
determinism
  causal, 6–7, 36, 49, 113–16, 171–72, 179
  free will and, 6–8
  initial conditions and, 6, 20n2
  knowledge level and, 6, 8
  material, 6
  predetermined decisions and, 8
dice, 14, 23, 44–45, 94
discontinuity axiom, 148–49
disposition effect, 155–56
distribution
  binary, 14–17 (*see also* binary distribution)

Cantor's theorem and, 51–55, 59–67
central limit theorem and, 21
classical vs. Bayesian statistics, 40–48
confidence and, 44–46
dominance argument and, 67, 87, 113–15, 158n5
exchangeability and, 42–44
law of large numbers and, 20–21, 36, 41–44
lotteries and, 79–82 (*see also* lotteries)
qualitative beliefs and, 173–79
Savage's theorem and, 94–112
uniform, 15–19
von Neumann-Morgenstern theorem and, 79–88
diversity axiom, 174
dominance
  definition of states and, 113–15
  first-order stochastic, 158n5
  Pareto, 67
  von Neumann-Morgenstern theorem and, 87
Dow, J., 168
Dreze, J. H., 126n2, 127
Dubins, Lester, 106
Duhem, 59

economics, 7
  Cantor's theorem and, 59, 71
  di Finetti's theorem and, 90
  maxmin expected utility and, 165n8
  prospect theory and, 154
  role of theories and, 75
  von Neumann-Morgenstern theorem and, 78
Eichberger, J., 186n6
Einstein, Albert, 59
Ellsberg's paradox
  Choquet expected utility and, 147, 151
  maxmin expected utility and, 167–68
  Savage's theorem and, 133–36, 140
embarrassment, 139–40
empirical similarity, 180–81, 184–88
empty sets, 118n3
endowment effect, 155–56
epistemology, 59
Epstein, L. G., 165, 168–69

equations
  Choquet integral, 150
  Goodman's grue-bleen paradox, 28–29
  kernel estimation, 181
  maxmin expected utility, 162, 167
  maximization of utility, 51, 54, 67–68
  probability transformation model, 156
  qualitative beliefs, 175
  Savage's theorem, 105, 109–11
  von Neumann-Morgenstern theorem,
    83
  Weber's law, 65
equilibrium, 73–75, 79
Euclidean space, 175n2
evolutionary psychology, 31–34
exchangeability, 42–44
exemplar learning, 181
experience
  defined, 20
  evolutionary psychology and, 31–34
  Goodman's grue-bleen paradox and,
    22–23, 26–34
  Kolmogorov's complexity and, 23–26
  law of large numbers and, 20–21
  simplicity and, 23–30, 33–34
  Tversky-Kahneman experiment and,
    37–38
  Wittgenstein and, 24

faith, 39–40
Fate, 7
Fechner's law, 65n14, 66n15
Feller, W., 20n1
fineness, 111–12
finitely additive measures, 105–7
Fishburn, P. C., 68, 79, 109n11, 142, 144,
    158n5
Fisher, 40
Foucault, 76
framing effects, 140, 155
Frechet, 106n10
free will, 4
  belief and, 5–7, 8n4
  decision matrix and, 12–13
  determinism and, 6–8 (*see also*
    determinism)
  Heisenberg's principle of uncertainty
    and, 6–7
  as illusion, 10–12

inferences of, 5
knowledge and, 6–12
observableness of, 6–7
predetermined decisions and, 8
predicting behavior and, 5
problem of, 7–10
psychological, 7
rationality and, 10–12
subjective approach and, 7
frequentist approach, 3, 49, 89
  axiomatic approach and, 182–86
  Billot-Gilboa-Samet-Schmeidler
    theorem and, 182–84, 186
  central limit theorem and, 21
  cognitive approach and, 180–89
  coin tossing and, 34
  combination and, 176, 183, 188–89
  concatenation and, 186
  concept of, 21
  empirical similarity and, 180–81,
    184–88
  evolutionary psychology and, 31–34
  geometric approach and, 184
  Goodman's grue-bleen paradox and,
    22–23, 26–34
  Hume's critique and, 21–22
  induction and, 21–34, 180–81
  intuition and, 181, 185
  kernel estimation and, 181
  Kolmogorov complexity and, 23–26
  language dependence and, 23–26,
    31–34
  law of large numbers and, 20–21
  objective probabilities and, 184–87
  problems with, 21–36
  relative frequencies and, 20–36
  Savage's theorem and, 133
  Schmeidler and, 133
  similarity-weighted empirical
    frequencies and, 180–81
  simplicity and, 23–30, 33–34
Friedman, 74

gain-loss asymmetry, 154–56, 158n7
Gajdos, T., 165
gambler fallacy, 41–42
game theory
  convex games and, 160–62, 164
  maxmin expected utility and, 160–69

maxmin theorem and, 78–79
Monty Hall three-door game and, 120–22
transferable utility game and, 147n1
value of game, 79
geometric approach, 84–85, 94–95, 184
Ghiradato, P., 98, 165
Gibbard, A., 72n2, 114n1
Gigerenzer, G., 124
Gilboa, Itzhak, i, xiii-xiv
 Cantor's theorem and, 57n6
 empirical similarity and, 185
 frequentist approach and, 33n13, 182
 future research and, 188, 189n1
 interpersonal comparisons of utility and, 71n21
 Luce's theorem and, 68n18, 69
 maxmin expected utility and, 163, 166n9, 167n10
 objectivity and, 138–39
 qualitative beliefs and, 174n1, 175, 179
 role of theories and, 74–75
 Savage's theorem and, 130n4, 132n7
God
 Bayesian statistics and, 41
 free will and, 7, 12–13
 Pascal's wager and, 38–40
Good, I. J., 118–19
Goodman's grue-bleen paradox
 artificiality of, 26–31
 evolutionary psychology and, 31–34
 generalizations and, 26–30
 induction and, 22–23, 26–34
 language dependence and, 22–23, 26–34
 projection problem and, 27n11
 sequences and, 26–30
 simplicity vs. complexity, 27–30, 33–34
 social science and, 59
 theory of entrenchment and, 27n10
 value names and, 30–31
Guerdjikova, A., 186n6

Halmos, P. R., 20n1
handwriting, 178
Hansen, L. P., 169

Hanson, N. R., 76
Harper, W. L., 114n1
Hart, P., 177n3
Heisenberg's principle of uncertainty, 6–7, 60n10
Helson, H., 154n1
Hempel's paradox of confirmation
 Bayesian statistics and, 117–20
 Good's variation and, 118–19
 space formulation and, 117
 states and, 116–20
Herstein, I. N., 86n9, 153
Hodges, J., 177n3
Hoffrage, U., 124
Hume, David, 21–22, 27, 178
hyperplane, 84–85, 94–95

independence axiom
 Anscombe-Aumann theorem and, 143
 Choquet expected utility and, 152
 maxmin expected utility and, 163, 166–67
 Savage's theorem and, 123–24, 126
 von Neumann-Morgenstern theorem and, 80, 82, 157n4
induction
 Cantor's theorem and, 54
 deduction and, 22n4, 186
 evolutionary psychology and, 31–34
 frequentist approach and, 180–81
 Goodman's grue-bleen paradox and, 22–23, 26–34
 Hume's critique and, 21–22
 Kolmogorov complexity and, 23–26
 language dependence and, 23–26, 31–34
 simplicity and, 23–30, 33–34
 transfinite, 54
 William of Occam and, 23–24
inference
 free will and, 5
 frequentist approach and, 27, 31, 34
 maxmin expected utility and, 167
 qualitative beliefs and, 172–73
 rationality and, 10
 Savage's theorem and, 132
 subjective probabilities and, 37, 40, 45–47
infimum expected uncertainty, 161n2

information
  cognitive approach and, 171–87
  confidence and, 5, 21, 34, 40, 44–46,
    162
  confirmation and, 116–20
  determinism and, 6
  embarrassment and, 139–40
  evolutionary psychology and, 31–34
  Hempel's paradox and, 116–20
  Hume's critique and, 21–22
  induction and, 21–34
  inference and, 5, 10, 27, 31, 34, 37, 40,
    45–47, 132, 167, 172–73
  initial conditions and, 6, 20n2
  intransitive indifference and, 66
  Kolomogorov complexity and, 23–26
  language dependence and, 23–26,
    31–34
  law of large numbers and, 20–21
  measure theory and, 105–8
  Monty Hall three-door game and,
    120–22
  overfitting and, 34
  perfect measurement and, 6n2
  Received View and, 60, 76
  simplicity and, 23–30, 33–34
  subjective approach and, 37–48
  Tversky-Kahneman experiment and,
    37–38
  updating and, 47
  Weber's law and, 65–66
initial conditions, 6, 20n2
intersubjectivity, 138
interval relations, 68
intuition
  Choquet expected utility and, 147–49
  confirmation and, 116–20
  frequentist approach and, 181, 185
  Monty Hall three-door game and,
    120–22
  nonatomicity and, 107–9
  normative interpretation and, 56–58
  null events and, 99–100
  Savage's theorem and, 133 (*see also*
    Savage's theorem)
  simplicity and, 56n5
  von Neumann-Morgenstern theorem
    and, 79–88
invariance axiom, 182–83

irrationality
  maxmin expected utility and, 167
  prospect theory and, 155–56
  subjective rationality and, 139–41

Jamison, D. T., 72n1
Jeffrey, R. C., 114n1
Jensen, N.-E., 79

Kahneman, Daniel, 124
  framing effects and, 140
  gambler fallacy and, 41–42
  prospect theory and, 154–57, 158n5
  subjective probabilities and, 37–38
Kane, R., 8n3
Kannai, Y., 165n7
Karni, Edi, 82, 128, 129n3
kernel methods, 171, 176–77, 181
Keynes, J. M., 14n2, 79n3
Klibanoff, P., 165
Knight, F. H., 79n3
knowledge
  canonical state space and, 14–15
  decision matrix and, 12–13
  exemplar learning and, 181
  free will and, 6–12
  inference and, 5, 10, 27, 31, 34, 37, 40,
    45–47, 132, 167, 172–73
  intransitive indifference and, 66
  language dependence and, 23–26,
    31–34
  rationality and, 10–12
  Received View and, 60, 76
  self, 8–10
  smooth beliefs and, 18–19 (*see also*
    beliefs)
  von Neumann-Morgenstern theorem
    and, 79–88
  Weber's law and, 65–66
  zero-probability and, 8n4
Kolmogorov's complexity, 23–26, 28n12
Kraft, C. H., 111
Krantz, D. H., 98
Kreps, D., 51, 52n2, 83, 95, 123, 144
Kuhn, T. S., 76

language
  Church's thesis and, 25n9
  evolutionary psychology and, 31–34

Goodman's grue-bleen paradox and, 22–23, 26–34
Kolomogorov complexity and, 23–26
law of large numbers and, 20–21, 36
rhetorical devices and, 72
simplicity and, 23–30, 33–34
value names and, 30–31
William of Occam and, 23–24
Laplace, 14
Lapson, R., 71n21
Latour, 76
Lau, L. J., 72n1
law of large numbers, 36
Bayesian statistics and, 41–44
exchangeability and, 42–44
frequentist approach and, 20–21
gambler fallacy and, 41–42
Lebesgue, 16, 106
Leshno, J., 181n1
Levi, I., 161n3
logic
Allais's paradox, 157
de Finetti's theorem, 89–93
Ellsberg's paradox, 133–36, 140, 147, 151, 167–68
evolutionary psychology and, 31–34
gambler fallacy, 41–42
general analogical reasoning, 177–79
Goodman's grue-bleen paradox, 22–23, 26–34
Hempel's paradox of confirmation, 116–20
Hume and, 21–22
induction and, 21–34
Kolmogorov complexity, 23–26
Monty Hall three-door game, 120–22
Newcomb's paradox, 113–15
preference theory and, 67–69
projection problem and, 27n11
St. Petersburg paradox, 70, 78–79, 109
Savage's theorem, 94–112
simplicity and, 23–30, 33–34
theory of entrenchment and, 27n10
Turing machines and, 24–25, 31
von Neumann-Morgenstern theorem, 79–88
William of Occam and, 23–24
logical positivism
Cantor's theorem, 59–61

as metaphor, 76–77
Received View, 60, 76
logistic regression, 180
lotteries
Anscombe-Aumann theorem and, 142–44
Choquet expective utility and, 152
gain-loss asymmetry and, 158n7
prospect theory and, 156–59
Savage's theorem and, 109, 137n9
semiorders and, 70
von Neumann-Morgenstern theorem and, 79–88, 142–44, 152
Luce, R. D., 66, 98
Luce's theorem, 66–69

Maccheroni, F. M., 165
Mach, 59
Machina, M. J., 18, 84–85, 94, 109–10, 134
Marinacci, M., 165
Markowitz, H. M., 154n1
Marks, L. E., 65nn14, 15
Marschak-Machina triangle, 84–85, 94
Mas-Colell, A., 52, 83
maxmin expected utility
applications and, 168–69
axiomatic approach and, 163, 166–68
Bayesian statistics and, 169
Bewley and, 165, 167
Choquet expected utility and, 161–62, 164
coalition and, 160–61
confidence and, 162
consistency and, 167–68
convex games and, 160–62, 164
Ellsberg's paradox and, 167–68
formal statement of, 163
independence and, 166–67, 173
irrationality and, 167
measurement and, 164
model of (MMEU), 162–65, 168–69
no-trade theorem and, 169
objectivity and, 166–68
preference theory and, 165
status quo and, 165
subjective rationality and, 166–68
transitivity and, 167
uncertainty aversion and, 160, 163

maxmin expected utility (*cont.*)
  variations of, 165
  von Neumann-Morgenstern theorem
    and, 165n7
maxmin theorem, 78–79
Maxwell's demon, 6n2
measure theory, 6n2
  atoms and, 105–7
  Lebesgue and, 106
  maxmin expected utility and, 164
  nonatomicity and, 107–9
  qualitative probability and, 110–11
  Savage's theorem and, 105–8
median, 79, 87, 110
meta-scientific interpretation
  Cantor's theorem, 59–62, 64
  de Finetti's theorem, 92
  von Neumann-Morgenstern theorem,
    86–87
Miao, J., 168
Milgrom, P., 169
Milnor, J., 86n9, 153
model of maxmin expected utility
  (MMEU), 162–65, 168–69
Mongin, P., 128
monotonicity axiom, 90–91
  Anscombe-Aumann theorem and,
    143–44
  Choquet expected utility and,
    149–52
  comonotonicity and, 150–52
  independence and, 152
  Savage's theorem and, 100–1, 144
  violation of, 149
Monty Hall three-door game, 120–22
Morgenstern, O., 79, 90
Mosteller, F., 156
Mukerji, S., 169
multiple priors, 40, 145, 168–69, 186n6.
  See also maxmin expected utility
Muslims, 40
Myerson, Roger, 122n5

Napoleon, 22n3
Nash equilibrium, 74–75, 79
Nature, 12, 33
  gambler fallacy and, 42
  human, 8–9 (*see also* behavior)
  Savage's theorem and, 96–97

von Neumann-Morgenstern theorem
    and, 82
nearest neighbor approach, 177n3
neurobiology, 7–8
Newcomb's paradox, 113–15, 122
Newtonian physics, 6–11
New York Stock Exchange, 3
Neyman, 40
Niebuhr, Reinhold, 12–13
Nishimura, K., 168–69
Nogee, P., 156
nonadditive probability, 188
  Choquet expected utility and, 147–49,
    161–62
  maxmin expected utility and, 160–62,
    169
nonatomicity, 107–9
nontriviality axiom, 90–91, 143
non-zero-sum games, 79
normative interpretation
  Cantor's theorem and, 52, 62–63
  classification problem and, 57
  de Finetti's theorem and, 93
  defining, 56–57
  logical positivism and, 76–77
  social science and, 56–58
  von Neumann-Morgenstern theorem
    and, 87–88
no-trade theorem, 169
Nozick, R., 113
null events, 99–100, 125–26
null set, 118n3, 181
null space, 104

objectivity
  empirical similarity and, 184–87
  frequentist approach and, 184–87
  maxmin expected utility and, 166–68
  rationality and, 139–41
  subjective approach and, 138–41
Odean, T., 155
omniscient predictor, 113
ontology, 58–59
order axiom, 174
outcomes
  definition of states and, 114–15
  frequentist approach and, 182–84
  probability transformation model and,
    156–58

prospect theory and, 156–58
qualitative beliefs and, 177–79
Savage's theorem and, 95–97, 105–9,
    126–27
overfitting, 34
Ozaki, H., 168–69

Pareto optimality, 67, 74
Parzen, E., 176
PASCAL, 25, 28, 78n1
Pascal's wager, 38–40
payoffs
    anscombe-Aumann theorem and,
        143
    combination axiom and, 178
    de Finetti's theorem and, 89–93
    definition of states and, 114
    frequentist approach and, 183
    maxmin expected utility and, 160
    Pascal's wager and, 38–40
    Savage's theorem and, 94–97, 100–1,
        124, 127
    von-Neumann-Morgenstern theorem
        and, 79
Pearl, J., 188
Pearson, 40
Penrose, R., 7
pharmaceuticals, 47–48
philosophy
    logical positivism and, 59–61, 76–77
    Received View and, 60, 76
    as social science, 58–59
    See also specific concept
physics
    determinism and, 6
    Heisenberg's principle of uncertainty
        and, 6–7
    logical positivism and, 59–60
    Newtonian, 6–11
    psychophysics and, 65–66
    Received View and, 60, 76
Poincare, Henri, 18
Popper, K. R., 60, 81n6, 124
prediction
    omniscient, 113
    problem of, 173, 176–79
preference theory
    Cantor's theorem and, 67–69
    maxmin expected utility and, 165

role of theories and, 73
Savage's theorem and, 97–103, 131–32
Preston, M. G., 156
principle of indifference, 49, 89
    arbitrariness and, 14–17
    beliefs and, 18–19
    canonical state space and, 14–17
    coin tossing and, 14–17
    difficulties with a uniform prior on
        [0,1], 15–16
    intransitive indifference and, 65–66
    symmetry and, 14, 17–18
probability
    Bayesian vs. classical statistics and,
        40–48
    canonical state space and, 14–17
    central limit theorem and, 21
    concept of, 1, 21, 36, 172
    confidence and, 44–45
    convex games and, 160–62, 164
    de Finetti's theorem and, 89–93
    distortion of, 156–58
    frequentist approach and, 3, 20–36,
        180–87
    future research for, 188–89
    inference and, 5
    kernel estimation and, 171, 176–77,
        181
    law of large numbers and, 20–21, 36,
        41–44
    Monty Hall three-door game and,
        120–22
    motivating examples of, 3–4
    nonadditive, 147–49, 160–62, 169,
        188
    null events and, 99–100, 125–26
    objective, 139–41, 166–68, 184–87
    Pascal's wager and, 38–40
    practical applications of, 3–4
    principle of indifference and, 14–19
    problem of induction and, 21–34
    prospect theory and, 154–59
    qualitative, 110–11
    rank-dependent, 158–59
    Savage's theorem and, 94–112
    subjective, 3, 7, 187 (*see also*
        subjective probability)
    symmetry and, 14, 17–18
    true randomness and, 6

probability (*cont.*)
  Tversky-Kahneman experiment and,
    37–38
  utility and, 147, 160–69 (*see also*
    utility)
  von Neumann-Morgenstern theorem
    and, 79–88
  zero, 8n4, 99–100
probability transformation model, 156–58
projective geometry, 184
prospect theory, 145
  Allais's paradox and, 157
  behavioral economics and, 154
  Choquet integration and, 154, 158–59
  disposition effect and, 155–56
  distortion of probabilities and, 156–58
  endowment effect and, 155–56
  framing effect and, 155
  gain-loss asymmetry and, 154–56,
    158n7
  irrationality and, 155–56
  rank-dependent probabilities and,
    158–59
  von Neumann-Morgenstern theorem
    and, 157
psychoanalysis, 60n11
psychology
  behaviorist, 60n11 (*see also* behavior)
  exemplar learning and, 181
  free will and, 7
psychopysics, 65–66

qualitative beliefs
  Archimedianity and, 174, 177n3
  axiomatic approach and, 173–79
  causality and, 179
  classification problems and, 178
  combination and, 174, 177–79
  diversity and, 174–75
  formal statement of, 175
  four techniques for, 175–77
  general analogical reasoning and,
    177–79
  kernel methods and, 176–77
  order and, 174
  outcomes and, 177–79
  randomness and, 177
quantum mechanics, 60n10
Quiggin, J., 158

Quine, W. V., 22, 76

Raiffa, 81
Ramsey, F. P., 89, 103, 130, 145
randomness
  classical vs. Bayesian statistics, 40–48
  coin tossing and, 6 (*see also* coin
    tossing)
  determinism and, 6 (*see also*
    determinism)
  Goodman's grue-bleen paradox and, 28
  Hempel's paradox of confirmation and,
    116
  knowledge level and, 6
  qualitative beliefs and, 177
  simplicity and, 23–30, 33–34
  smooth beliefs and, 18–19
  true, 6
rank-dependent probabilities, 158–59
ranking statements, 37–38, 102
rationality
  decision matrix and, 12–13
  definition of states and, 113–20
  dominance argument and, 67, 87,
    113–15, 158n5
  embarrassment and, 139–40
  empirical similarity and, 180–81,
    184–87
  framing effects and, 140
  free will and, 10–12
  gambler fallacy and, 41–42
  illusion of, 10–12
  irrationality and, 139–41
  maxmin expected utility and, 166–68
  Monty Hall three-door game and,
    120–22
  objectivity and, 139–41
  reasoned choices and, 131–32
  Savage's theorem and, 131–32
  subjective approach and, 37–48,
    166–68
  Tversky-Kahneman experiment and,
    37–38
Received View, 60, 76
relative frequencies
  central limit theorem and, 21
  evolutionary psychology and, 31–34
  Goodman's grue-bleen paradox and,
    22–23, 26–34

language dependence and, 23–26,
31–34
law of large numbers and, 20–21
problem of induction and, 21–34
See also frequentist approach
reverse engineering, 103
rhetorical devices, 72
Riemann integral, 148, 150
risk, 1, 145
additivity axiom and, 94
de Finetti's theorem and, 91, 93
maxmin expected utility and, 167–69
prospect theory and, 155, 159n8
Savage's theorem and, 94–95, 101
von Neumann-Morgenstern theorem
and, 78–79, 81
Rosenblatt, M., 176
Rostek, M., 110
roulette wheels
Anscombe-Aumann theorem and, 143
de Finetti's theorem and, 93
gambler fallacy and, 41–42
principle of indifference and, 18
Savage's theorem and, 94–95
Rubinstein, A., 157n4
Russell, B., 24

St. Petersburg paradox, 70, 78–79, 109
Samet, D., 182
Samuelson, 33n13
Sargent, T. J., 169
Savage, L. J., 90, 95, 126–27
Savage's theorem, 138, 145, 171
acts and, 96–97
additivity and, 105–7
Anscombe-Aumann theorem and, 142,
144
Archimedeanity and, 103–4, 111–12
axiomatic approach, 97–107, 111–12,
123–32, 136–37
background for, 94–96
Bayesian statistics and, 130–33
cancellation and, 110
causality and, 114n1, 115–16
completeness and, 132
complexity problems and, 137
consumer theory and, 96
continuity and, 106, 111–12
critiques of, 123–37

decision matrices and, 134–35
Ellsberg's paradox and, 133–36, 140,
147, 151
empirical similarity and, 185
fineness and, 111 12
finite events in partition, 103–4
formal statement of, 108
frequentist approach and, 133
generated state issues and, 115–16
independence and, 123–24, 126
Jeffrey and, 114n1
measure theory and, 105–8
model of maxmin expected utility
(MMEU) and, 163
monotonicity and, 100–1, 144
nonatomicity and, 107–9
null events and, 99–100, 125–26
observability of states and, 136–37
outcomes and, 95–97, 105–9, 126–27
preference theory and, 97–103, 131–32
primitive language of, 95
proof, 110–12
qualitative probabilities, 110–12
rationality and, 131–32
raw preferences and, 131–32
reasoned choice and, 131–32
representation and, 129
Schmeidler and, 109–10, 128, 132–34,
136
splicing functions and, 99
state-dependent utility and, 127–30
states and, 96–97
subjective probability, 95, 102–3,
128–32
sure-thing principle (STP) and, 98–99
"technical" axioms of, 103–5, 108, 123
tightness and, 111–12
utility median and, 110
weak order and, 97
Schmeidler, David
Cantor's theorem and, 57n6
Choquet expected utility and, 147–49,
151–52, 159n8
convex games and, 161
frequentist approach and, 22n5, 182
future research and, 188, 189n1
maxmin expected utility and, 161, 163
objectivity and, 138–39
qualitative beliefs and, 174n1, 175, 179

Schmeidler, David (*cont.*)
  role of theories and, 74–75
  Savage's theorem and, 109–10, 128,
    132–34, 136
  von Neumann-Morgenstern theorem
    and, 82
Schneider, M., 165
science
  determinism and, 6
  Heisenberg's principle of uncertainty
    and, 6–7
  logical positivism and, 59–60
  Newtonian, 6–11
  psychophysics and, 65–66
  Received View and, 60, 76
Scott, D. W., 176
Searle, J. R., 7–8
semiorders, 65–71
separability axiom, 51–54, 61, 68–69
separation argument, 85–86
sequences, 33–34
  canonical state space and, 14–17
  coin tossing and, 104n7 (*see also* coin
    tossing)
  Goodman's grue-bleen paradox and,
    26–30
  Kolmogorov's complexity and, 23–26
  preference theory and, 68–69
  projection problem and, 27n11
  Savage's theorem and, 104n7
  Turing machines and, 24–25, 31
  von Neumann-Morgenstern theorem
    and, 83–84
"Serenity Prayer" (Niebuhr), 12–13
Shafer, G., 130n4
Shapley, L. S., 160
Shefrin, H., 155
Silverman, B. W., 176
similarity
  future research and, 188
  qualitative beliefs and, 176, 178–79
  weighted empirical frequencies and,
    180–81, 184–87
Simon, H. A., 139n1
simplicity
  Goodman's grue-bleen paradox and,
    27–30, 33–34
  induction and, 23–30, 33–34
  intuition and, 56n5

overfitting and, 34
  stability and, 33n13
  William of Occam and, 23–24
  Wittgenstein and, 24
Simpson's paradox, 179n5
Sober, E., 23n6
social science
  choice theory and, 57, 71, 124, 138–41,
    158n6
  normative interpretation and, 56–58
  philosophy as, 58–59
splicing functions, 99
stability, 33n13
state-dependent utility, 127–30
states
  Bayesian statistics and, 114
  canonical space and, 14–17
  causality and, 113–16
  confirmation and, 116–20
  defining, 113–20
  dominance argument and, 67, 87,
    113–15, 158n5
  as functions from acts to outcomes,
    114–15
  Hempel's paradox and, 116–20
  Monty Hall three-door game and,
    120–22
  Newcomb's paradox and, 113–15, 122
  observability of, 136–37
  omniscient predictor and, 113
  Savage's theorem and, 96–97
state space, 40–41, 44–45
statistics
  Bayesian, 40–48 (*see also* Bayesian
    statistics)
  central limit theorem and, 21
  classical, 3, 40–48
  confidence and, 44–46
  future research for, 188–89
  kernel methods and, 171, 176–77,
    181
  law of large numbers and, 20–21, 36,
    41–44
  overfitting and, 34
  qualitative beliefs and, 173–79
Statman, M., 155
status quo, 165
Stevens, S. S., 65n15
Stokey, N., 169

subjective probability, 3, 49, 187
    Bayesian statistics and, 40–48
    de Finetti's theorem and, 89–94
    definition of, 128–29
    free will and, 7
    maxmin expected utility and, 166–68
    objectivity and, 138–41
    Pascal's wager and, 38–40
    psychophysics and, 65–66
    Savage's theorem and, 95, 102–3,
        128–32
    Tversky-Kahneman experiment and,
        37–38
subjective sensation, 65n14
sure-thing principle (STP), 98–99
symmetry
    Choquet expected utility and, 152
    defining, 17
    gain-loss asymmetry, 154–56, 158n7
    principle of indifference and, 14, 17–18
    Savage's theorem and, 133, 136

Teicher, H., 44n9
theories
    assumption and, 73–74
    conceptual frameworks and, 74–76
    deviation dangers and, 124
    falsehood of, 60, 124–25
    future research and, 188–89
    logical positivism and, 76–77
    Popper on, 60, 124
    role of, 72–77
    transitivity and, 72–73
    utility and, 72–77
theory of entrenchment, 27n10
thought experiments, 61n12, 81, 133
tightness, 111–12
transferable utility game, 147n1
    convex games and, 160–62, 164
    maxmin expected utility and, 160–69
transfinite induction, 54
transitivity axiom
    Cantor's theorem and, 51–52, 60–61
    maxmin expected utility and, 167
    role of theories and, 72–73
trigonometry, 25
Turing machines, 24–25, 31
Tversky, Amos, 124, 139n2
    framing effects and, 140

gambler fallacy and, 41–42
prospect theory and, 154–57, 158n5
subjective probabilities and, 37–38

uncertainty
    Anscombe-Aumann theorem and,
        143–44
    aversion of, 160–64, 168
    behavioral definitions and, 49 (see also
        behavior)
    Bewley's approach and, 165
    classical approach and, 3
    cognition and, 171–89
    comonotonicity and, 151–52
    free will and, 4–13
    frequentist approach and, 3, 20–36
    future research for, 188–89
    Heisenberg's principle of, 6–7, 60n10
    labor market and, 169
    nonadditive probabilities and, 160
    principle of indifference and, 14–19
    subjective probabilities and, 37–48,
        167
uniform distribution, 15–19
updating, 47
utility
    alternative measurement methods for,
        71
    Anscombe-Aumann theorem and,
        142–44
    axiomatic approach to, 51–55
    Cantor's theorem and, 51–55, 59–67
    cardinal, 61, 65, 70n19, 86, 101, 116,
        182
    characterization of, 51–53
    Choquet expected utility and, 147–53,
        161–62
    completeness and, 51–52
    conceptual frameworks and, 74–76
    continuity and, 53
    convex games and, 160–62, 164
    defining, 1
    elicitation of, 83, 87–88
    Ellsberg's paradox and, 133–36
    intransitive indifference and, 66
    Luce's theorem and, 66–69
    maximization of, 38–40, 49, 51–71,
        78–79, 102, 124, 127–30
    maxmin expected, 160–69

utility (*cont.*)
median and, 110
meta-scientific interpretation and,
59–62, 64
ordinal, 61, 64, 70–72, 87n10, 101,
144, 148
Pascal's wage and, 38–40
preference theory and, 67–69
prospect theory and, 154–59
quantile of, 110
rank-dependent, 159
role of theories and, 72–77
St. Petersburg paradox and, 70, 78–79
Savage's theorem and, 94–112, 123–44
separability and, 51–54
state-dependent, 127–30
transferable, 147n1, 160–69
transitivity and, 51–52
uniqueness of function, 69–71
von Neumann-Morgenstern theorem
and, 79–88
Weber's law and, 65–66

value of game, 79
variables
Archimedeanity and, 174
classical vs. Bayesian statistics, 40–48
exchangeability and, 42–44
independent, 21
indicator, 20
law of large numbers and, 20–21, 36,
41–44
random, 16, 20, 175 (*see also*
randomness)
simplicity and, 34
value names and, 30
Varian, H., 72n2
Villegas, C., 107
von Kries, 14n2
von Neumann, J., 78–79, 90
von Neumann-Morgeanstern theorem
algebraic approach and, 83–84
Anscombe-Aumann theorem and,
142–44
axiomatic approach, 83–88

Choquet expected utility and, 152–53
consumer theory and, 80
continuity and, 80–81
di Finetti's theorem and, 93n3
formal statement of, 82
geometric approach and, 84–85
independence and, 80, 82, 157n4
lotteries and, 79–88, 142–44, 152
maxmin expected utility and, 165n7
meta-scientific interpretation and,
86–87
normative interpretation and, 87–88
proofs, 83–86, 91
prospect theory and, 157
Savage's theorem and, 94–96, 109, 112
separation argument, 85–86

Wakker, Peter, 1, 107, 109, 156, 164n6
Wang, T., 169
wars, 3, 49
frequentist approach and, 23, 35–36,
187
principle of indifference and, 17
observability of states and, 136
qualitative beliefs and, 179
role of theories and, 77
weak order axiom
Anscombe-Aumann theorem and, 143
di Finetti's theorem and, 90
Savage's theorem and, 97, 110
von Neumann-Morgenstern theorem
and, 80
Weber, E. H., 65
Weber-Fechner law, 65n14
Weber's law, 65–66
Werlang, S. R. C., 168
Weymark, J. A., 158n6
William of Occam, 23–24
Wittgenstein, L., 24

Yaari, M. E., 158

Zajonc, R. B., 132n6
zero-probability events, 8n4, 99–100
zero-sum games, 79, 120n4

Other titles in the series *(continued from page iii)*

Eric Ghysels, Norman R. Swanson, and Mark Watson, Editors, *Essays in econometrics: Collected papers of Clive W. J. Granger* (Volume II), 0 521 79207 X, 0 521 80407 8, 0 521 79649 0, 0 521 79697 0

Cheng Hsiao *Analysis of panel data,* second edition, 0 521 81855 9, 0 521 52271 4

Mathias Dewatripont, Lars Peter Hansen, and Stephen J. Turnovsky, Editors, *Advances in economics and econometrics – Eighth World Congress* (Volume I), 0 521 81872 8, 0 521 52411 3

Mathias Dewatripont, Lars Peter Hansen, and Stephen J. Turnovsky, Editors, *Advances in economics and econometrics – Eighth World Congress* (Volume II), 0 521 81873 7, 0 521 52412 1

Mathias Dewatripont, Lars Peter Hansen, and Stephen J. Turnovsky, Editors, *Advances in economics and econometrics – Eighth World Congress* (Volume III), 0 521 81874 5, 0 521 52413 X

Roger Koenker *Quantile regression*, 0 521 84573 4, 0 521 60827 9

Charles Blackorby, Walter Bossert, and David Donaldson, *Population issues in social choice theory, welfare economics, and ethics*, 0 521 82551 2, 0 521 53258 2

John E. Roemer, *Democracy, education, and equality*, 0 521 84665 X, 0 521 60913 5

Richard Blundell, Whitney K. Newey, and Thorsten Persson, *Advances in economics and econometrics – Ninth World Congress* (Volume I), 0 521 87152 2, 0 521 69208 3

Richard Blundell, Whitney K. Newey, and Thorsten Persson, *Advances in economics and econometrics – Ninth World Congress* (Volume II), 0 521 87153 0, 0 521 69209 1

Richard Blundell, Whitney K. Newey, and Thorsten Persson, *Advances in economics and econometrics – Ninth World Congress* (Volume III), 0 521 87154 9, 0 521 69210 5

Fernando Vega-Redondo *Complex social networks*, 0 521 85740 6, 0 521 67409 3